GREAT HARRY

CLASSIC
Sailing Ships

KENNETH GIGGAL
with paintings by
CORNELIS de VRIES

LONGMEADOW
PRESS

First published in 1988 by Webb & Bower (Publishers) Limited

This 1994 edition published by Longmeadow Press,
201 High Ridge Road, Stamförd, CT 06904

Longmeadow Press and the colophon are registerd trademarks

Designed by Malcom Couch

ISBN 0-681- 21881 - 9

Printed and bound in Italy by New Interlitho Italia SPA

Edition
0 9 8 7 6 5 4 3 2

Contents

Foreword

There have been many books about sailing ships but possibly only two, both published more than fifty years ago by artist Jack Sperling and writer Basil Lubbock, were the work of a single artist and a single writer, every part of the text and every original painting executed especially for this purpose. Cornelis de Vries has a wonderful eye for detail, and the writing of sailor and author Kenneth Giggal evokes an atmosphere of the great age of sail which brings it most vividly to life.

John Worsley
President of the Royal Society of Marine Artists

Author's note

Cees de Vries has made a lifelong study of sail, and is widely celebrated in his native Holland for his beautiful and extremely accurate ships' portraits. He works wherever possible from archive collections of original designs and sail-plans, but it must be borne in mind that no two (even contemporary) paintings of any one ship are ever quite the same. Two early 16th century models of the *Henri Grace de Dieu*, one in the Maritime Museum at Greenwich and the other in a German museum, differ considerably. This is not to suggest that either is inaccurate; great ships of that period were often subjected to extensive reconstruction, the removal of unwieldy superstructure being almost commonplace. In fact, and as will be made clear, conversions of sailing ships continued up to and even after 1900.

Much the same contradictions occur in the sphere of weights and measures. In the early days of English merchant sailing, when trade with the Continent was largely in wine, ships were listed according to the number of *tuns*, or casks, they could carry,

and there was no separate word for a measure of weight until *ton* began to appear in the language around 1688. Later, the Continental near-equivalent was of course the metric *tonne* of 1,000 kilogrammes, or 2,204.6 pounds, as against the English ton of 2,240 pounds and the American ton of 2,000 pounds. But so far as shipping was concerned even this did little to obviate confusion because originally a ton was still taken to indicate the amount of space previously taken up by a tun of wine. There was an attempt at uniformity in 1718, when one ton of cargo began to be generally accepted as meaning one hundred cubic feet of 'tween-decks cargo space. However, it was not until much later that ships and shipping adopted the actual one ton weight although, according to the Oxford English Dictionary, the word *displacement* appeared in this context as early as 1802.

Linear measurements are similarly complicated, and a further explanatory note will be easier on the eye than a litter in the text of conversions in parentheses. Most British readers are familiar

now with the metric system, and where my researches have taken me to Continental sources I have made no attempt to list metric equivalents in feet and inches. Dutch shipbuilders used always to measure their ships in multiples of feet, and some do even to this day, but whereas the archaic 'Amsterdam' or 'Antwerp' foot was a measurement of 28.31 centimetres it is now, at 30.48 centimetres, the same as an English foot. Unless otherwise stated, all 'miles' in the text refer to the nautical mile of 6,080 feet as opposed to the English land mile of 5,280 feet.

Finally, although I hope my text will stand scrutiny by the expert, I have tried wherever possible to avoid the use of esoteric terminology. I have run no risk of dulling enthusiasm in the interested layman by 'blinding him with science'.

London Amsterdam Hamburg 1985–88.

Acknowledgements

I am enormously indebted to Gien de Vries, sister of the artist. Throughout the three years it took to write this book, she worked without stint on translations from the Dutch and German, and was always available for the response to any query. Lacking prior assurance of her assistance, I might never have

embarked upon the project. I must also thank the staffs of Maritime Museums in London (Greenwich), Amsterdam and Hamburg, in all of which institutions I met with help and kindness. Those of my sailing mates too numerous to mention by name will, I am sure, forgive me for singling out Ted Dickinson,

who not only offered advice but actually *gave* me his own treasured copy of Basil Lubbock's *The Down Easters*. I must, too, thank my old friend Patrick Ross-Tuppin for some marvellous blue-water sailing in his beautiful boat *Tilly Witch*.

ROYAL PRINCE

A Short History of Sail

Early Sailors – Explorers and Navigators
Merchant Adventurers – Fighting Ships

EARLY SAILORS

I⊤ SEEMS ODD that in English, the language of two great seafaring nations, the words *sail*, *sailor*, and *sailing* are often wrongly used. Those technicians who man the oil and nuclear-powered monsters of our present day might reasonably be called seamen, but they are certainly not sailors. Nor, at the other end of the time scale, were the Phoenicians who traded along the south coast of Britain before the birth of Christ. Even the Vikings, who ranged across oceans so distant as those around Iceland and Greenland and possibly North America were not true sailors, because sail for them was merely an occasional adjunct to human muscle power. As did the galleys of ancient Greece and Rome, voyages by Viking longboats depended primarily upon the stamina of their oarsmen, and with only two known exceptions the same remained largely true until, around 1575, the galleas (an ungainly cross between a galley and a sailing vessel) with its banks of oars, gave way to the all-sail galleon. The reason for this enormous hiatus in evolution is both mystifying and obvious: most seafarers remained incapable of understanding, much less controlling, the variable forces of wind. So the Viking longboat hoisted its single square sail only in the event of a breeze astern, and lowered it when the wind turned around. There is indeed plenty of evidence to suggest that many Norse drakken, or fighting ships, were nothing more than huge, open, rowing boats up to 150 feet long and 50 feet wide, propelled by 30 or 40 oars on each side. They were clinker-built and of such shallow draught as to permit raiding far up-river.

There is much less evidence to support the chronicles we have of the voyage of St Brendan – or, more correctly, St Brenaind. No account was written down until some four hundred years after his death in AD 578 and the oldest surviving manuscript, now in the British Museum, dates from the 11th century. More than one hundred copies of the *Navigatio Brendani* still exist, and these have been translated into many languages. Most are contradictory, and all owe much more to fancy than to fact. There undoubtedly *was* a Benedictine abbott named Brenaind and he *did* embark in about the year 540, along with seventeen other Irish monks, on a voyage in search of the fabled Atlantic islands. Their open boat had a wooden frame covered with cowhides and they were away in it, so the legend goes, for seven years. Being at the mercy of wind and waves, this last might easily be true, but Brenaind could have had no possible idea as to where his landfalls lay, and the vast bulk of his handed-down story is patently mythological.

Among the very earliest of ships dependent entirely on sail are those which originated on the coast of North Africa, and on the River Nile. The Arab dhow, still very much in constant service, is constructed today as it always was by native craftsmen using rule of thumb and has changed little, if at all, over many centuries. Very sturdily built, it varies in size between 90 and 200 tons. Most have a long sloping stem and a single mast which carries an enormous lateen sail. (The word 'lateen' is a corruption of 'latin-er', the name applied to this kind of rig by the north Europeans who first came across it.)

Down the years there have been several variations of the dhow – feluccas, xebecs, polacres, etc – but significantly, only the original single-masted mode has withstood the test of time. The dhow's main advantage over ships of other nations was its ability to sail close to the wind and to get out of harbour at times when the square-rigged cogs and nefs remained land-bound by unfavourable conditions. One big disadvantage was that the heel of the massive lateen yard, often longer than the ship itself, needed to be hauled in close to the base of the mast and swung across to port or starboard with every new tack. Likewise the heavy shrouds, which supported the mast only on the weather side. Given a good following wind, the much larger two- and three-masted polacres, some of them well over 1,000 tons, hoisted a huge, square sail on the main; but such an evolution was extremely laborious and demanded the use of many strong hands.

Built predominantly by the Arabs, many of these fine Mediterranean ships were engaged in the slave trade, bartering and raiding for their human cargoes all up and down the coast of east Africa. They were easily the most seaworthy of sailing craft up to and beyond the 13th century and in 1265, when King Louis IX of France was planning his Great Crusade, he ordered his transports built in Genoa and Venice. These were big two-masted lateeners with two full decks running stem to stern, and half-decks fore and aft. The masts were all of one piece and the taller foremast, set well for'ard and raked sharply towards the bows, carried a much bigger sail. The shorter mast had no rake and was set amidships. These heavy broad-beamed vessels required a crew of 25 to 30 to handle the huge spread of canvas.

By comparison, the ships of northern Europe seemed small and inadequate. Manned by a crew of eight or ten, the ubiquitous cog rarely exceeded around 120 tons. The hull, some 80 feet long and 25 feet wide, was made up of lapped strakes set into a flat bottom of planks laid edge to edge and the one mast, stepped amidships, normally carried a single square sail. There was, however, one very important innovation: cogs introduced the straight sternpost. This allowed for the hanging of a central rudder, a device which replaced the great clumsy steering oars and so made the task of the helmsman infinitely easier. Unfortunately, it would seem that this major leap forward exhausted the late medieval shipwrights' inventive powers, because they made no further advance over the following 200 years. Then, towards the end of the 15th century, the caravel emerged.

First, though, a look at another unique type of vessel, one which certainly preceded the caravel and possibly even the dhow; one which, like the dhow, has survived in its essentials up to the present day. The Far Eastern junk was first seen by travelers from the West – most notably, Marco Polo – during the last

quarter of the 13th century, when it was obvious that the basic design had then been perfected for a very great many years. The word 'junk' is a generic term deriving from the Javanese 'djhong', meaning any large seagoing vessel. Junks ranged all over the Far East and so embraced different forms, but that version developed by the Chinese might fairly be regarded now as definitive. It was, and remains, a remarkable oddity: a sturdy and sizeable ocean-going ship which, in the view of a European observer, seems always to be moving astern. The heavy bows are square, with a pronounced overhang, and the stern is high and pointed. The bottom is flat, but construction of its ungainly hull showed advances far ahead of the times. Quite unlike any other in the world, the interior of those earliest known junks was divided by transverse bulkheads into a series of watertight compartments, each one capable of being sealed off in the event of its being holed.

Junks are rigged now pretty much as they were when Marco Polo described the fleet which carried his party from Cathay to India in 1298, although the Chinese ships then had two masts whereas later they commonly stepped three. The canvas, however – carried in a curious form of lug-sail – remains unchanged with its distinctive lateral bracing of fan-like bamboo poles. The overall effect might well be that of a ship designer's nightmare, but there is no doubt whatever that the junk is a highly successful craft, and was the one best suited to those conditions of wind and water facing sailors in that part of the world. Chinese sailors were making long and hazardous voyages to India down the South China Sea, through the reef-ridden waters around the Malaysian Peninsula, and across the Bay of Bengal, long before English sailors had properly mastered the Channel. Similarly, dhows were ranging the Mediterranean and scouring the east coast of Africa at very least two hundred years before the explorers of Spain and Portugal set out in search of new worlds.

In comparison, the development of sail in the whole of Europe was painfully slow. In the northern countries, cogs and nefs showed little advance in design until, in the early part of the 16th century, the Portuguese led the rest of Europe by introducing the caravel. In the meantime, and due to the age-old Viking influence, cogs retained their high sternposts, so that the tiller needed to be curved around it in order to steer the ship. With the nef the high sternpost disappeared, although this appears to have been a very gradual process.

The caravel of the late 15th century represented a great leap forward in European design, but it was based very firmly on its Mediterranean counterpart, the dhow. With three raked masts and lateen rigged overall, the main improvements were the straight sternpost and central rudder, and a bowsprit by means of which the big foresail might more easily be re-set closer to the wind. An outrigger astern facilitated this service for the sail on the mizzen, and so it was that the Portuguese caravel was the first European vessel capable of beating back home up the coast of Africa against the constant prevailing blow.

It was as if the seamen of Europe had awakened from a centuries-long sleep. The limitations of the caravel – it was a small ship with very shallow draught, difficult to handle in changing weather and unable to take advantage of a following wind – were rapidly overcome, and the caravel redonda emerged. There was little or no difference in hull design, but a major change in the rigging. The three masts, no longer raked, were re-stepped into what was to become the standard European form of fore, main, and mizzen, with a single square sail on the fore and main. The redonda was soon superseded by the nao, or carrack, a full-rigged ship so far ahead of its immediate progenitor as to seem like a whole new breed. With a spritsail under the bowsprit and a topsail on the mainmast, this was a ship for distant waters, the ship which inspired Portuguese explorers to challenge the great unknown.

Marine historians disagree as to which type of hull or rig did or did not accurately merit the description of cog or nef or caravel or carrack. Late medieval and middle-ages shipwrights worked without drawings or plans, each to the limit of his knowledge and skills. They were bound by the specifications of their patrons and limited by available materials. In short, there was no set *design*.

EXPLORERS AND NAVIGATORS

SO FAR AS ocean exploration is concerned, there was never a nation in history to rival the Portuguese. Where they led, others followed, and perhaps to greater effect, but in 1497 Vasco da Gama was the first European to sail around Africa to Asia; a triumph only made possible by a voyage made ten years earlier by his countryman Bartolomeu Dias. Dias traversed the Cape of Good Hope and returned with the knowledge of an open sea route leading to the Orient. Magellan, too, was Portuguese, although when he set out from Seville in 1519 to circumnavigate the globe his ships flew the flag of Spain. Columbus was an Italian from Genoa but he, too, served the rulers of Spain. It is doubtful, however, that any of their momentous enterprises would ever have been embarked upon had it not been for the work of one man: Henry, Prince of Portugal.

Known now as he was in his lifetime as Henry the Navigator, Henry never went to sea. All of his far distant voyages were conducted in an original, far-seeing mind. He was a theoriser *par excellence*. Born in Oporto on 4 March 1394, Henry's earliest destiny was that of a soldier. In 1418 he led a Portuguese army in the relief of Cueta, then besieged by Musselman forces, and was rewarded by his father with the governorship of Algarve, Portugal's southernmost province. He made his home at Sagres, near the rocky headland of Cape St Vincent, where he began in 1437 to build his famous naval arsenal. This massive structure, set four-square atop towering rocks lashed by the Atlantic, looks today exactly as it must have looked when first completed. Henry devoted the rest of his life to the study of navigation and his great arsenal became observatory, naval college, and his own main residence.

In 1444, ten years after one of his captains, Gil Eannes, had been first to double Cape Bojador, Henry's licence covered more than thirty ships. Exploration fever raged throughout Portugal and captains flocked to Sagres to learn the latest skills and to volunteer their services. In 1445 both Diniz Dias and Nuno Tristam reached the Senegal, and Dias went on to round Cape Verde. That same year saw the colonization of the Azores. In 1446, Alvaro Fernandez ventured 100 leagues beyond the point at which Dias turned back, and in 1456 Alvise de Cadamosto discovered the Cape Verde Islands before pressing on to make maps and charts of a considerable stretch of the mainland further south. When he died in 1460, the Navigator was actively planning the great expedition of Pedro de Sinta which began in 1461.

Henry devoted the greater part of his life to the task of creating at his arsenal the world's foremost school of navigational science. He was determined to provide his pilots and captains with the finest maps, charts and instruments, and with instruction as to their use. To this end he recruited teachers from all around the Mediterranean; Jews, Italians, Arabs and Spaniards, each of them a master of his craft. His court was renowned world-wide as the premier seat of mathematical and geographical studies, the envy of northern Europe. A devout Christian, one who habitually wore a hair shirt, Henry was buried in the church of St Mary in Lagos, but his body was later removed to the monastery of Batalha.

Portuguese expansion did not die with Henry, but it waned for twenty years. Explorers continued to press slowly towards Africa's southernmost tip, but they were severely hampered by the limits of their as-yet inadequate ships. Their small caravels, never more than 60 feet in length, needed crews of around 35, and the ordinary seaman suffered apalling hardship. He lived on deck, seeking relief from the blazing sun in the shadow of a sail, and shelter from the raging storm in whatever lee corner he could find. Food rotted quickly in the stinking holds, fouled by the excretions of swarming rats and infested with maggots and worm. These and other depredations were only bearable in the light and fire of inspired direction, and Henry's nephew King Alfonso V was a landsman first and foremost, interested mainly in waging a twenty years war with the rulers of Morocco. Fortunately, however, Alfonso's son and successor João (or John) the Second was a man cast in the mould of his famous great uncle, and when in 1481 he succeeded to the throne he began with vigour to take up where Henry the Navigator left off. The best of his captains, Diogo Cão, became the most intrepid Portuguese explorer of that time.

Apart from sparse details of his momentous voyages, little is known of Cão's life and personality. He added a further 1,500

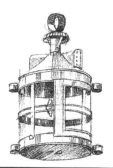

miles to the then-known map of Africa's coastline, sailing up and into the mouth of the Congo before returning seawards to press further south. A well-advised Portuguese passion for secrecy has left present-day chroniclers with no useful account of Cão's fascinating voyages, but it is recorded that in 1486 his explorations reached their most southerly point at Cape Cross, a comparatively short distance to that other Cape at the very tip of the continent. Cão died on his way home to Lisbon, cause of death not known, and his mantle as Portugal's most famous explorer was adopted by one Bartolomeu Dias.

Just as those of Cão, the life and achievements of Bartolomeu Dias remain much of a mystery. He might or might not have been a descendant of the Diniz Dias who served Henry the Navigator. No matter. What we do know is that in 1487 his king, John II, commissioned him to embark upon the most ambitious voyage of exploration ever contemplated. Dias was given three ships; two well-armed caravels and a third vessel, heavily laden with food and supplies, to be regarded as expendable once its cargo was exhausted. The far-seeing John had previously dispatched an emmissary overland to Asia, in the mind-boggling hope that the landsman and the seafarer might somehow come together in India. It was an enterprise of almost unimaginable vision.

Dias sailed south out of Lisbon in August 1487, left his empty supply ship together with nine men in a comfortable anchorage near Angra das Aldeias on the coast of Angola, and pressed on in the two caravels. He passed Cão's monument at Cape Cross on 1 December and anchored on the eighth in Walvis Bay. After taking on fresh water and provisions his ships ran into fierce southerly gales which drove them to seek shelter in the natural harbour now known as Lüderitz, but which Dias named Angra das Voltas. Once back at sea the ships were soon plagued again by hard southerlies, and Dias abandoned his hugging of the coastline to look for favourable winds offshore. Although he did not know it, this was to be his last sight of the west coast of Africa because he was in fact only 200 miles short of the Cape. The mountainous seas of the Roaring Forties drove the little vessels south-south-west for two whole weeks before Dias was able to turn east and, he thought, towards the west coast. When he was forced to realise that there no longer *was* a west coast, Dias changed course to head north, the first man to round the southern tip of Africa. It was now late February, towards the end of summer in South Africa, and the friendly landscape reminded the caravels' crews of their native Portugal. Dias sailed leisurely eastwards along shores abundant with fresh foods and water, past Algoa Bay and the site of what is now Port Elizabeth, and probably as far as present-day East London.

It was there, with the coast running firmly north-east, that Dias was persuaded by his officers to put up the helm and turn back. Having agreed, he explored and charted that part of the great cape he had over-run on his month-long tack to the south. At the end of April 1488 he put into Struys Bay, and spent the greater part of the following month overhauling and re-stocking his ships in preparation for the long passage home. On 6 June he sighted 'that great and noble cape' dominated by Table Mountain, then as now one of the world's most magnificent landfalls. Continuing north, he was back at the end of July at the anchorage in which he had left his supply ship. Six of the skeleton crew had been killed in an attack by natives, and a seventh man died soon afterwards. Dias stripped and burned the supply ship before pressing on, and was sailing into the Tagus up to Lisbon in December 1488. He and his men had been away for 15 months, and their voyage of 16,000 miles had taken them across the meeting point of Atlantic and Pacific, thus opening up a sea route to Asia and the Far East. Dias had charted his momentous traverse as the Cape of Storms, but his far-seeing monarch John II preferred to call it the name by which it is known today – the Cape of Good Hope.

Although it marked a spectacular peak in the history of Portuguese exploration, Dias' voyage was soon to be eclipsed by even greater feats of endurance and discovery. John II was succeeded in 1495 by Manuel I, a monarch whose interest in the sea equalled that of the Navigator himself. During his 26-year reign – he died in 1521 – Manuel's captains and pilots established themselves as easily the most adventurous mariners the world had ever known. This was an era dominated by giants such as Vasco da Gama and Ferdinand Magellan, (whose stories appear elsewhere in these pages), an era during which Portuguese explorers discovered South America, circumnavigated the globe, became rulers of the sea lanes between Europe and China, and began the first colonization of India.

But it was an era, also, which aroused the powerful jealousy of Portugal's nearest neighbour, Spain. Rivalry between the two nations burgeoned so rapidly, and became so fierce, that both sought adjudication by Pope Alexander VI. Exercising his infallibility, the Pope decreed in 1493 that an imaginary line be drawn, a line running north to south and passing through a point some 350 miles west of the Cape Verde Islands. All new lands to the west were to be ceded to Spain, all those to the east to Portugal. Knowing that Columbus had meantime sailed west to plant the Spanish flag in what he, albeit erroneously, assumed to be the Indies, an old and failing John of Portugal objected strongly to the papal bull, and the imaginary line was moved almost 1,000 miles to the west. This assured Portugal's monopoly of the African trade and firmly preserved her already-discovered sea route east to India.

This final decade of the 15th century heralded a whole new concept in the use of sail. Small, coast-hugging caravels were no good for the crossing of vast oceans and so, necessity being the mother of invention, the full-rigged ship was born. Called a nao by the Portuguese, and a carrack by almost everyone else, this was a somewhat ungainly mutation of all that was best in the caravel and the cog. With four square sails – spritsail, fore, main and top – and a lateen on the mizzen, its carvel hull was big and full-bellied for the carrying of many stores, and rounded at the stern. It was an excellent design, much enlarged and improved upon but basically unchanged over the next 300 years.

Sadly, the development of aids to navigation did not keep pace with that of ships, hence Columbus' grossly mistaken belief that in reaching the islands off the east coast of America he had discovered a western passage to India. The late 15th century explorers had a reasonably accurate compass to point the direction in which they were sailing, and were able by means of either quadrant and/or astrolabe fairly to determine their latitude north or south of the equator. But any calculation of longitude, the one most vital factor required to indicate exact position, evaded all efforts of pilots and cosmologists until the invention in the 18th century of the ships' chronometer. Nevertheless, far distant shores were reached, and charted, and the limits of the known world were enormously extended within the span of only thirty years.

However, in spite of then being a world power holding sway in Europe as far north as, and including, Holland, Spain with all of its ports and long coastline never produced really great mariners. Spain was a colonizer on an unprecedented scale but her people, perhaps best personified in Cortez, were much better soldiers than sailors. Once Columbus and Magellan had shown them the way, the conquistadores were able to indulge their boundless lust for land and gold, and converts to the Christian faith. As they proceeded with the rape of Central America their neighbours the Portuguese, in observance of Pope Alexander's bull, sailed ever farther eastwards towards the Orient.

Vasco da Gama (1460–1524) was the first of the last of the great Portuguese explorers. Born at Sines in the year which marked the death of Henry the Navigator, he was appointed by Manuel I to command a fleet of four vessels on a voyage of exploration far beyond the eastern limits reached by his famous predecessor Dias. Sailing his flagship the nao *San Gabriel* with Gançalo Alveres as captain, he set out in July 1497 on a 27,000-mile voyage which carried him via the Spice Islands to India, where he was well received at Calicut on the Malabar Coast by the local zamarin, or king. Later, in 1502, he returned there in order to wreak a terrible punishment on the native Muslims for their massacre of the Christian settlement, and proceeded afterwards on to Cochin, there to set up a trade agreement which benefited Portugal enormously and which made for da Gama himself a personal fortune which rivalled that of his monarch.

In spite of all efforts, Spain and Portugal were unable for long to hide their vast expansion of influence from the eyes and ears of their northern neighbours. As early as 1484 the merchants of Bristol had recruited the Venetian navigator and explorer Giovanni Caboto, and had charged him to prove himself worthy. Caboto changed his name to John Cabot, swore allegiance to King Henry VII of England, and sailed out in 1497 to discover Greenland and Newfoundland, mistaking the latter for the eastern mainland of North America. Just like Columbus, Cabot was looking for a western passage to India, and England's curious neglect of his discoveries might perhaps have been due to the stories he brought back of freezing cold, iceberg-filled seas. In any event, immediate further exploration of those northern latitudes was left to the Portuguese and the French.

Pope Alexander's equal sharing between Spain and Portugal of the as-yet undiscovered world lasted almost one hundred years. Then, in 1580, Francis Drake returned to England after a circumnavigation of the world which included a mighty detour up the western coasts of both South and North America. Prot-

estant England had no intention of observing the papal bull of 1493 and neither, once it had thrown off Spanish rule, had Holland. By the middle of the 16th century, even Catholic France was disputing Alexander's bull: in 1540 King Francis I said 'I should like to see Adam's will wherein he left the whole world to be divided between Portugal and Spain.' Nevertheless, those two Iberian countries grew fabulously rich from their respective east/west monopolies before, towards the end of the century, England, Holland, and France stepped in to end their golden franchise. In the main, the early French colonizers sailed west, the Dutch sailed east, and the English sailed everywhere.

Permitting the least to be first, and dauntless venturers over unknown lands as they were, the French came late to ocean exploration. Prior to the Seven Years War of 1756–63, the mariners of France simply followed on in the wakes of Columbus and Cabot and set men ashore to explore the hinterlands of Canada and North America. In 1603 Samuel de Champlain sailed up the St Lawrence river and in 1604 he established at Port Royal, now Annapolis Royal, the first French colony. He founded Quebec in 1608, before pressing on up the St Lawrence in the forlorn hope of finding that north-west passage to China which was to elude and bedevil explorers over the next two hundred years. He did eventually reach Lake Huron and Lake Ontario, but died in 1635 with his quest still no more than a dream.

Far to the south, Louis de Saint Denis set out in 1714 to cross Texas, and in 1722 his countryman La Harpe had reached the Red River in Arkansas. Bourmont explored Kansas in 1723, and the Mallet brothers roamed Colorado and Nebraska in 1739. Four years later, in 1743, Pierre de la Verendraye had discovered Lakes Winnipeg and Manitoba and had trekked south of the Missouri and on to the Rocky Mountains.

It was not until 1763, however, that French ships ventured widely into the Pacific. Soon afterwards, in 1768, Louis Bouganville claimed Tahiti for France, also Samoa, the New Hebrides and New Guinea. The French explorer Marion-Dufresne discovered the Crozet Islands in 1768, naming them after one of his officers, who went on four years later to take short-lived possession of New Zealand. Latest of all, La Perouse followed on after England's Captain Cook to ascertain in 1785–89 that no important stretch of land existed between the east of Paumotu and the Marquesas.

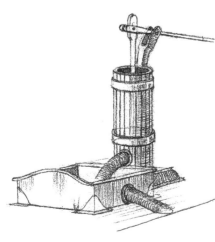

Holland produced a number of famous explorers far disproportionate to that country's tiny size. Among the earliest were Willem Barentsz (1550–97) and Jacob Lamaire (1585–1616), both of whose stories are told together with those of their ships, the *Nova Zembla* and the *Eendracht* respectively. Another bold Dutch seafarer of that same period was Willem Jansz who, in 1605, set out in his ship *Het Duyfken* to explore the southern coast of New Guinea before sailing on to find 'a great land in the south', and ironically actually succeeded without ever having realised that he had in fact done so. He sailed into the Gulf of Carpentaria believing that the land on his port side was still the coast of New Guinea, and put a visiting party ashore on the mainland of Australia before turning back for want of supplies. Ten years later Captain Dirk Hartogsz gave his name to a group of islands off the western coast of Australia, and in 1616 Frederik de Houtman, whose ship was wrecked on the west coast of the continent, gave his name to the dangerous Houtman Rocks. Another avid seeker after the 'great south land' was Jacob Roggeveen (1659–1729), but his main claim to fame appears to be the discovery in 1722 of Easter Island.

Few would argue, though, that the greatest of all Dutch explorers was Abel Janszoon Tasman (1603–59). Tasman began his service with de VOC (the Dutch East India Company) in 1633, and was elected in 1642 to command a voyage of discovery which proved to be the most successful and far-reaching of all Dutch exploration of the southern hemisphere. His orders were to explore the Indian Ocean from east to west in latitudes far to the south of any then known, and to find a passage eastwards to South America. He left Batavia in the August of that year with two small ships, the *Heemskirk* and the *Zeehaen*, and reached his most southerly latitude of about 49° south and in what he reckoned to be about 94° east. Turning north, he explored the group of islands now known as Tasmania, but missed a golden opportunity to navigate Bass Strait when his officers voted against him and opted to sail on east rather than investigate the landfall further. When in December of 1642 his ships fetched the coast of New Zealand's South Island he explored it to the north and entered the strait between the two islands. Supposing the strait to be a bay, he left New Zealand in January 1643 under the false impression that he had discovered the western coast of a new southern continent. Turning to the north east on his quest for a passage to Chile, he came upon Tonga and the Fiji Islands before conditions on board forced his return to Batavia on the 15th of June 1643. In that momentous 10-months voyage, Tasman had circumnavigated the continent of Australia without once having sighted its shores. He set out again from Batavia on the last day of February in the leap year of 1644 and sailed south east into Torres Strait, which he mistook for a wide shallow bay. He followed the Gulf of Carpentaria and coasted the shores of southern Australia to a latitude of about 22° south. He then went back to Batavia where the council of de VOC, disappointed by his failure to discover lands of potential exploitation by trade, decided to send him on no further voyages of discovery. Instead, the council put him in command of a trading fleet sailing to and from Siam, and in 1648 of a war fleet sent to fight in the Phillipines against Spain. Tasman quit de VOC in 1653 and died at home in Holland between October 1659, exact dates not known, and February 1661.

Although not primarily an explorer, Sir Francis Drake of England was certainly a fearless adventurer and his 1577–80 circumnavigation of the globe included a voyage of discovery up the western coast of America as far as the place he named New Albion, known now as San Francisco. This was a time, however, when, with sea routes around both of the southern capes already established, the English turned their attention to the possibility of there being a northern passage to the Orient; and among the most notable of English explorers in the Arctic were Martin Frobisher (1535–94), Sir Humphrey Gilbert (1539–83), Henry Hudson (died 1611) and William Baffin (1584–1622).

Frobisher, an almost exact contemporary of Drake, was a man cast in the same mould. A blunt and somewhat uncouth Yorkshireman, he was nevertheless a brilliant navigator, and one of the most fearless seamen of his day. On his second voyage to Guinea, when he was fifteen years old, he was captured by the Portuguese and held prisoner. He eventually escaped, and turned up five years later on the Barbary Coast. Accused in the 1560's of piracy, he evaded the charge by volunteering to serve the Queen and, later, the Earl of Warwick, who put him in charge of an expedition in search of a north-west passage to Cathay and India. Frobisher's command – two tiny barques, the *Michael* and the *Gabriel* accompanied by a pinnace – sailed from Blackwall in June 1576. The expedition was no great success. The pinnace was lost, the *Michael* deserted and the *Gabriel* was forced to turn back out of the great bay which Frobisher discovered, by floating ice. An expedition the following year fared little better, but when in 1578 Frobisher set out a third time it was under the auspices of Queen Elizabeth, who believed in the value of the northern territories and was determined to establish a colony there. Appointed as High Admiral of all Lands and Waters discovered by him, Frobisher sailed in May 1578 at the head of fifteen ships. A new strait was discovered (Hudson Strait) before ice and storm drove the fleet back into Frobisher Bay, where work began on the setting up of the colony. The venture failed, and Frobisher returned to England, still in the service of the queen. In 1580 he commanded the *Foresight,* and in 1585 he sailed in *Primrose* as vice admiral to Sir Francis Drake on his expedition to the West Indies. He was knighted in 1588 for his bravery against the Spanish Armada, and 1594 saw him in command of a squadron sent to aid the defence of Brest. He was wounded in that action and died at Plymouth on 22 November.

Sir Humphrey Gilbert, soldier, scholar, and astronomer whose long advocacy of a north-west passage inspired the voyages of Frobisher, became a man of action when he set out from Plymouth in 1583. His fleet of five small ships arrived off what is now St John's, and successfully established the first-ever

English settlement on the continent of North America. Before returning to England he sailed south to Cape Breton with the only two remaining ships, *Golden Hind* and *Squirrel*, very small vessels of no more than 40 and 10 tons respectively. Gilbert chose to re-cross the Atlantic in *Squirrel* and was lost, together with all hands, when the tiny ship disappeared during a violent storm off the Azores.

Like Frobisher, but unlike Gilbert, Henry Hudson was first and foremost a tough, practical mariner. Most of his early life remains a mystery, but he made four momentous Arctic voyages in search of passages, both east and west, for a short sea route to China. His first, in 1607, traced the boundary of sea ice east, and well beyond Spitsbergen. He also discovered the island now known as Jan Mayen Island, and laid the foundations for the setting-up at Spitsbergen of the English whale fisheries. He next sailed, and again for the Muscovy Company, in April 1608, but, after roving the Barents Sea, became disenchanted with the idea of finding a passage to the east. He made one final effort, this time in the service of Holland, sailing from the island of Texel on 6 April 1609. By 5 May his ship, the *Halve Maan* (*Half Moon*), with its mixed Dutch and English crew, was well into the Barents Sea and up against ice off Novaya Zemblya. Threatened with mutiny, Hudson needed little persuasion to put up the helm and sail across the North Atlantic in search of that north-west passage in which he had come more firmly to believe. He sailed 150 miles up the river which bears his name before deciding that the channel offered no sea route to China, and returned to Holland via Dartmouth in England, where he was told that any of his future voyages must be made in the service of his own native country. However, this expedition he made for Holland was one of great importance: it confounded for all time the wrongly-held notion that, at or near the latitude of 40° north, only a narrow strip of land separated the Atlantic and Pacific oceans. Hudson's fourth and final voyage ended in personal disaster. His ship the *Discovery*, of 55 tons, sailed out of London's river on 17 April 1610. He reached Hudson's Bay in the early part of August, spent three ice-free months exploring its eastern shore, and was frozen-in by early November near the south-west corner of James Bay. It was a hard and terrible place in which to winter, and the spring thaw of 1611 saw his crew determined on mutiny. On 22 June Hudson and eight others, including his young son, were set adrift in an open boat, never to be seen or heard of again. So Henry Hudson passed into oblivion, but not before he had far extended the limits of previous explorers, giving his name to bay, strait, and river.

William Baffin (1584–1622) was chief pilot under Captain James Hall of an expedition to find a north-west passage launched in 1612. Captain Hall was killed early in a fight with natives on the west coast of Greenland, and Baffin spent the next two years in the service of the Muscovy Company at their whaling station on Spitsbergen. This must have been a time of frustration because Baffin, apart from his excellence as a navigator, possessed a scientific mind capable of making tidal and astronomical observations which were proved remarkably accurate after the passing of two hundred years. In 1615 he served as pilot to Captain Robert Bylot, and made a masterly survey of Hudson Strait. In 1616, he acted again as pilot when *Discovery* sailed more than 300 miles further north west than any previous explorer,

and was responsible for the discovery, beyond the Davis Strait, of the great bay which now bears his name. He also mapped and charted the series of straits which he named after his patrons – Lancaster, Smith, and Jones – and no-one sailed farther north in those seas during the next 236 years. Following this huge triumph, Baffin made surveys of the Red Sea and the Persian Gulf for the East India Company, and died in January 1622 from a wound received in the Anglo-Persian attack on Kishm. He left behind a mass of scientific data, including a proposition by which longitude at sea might be determined by means of lunar observation, the first of its kind ever recorded.

In spite of his comparitively late appearance in the annals of world exploration, it might reasonably be said that James Cook (1728–79), son of a poor Yorkshire farm labourer, made as great a contribution to the charting of oceans as all of his English predecessors put together. Explorer, circumnavigator, hydrographer, cartographer, geographer and oceanographer, his vast and accurate recording of the entire southern hemisphere was a legacy which remains inestimable. A brilliant and largely self-taught theoretician, Cook first went to sea when he was 18 years old, sailing before the mast in a Geordie Brig, or coal-boat, plying up and down the treacherous waters of England's east coast. It was the best possible training and in 1755, after several years in the Baltic trade, he was offered a ship of his own. But with rumours flying of an imminent war with France, he chose instead to join the Royal Navy. He enlisted as Able Seaman, was promoted in a matter of weeks to Master's Mate and incredibly, after only two more years, to the command of HMS *Pembroke*, a ship of 64 guns. In 1758 he took *Pembroke* across the Atlantic to take part in the naval assault on Quebec, and made a vital contribution to the exercise by his masterly charting of the St Lawrence river in preparation for the moving-up of the fleet. Having thus laid the foundations of his reputation as a marine surveyor, Cook went on in 1763 to make a detailed survey of Newfoundland; and in 1767 the Royal Society of England published an account of his observation of an eclipse of the sun and his accurate calculation therefrom of his ship's exact position off the Burgeo Islands. In 1768 Cook was given command of the bark HMS *Endeavour,* and sent by the Admiralty out to Tahiti, first to make certain astronomical observations there before sailing on to a voyage of discovery in the oceans of the far south. This was to be the first of three great voyages of exploration carried out by Cook before he was killed in an unimportant scuffle with Hawaiian natives, in 1779. An account of these three voyages appears elsewhere in this book.

MERCHANT ADVENTURERS

SOME HISTORIANS believe that Phoenician galleys ventured out through the Straits of Gibraltar to trade for tin along the south coast of England many years BC, and it is certainly true that commerce all around the shores of the Mediterranean had already been long established. It is a fact, too, that oriental junks sailed across vast expanses of ocean long before Marco Polo took passage from China to India in 1298, and this at

a time when European trade was largely confined to a shuttling between the channel ports of little cogs and nefs.

The emergence of the world's great merchant fleets coincided almost exactly with that of the 17th century. Before 1600, and indeed for some years afterwards, Spain's huge traffic with the New World was somewhat one-sided, with the export only of religion and the import of prodigious loot. The Portuguese were much less rapacious in their dealings with Africa and India; but it was not until the formation in Europe of the various East India companies that East and West came properly to meet. Such companies were formed in England, Holland, Scotland, Denmark, France, Spain, Austria and Sweden, but compared to the first two, all others were insignificant.

On the very last day of the year 1600 Queen Elizabeth of England signed a royal charter which assigned to 'The Governor and Company of Merchants trading in the East Indies' (the Honourable East India Company) sole rights of all trading beyond the Cape of Good Hope and the Straits of Magellan, any unauthorised interloper to forfeit both ship and cargo. Initially, the charter was to have expired in 1615; in fact it ran – by progressive extension – for 258 years. Holland followed hard on the heels of England with the establishment in 1602 of the Verenidge Oostindische Compagnie, familiarly known as *de VOC*. Brainchild of Johan van Oldebarnaveldt (1547–1619) *de VOC* represented the getting-together of six independent shipping cohorts in Amsterdam, Middelburg, Delft, Rotterdam, Hoorn, and Enkhuizen. The central committee, or board of directors, was known as De Heeren Zeventien, or The Seventeen Gentlemen. *De VOC* flourished for 196 years before being taken over by the government in 1798.

These two great East India companies, and particularly that of England, began very quickly to exercise the most enormous influence. They came, in little time, to organise and command their own private armies and navies, and actually to administer the government of those eastern countries over all of whose trade they held franchise. Officers of the Honourable East India Company were the virtual rulers of India up to and until the Mutiny of 1857, relinquishing their absolute dominance only when, in 1858, it ceased to be a trading concern and administration of the sub-continent passed to the British Crown. Even then transfer of power was little more than nominal, because and perforce the same expatriots remained in precisely the same positions of authority, the only real difference being that they no longer wore the company's distinctive uniforms. In the long meantime there had been recurring unease in the parliaments of both England and Holland that such was the power of these huge private companies it constituted a challenge, if not a threat, to the sovereign rules of Law, and Land. (There is a parallel today in the strengths of the big multi-nationals.) Even so, and in spite of that insatiable greed for dividends which ultimately brought about their downfall, there is no question that the East India companies of England and Holland made an incalculable contribution to their respective countries' expansion and prestige.

The Blackwall Yard

No history of merchantmen under sail could ever be complete without some account of the yard on London's river which gave its name to that unique series of ships, some of which were designed in London for construction in Bombay, the fabulous Blackwall frigates. At the outset all were well-armed vessels built for the East India Company and the first to be launched, the *Globe*, sailed for India in 1611. Later, between 1651 and 1680, a number of naval frigates – *Dreadnaught, Yorke, Essex, Kent* and *Suffolk* – were built for King Charles II who, together with his cousin Prince Rupert, took a great interest in shipbuilding and did much to promote the craft. Rupert was, in fact, a most expert sailor, far better able to handle a ship than most of Charles' regular captains. But this is a whole new story. Sufficient to state that the only naval ships at Blackwall at the end of the 17th century were two small fireships in 1695, and one 50-gun frigate, the *Burlington*, in 1696.

These marvellous Blackwall frigates of the 17th century were considerably faster and rather more weatherly than those of their greatest rivals, the Dutch, and could sail rings round all others including the Spanish, the Portuguese and the French. Oddly, too, something of their superior qualities seemed to exercise an effect on their masters. Many crews, even those in men of war, were much better fed and cared for than those of later years when harsh treatment, bad food, and scurvy were rampant. Much of the credit for this happy state of affairs must go to Samuel Pepys the diarist, who devoted the whole of his adult life to service with the Admiralty. A man of integrity and tireless industry, Pepys was finally elected in 1673 to the office of Secretary to the Lord High Admiral of England. He several times visited the Blackwall Yard, doing so on one occasion in 1661 when he went to inspect the newly-completed wet dock.

Viewed with hindsight it is not surprising that, after 1700, the Blackwall Yard was given no further royal commissions. Almost as though it had been waiting for the honest old watchdog to die, there began after Pepys' death in 1703 the most shameful period in British naval history. Graft and corruption spread like a festering plague, permeating every level of Admiralty administration. Fair dealing, enterprise and natural ability all were stifled in the interest of greed and self-advancement, and efficiency deteriorated with alarming consequences. Fighting ships built using cheap and inferior materials lost their clean sweet lines, and morale in the Royal Navy plunged to an all-time low.

But the privately-owned Blackwall Yard stood aloof from all this, with the inevitable result that the ships which slid down its ways were infinitely superior in every way to any then being built in yards belonging to the king. Jealous and worried Admiralty

officials introduced restrictions on the sale of English oak, but whilst this sanction enforced the building of smaller merchant ships, it also led to a burgeoning of innovation. Blackwall East Indiamen built up to and around the turn of the century rarely exceeded 700 tons, but the yard was first in England, if not in the world, to introduce iron knees and brackets and the capstans with iron spindles and pawls; and Blackwall frigates emerged with the round-headed rudder and flush upper decks long before naval constructors came around to adopting these important improvements.

At last, and after more than a hundred years of decay, the Admiralty diehards were forced to ask Gabriel Snodgrass, then chief surveyor of the East India Company, to inspect and report upon the state of Royal Naval dockyards. His masterly listing of defects gave rise in responsible government circles to serious concern, and a determined effort was made by the Admiralty to put its house in order. Promulgation of the Snodgrass Report coincided almost exactly with the beginning in the Blackwall Yard of its greatest-ever era.

In 1774 the yard had no fewer than seven fine vessels on its stocks, and in 1789 the yard's chief executive, John Perry, embarked upon the construction of his famous Brunswick dock. This huge dock incorporated two enormous basins, the largest of which could accommodate thirty first-class Indiamen, the other having berths for thirty smaller ships. Perry was the architect also of a splendid new mast house with the aid of which, on 25 October 1791, the big East Indiaman *Lord Macauley* was fitted out with her bowsprit and an entire suit of masts in three hours and forty minutes. A feat which, but for its being a matter of record, seems unbelievable.

The Blackwall Yard went on until 1836 to build and launch many of the finest sailing ships the world has ever known, and its fascinating two-hundred-years history has been the subject in its own right of several worthy books, perhaps the best of which being Basil Lubbock's *The Blackwall Figates* published in Glasgow in 1922.

> At the Blackwall docks we bid adieu
> To lovely Kate and lively Sue
> Our anchors weigh'd and our sails unfurled
> And we're bound to plough the wat'ry world
> Sing hay, we're outward bound
> Hurrah, we're outward bound

Anon

The Clippers

Having regard to a wide-ranging difference in tonnage, hull design, sail plan, masting and rigging, the clipper ship was a vessel most difficult to typify. Cees de Vries offers his own definition, and it is one which seems as good as any other: 'a clipper was any square-rigged merchantman capable of sailing very close to the wind, and thus well fitted to make very fast passages in any condition of weather'. But whatever the arguments *pro* and *con,* they were a breed of ocean greyhound the like of which were never seen before and will never be seen again.

Full justice to the story of these great ships would necessitate years of study and occupy several volumes. The yards of New England came late to the concept of very fast sailing ships, but when eventually they did (and the actual word *clipper* is probably of American origin), those they built were bigger and better than any others afloat; ships which, for a brief but glorious period, reigned virtually supreme. Some few historians hold to the opinion that the 500 ton *Anne McKim,* built at Baltimore in 1833 by the wealthy merchant Isaac McKim, was the first true clipper, but there is no hard evidence to suggest that she was anything more than a possible forerunner. In fact, the emergence of the Down Easters, or Cape Horners, was not a gradual process. Their twenty-five years of fame and glory began quite suddenly around the middle of the 19th century, and 1853 saw the launching in East Boston of Donald MacKay's *Great Republic* which, at 4,555 tons, was far and away the most enormous clipper ever built. This fact might better be appreciated by a comparison with W H Webb's record-breaking *Young America,* launched during that same year and, at only 1,439 tons, considered to be a big ship.

MacKay and Webb were fierce competitors, but whilst MacKay became perhaps more famous, the latter is still regarded by most experts as a designer of greater achievement. He built no fewer than 150 fine ships, always holding to a personal opinion that *Young America* was his masterpiece. Coincidentally, *Young America*'s most worthy rival in the Cape Horn trade, the 1,679 ton *David Crockett* built in the Connecticut yard of Greenman & Co., was also launched in 1853. The Greenman craftsmen were never to become noted as builders of clipper ships but this one, with its figurehead a large carved image of its frontiersman namesake, ranked high among the very best of all.

It is, of course, quite well known that the Puritan settlers of New England were seamen of the highest order, and that whalers from the north-east coast held world domination of that hazardous trade from as early as 1645. By the middle of the 19th century, however, a relentless process of over-fishing had resulted in the start of a decline in the industry, and so it was fortuitous that the advent of the yankee clipper happened to coincide with a surplus body of experienced master-mariners admirably competent to sail them. They needed to be. No passage in any ocean demands a traverse so extremely difficult and dangerous as that around Cape Horn. It was by no means uncommon for the rounding to take six weeks or more, and many ships' masters simply abandoned the attempt, preferring to put up the helm and sail east all around the world.

The parish records of some small New England towns now seem almost incredible. In 1899, and out of a total population of only 2,000 men, women, and children, there lived in Searsport (formerly called Prospect) over ten per cent of all American sea captains. Fifty years previously, in 1847, just one family of this little community, the Pendleton family, held what might appear to be an all-time record: fourteen of its members were masters of full-rigged ships. But, marvel upon marvel, nearby Thomaston was properly renowned as The Town of a Hundred Captains, twenty-five of whom were members of a single family, the Watts.

Small wonder then that those marvellous yankee clippers were the envy of the world. Inbred pride in seamanship led their masters to set standards almost impossible to maintain, standards not only of sailing but of pristine cleanliness. The second mates of yankees were literally fanatical, vying with each other – the rest of the world was hardly in the running – to display a ship at all times so immaculate as to defy any possible finding of fault. The yankee clippers might, in comparison with English ships, be somewhat lacking in fancy sternboards and gleaming, metal brightwork, but every inch of freeboard and top-hamper, every mast and spar and yard, was kept scoured and oiled, or varnished or painted. Hands off watch were sent aloft, even to scrub the sails. Nothing could be more descriptive of such passion for orderliness than this account by a contemporary British captain: '... at Port Chalmers in New Zealand there was lying at the wharf an American ship, the *General Maclellan.* She carried three skysail yards, and all her spars and masts etc from truck to deck were scraped and oiled. Her sails were all of white cotton, and stowed with a lovely harbour stow ... all her running gear was stowed up and down the shrouds and fastened with narrow strips of white canvas. The jibboom was rigged in, and all the head-stays set up taut to the bowsprit. The yards were squared as though with a tape-line, and there was not one slack rope or any other thing untidy or out of place from stem to stern ...'.

But to keep a ship so constantly spick and span demands unceasing, arduous effort, and hands who shipped aboard yankee clippers were driven terribly hard. That many of their albeit God-fearing officers were brutal almost beyond belief is a simple matter of fact. There are numerous recorded accounts of fearful beatings, not a few leading to death. The crusading *Red Record,* published at San Francisco between 1888 and 1895 as a supplement to the *Coast Seamen's Journal,* listed horrific details over that short period of sixty-four cases of cruelty and killings in the Cape Horn fleet alone. However, such was the power and influence of those old ships' masters that although first and second mates were quite often accused of maiming and murder, and tried in courts of law, not one was ever found guilty. Their cases were invariably dismissed 'for lack of evidence' or as 'justifiable discipline'.

The short but exciting saga of clipper ships revolved around a rapid sequence of various historical events. The discovery of gold in western America culminated in the Great Californian Gold Rush of 1849, which created an urgent and insatiable demand for ships capable of fast passages from New York to San Francisco all the way around Cape Horn. Also in 1849 repeal of the Navigation Acts ended all British monopoly of the China trade, and the Americans were not slow to take advantage. There was tremendous competition to be first ship home in England with a cargo of the new season's China tea, and in 1852 a yankee clipper, the *Witch of the Wave,* made the long east-west passage in an astonishing 90 days. In spite of every effort, the British did not better this time until *Sir Lancelot* clipped just one day off the record, in 1869. But yet another coincidence: 1869 saw the opening of the Suez Canal, and even as *Sir Lancelot* was making her record-breaking run, much shorter passages by steamers heralded the beginning of the end. Even so, the advantage of steam over sail afforded by the canal was one of distance only. The record for a 24-hour run (436 sea miles) set up on her maiden voyage by Donald MacKay's famous *Lightning,* remained unchallenged by any steamship for very many years.

In the meantime though, and although the yankees went on for more than a decade to set up very fast times, the honours for sustained speeds on long passages in all conditions of weather passed almost inevitably to the British. Some other European countries built justly-famous ships, but Britons' pride dictated that they, and they alone, must continue to dominate the traffic of every sea. Great Britain owned and sailed far more ships than any other country in the world, was determined to retain its lead, and all efforts made towards this end resulted in ships '... awe-inspiring in their beauty, filled with infinite grace, stately as a cathedral'. Their names are legion, and it is not possible here to record more than just a few, but the following account might serve as representative.

In 1866 three British clippers – *Ariel, Serica,* and *Taeping –* cleared Foochow harbour on the same tide, each bound for London with a cargo of tea. The three ships never came together again until they entered the English Channel. Then, a dawn light revealed *Ariel* and *Taeping* sailing almost side by side, and the pair of them raced neck and neck up the Channel with *Serica* barely an hour astern. *Ariel* docked a mere ten minutes before her closest rival, and the trio completed the passage in exactly 90 days.

These great little ships, all three built between 1863 and 1865, and all by Steele of Greenock, were echoes of a model first devised by Alexander Hall of Aberdeen. Hall was the man who introduced hollow cheeks and the long sharp entrance, veritable hallmarks of the extreme clipper. There was great rivalry between shipbuilders on the east and west coasts of Scotland, and although many fine vessels were devised and constructed in the yards of Sunderland, Liverpool and London, the vast majority of British tea clippers were out of yards well north of the border. They ranged in size from Alexander Hall's little *Chrysolite* of only 471 tons, to Connell's (of Glasgow) *Wild Deer* of 1,126 tons, and averaging about 780. Very few exceeded 900 tons, and all were quite small when compared with the heavy Black Ball-ers which later made the grain and wool runs between America and Europe and the Antipodes.

In mighty contrast to these ships on the China run, the *Schomberg* of 2,284 registered tons, designed and launched in 1855 by Alexander Hall at Aberdeen, was easily the biggest-ever British-built clipper. She had 60 staterooms on four decks, providing accommodation for 100 passengers. With five square sails on each of her three masts, she carried a huge spread of canvas and her main lower yard, at 116 feet 6 inches was the longest of any British merchant ship. Unfortunately, her beautiful fine lines were never the subject of a contemporary artist, and her true potential was never developed. She was wrecked towards the end of her maiden voyage out to Australia, after having done one especially notable day's work of 368 nautical miles.

There were two separate and distinct Black Ball shipping lines, a fact which leads to occasional confusion. A black ball on a red ground was the house flag of the American line, which came first. A black ball on a white ground was the house flag of James Baines of Liverpool, the owner in his day of many famous ships, some of them built for him in America, and including Donald MacKay's fabulous *Lightning,* the *Marco Polo,* the aptly-named *Champion of the Seas* (which made a record 24-hour run from noon to noon of 11 and 12 December 1854, of 465 nautical miles) and of course his famous namesake the *James Baines.* Baines made a vast fortune shipping emigrants out to, and wool and grain back from, Australia, but he squandered every penny of it and died impoverished in a miserable rented room.

Voyages out to Australia and New Zealand began leisurely enough in 1787, with the first small fleet of transports carrying convicts out to the penal settlements. In 1851, however, when news reached England of the discovery of gold in Australia, the great boom exploded and the demand for fast ships became insatiable. The greed for gold rapidly became a raging fever, and the British Commissioners for Emigration were inundated with requests for passage. In 1852 over 100,000 hopefuls shipped out to Australia in search of instant wealth, and within eighteen months the population of the continent more than tripled. This in spite of the fact that emigrants were packed into ships in conditions so apalling that a great many of them never survived the passage, perishing at sea from disease. Gold-hungry crews deserted in Melbourne and at Port Phillips, so that captains were forced to take on jail-birds and transportees, totally unseasoned hands, to work their ships on the passage home. All of which coincided almost exactly with a similar gold-rush situation on the western coast of America, and so was engendered an enormous ship-building programme on both sides of the Atlantic.

On an albeit-smaller scale, the boom extended to Holland, and

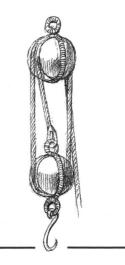

although the Dutch could not really compete in terms of size and speed and numbers, they built some justly-famous ships. Foremost among the great Netherlands shipbuilders were the Smit and Meursing families. An account of the dynasty founded by old Fop Smit, who built the *Noach* series, appears elsewhere in these pages. The Meursing family originated in the northern town of Groningen, where for many years they designed and built koffs, spritsails barges, and galliots. They also built some barks, schooners and brigantines, mostly for owner-captains trading with Britain, France and Scandinavia; and it was in such vessels that hundreds if not thousands of young men gained experience and training before moving on into berths in the big Dutch ships sailing far away over blue water.

Around the middle of the 19th century two brothers of the family, W H and A H Meursing, moved south to Amsterdam and set themselves up in the Nachtegaal Yard, hard alongside of the Blekerstraat. In 1856, and after having founded a second yard at Nieuwendam, they launched the brig-rigged clipper *Santo Rosa*. In 1860, A H Meursing branched out on his own under the name of Meursing & Co, and acquired the yard which then flanked Amsterdam's Oostenburgervoorstraat. It would seem that A H bit off rather more than he could chew, because in 1862 he was more or less forced into partnership with the old-established shipowning firm of Huygens & Van Gelder. Curiously, in view of the fact that in 1858 the Meursing family had built at Hoogenzand the first-ever Dutch iron ship, it was not until 1870 that they delivered a composite ship, the *Merapi*. It was already too late. By this time, the big shipping boom had passed and buyers were scarce, and in order to keep the workforce in full employment, the builders of Amsterdam were compelled to become owners. Also, due to high taxes in the capital, builders found it hard to compete with rivals such as Fop Smit, whose yards were way out in places like Kinderdijk.

In 1874 the Meursings built and launched, for themselves, the first of a famous series of ships all of which bore the same name, *Thorbecke*. It was the beginning of the end. The first *Thorbecke* made only one voyage under the Meursing house flag, after which she was sold to the shipping firm of Hendrichs & Co. The Meursings ceased then to be owners, but went on to build clippers for Hendrichs, perhaps the most famous of which, the

graceful *Slamat,* was launched in 1876. The Meursing family was never quite so renowned as that of old Fop Smit, but seen now against a background of history, the Meursings probably made a greater overall contribution to the building of ships in Holland. They were masters of the craft.

It would also seem, in retrospect, that Dutch shipbuilders went rashly overboard in the new-fangled use of iron and steel, materials not suitable for their traditional trade in the East Indies. Unlike the old copper-sheathed wooden hulls, iron in those tropical waters attracted an enormous fouling of marine growth, and passages home were disastrously slow. So, Dutch ships were compelled to seek work in cold or temperate seas already overcrowded by established competition.

Some few clippers, notably the famous *Vassa*, were built in Scandinavia, Denmark and Germany, but the number even in total was not significant. This wonderful breed of ship was born in New England, nurtured in Britain, and spawned progeny in Holland. Together, these three nations achieved absolute perfection in the art of harnassing the wind.

FIGHTING SHIPS

PERHAPS THE EARLIEST major sea battle of which we have any reasonably valid account was that fought in 31 BC off a promontory in northern Arcanania, the country we now call Greece. The combined fleets of Mark Antony and Cleopatra took on the forces of the Emperor Octavian, and suffered an utter defeat. The 400 vessels were fairly evenly divided, but whereas the galleys commanded by Antony were big and clumsy, those of Octavian were light, manoeuvrable and far better able to perform the tactics of hit and run. Realising this, Cleopatra ordered an early withdrawal of her ships, leaving Antony's fleet to be routed and burned. Actium was a monumental anachronism. It set a precedent in the history of human conflict, the vast importance of which was to be largely ignored for more than a thousand years. The fate of nations, and even of empires, continued to be determined by battles on terra firma, invaders by sea or river being permitted to disembark, muster their armies, and attack with impunity. Not until late in the ninth century was there any notable exception.

King Alfred, or Aelfred, known as 'The Great' (849–899) is popularly regarded as being the father of the English navy. He was certainly the first English king to fight his enemies at sea, and with no such previous experience he challenged and triumphed over the most ferocious pirates ever to scour the northern hemisphere. Alfred delivered England from the Danish raiders who had plundered her virtually at will for over a hundred years, and he did so by beating them soundly using skills traditionally their own. He ordered the building of a new and radically different fleet of ships and was ready, in the year 897, to employ that brilliant strategy which so surprised the Danes that they were scattered in confusion. Instead of battling on shore, he engaged the Norsemen afloat from ships with much more freeboard, and the tremendous advantage of a higher plat-

form was even further enhanced by a considerable superiority in overall size.

Dissenting historians insist that Alfred's sea victories were few in number and of small account, but there is little doubt that had the life of this most wise and learned of all English kings not been so tragically short the whole course of England's role at sea, and therefore its course in world history, might have been vastly different. As it was, his ships were dispersed after his death, and none of his immediate successors shared his interest in a navy until Edgar the Pious (959–975) occupied the throne. It is recorded that King Edgar could muster a fleet of 4,000 ships and if only, fewer than a hundred years later, Harold had been able to muster even half that number there might never have been a Battle of Hastings and England would have remained uninvaded since the Vikings broached her shores. In the event, William the Bastard disembarked all his knights, their horses and his men-at-arms at Pevensy totally unopposed, and took his leisure time in choosing the ground on which to fight, in 1066, the most crucial battle in the whole of English history.

Even then, William learned no lesson from his easy conquest and England, together with the rest of the world, showed little or no interest in the purpose-built fighting ship for almost half a millenium. In the interim, those few sea engagements which did take place – most notably those between English and French fleets in 1217 and again in 1340 – were fought by landsmen soldiers from crudely-converted merchant ships. These little cogs and nefs were hastily fitted fore and aft with flimsy platforms raised on wooden pillars, called fore-castles and stern-castles, most of which had low castellated ramparts painted to look like stone walls. All this makeshift top-hamper must have made the ships extremely liable to capsize in any measure of wind on the beam, and it is amazing to reflect that this cumbersome and dangerous adaptation actually became a feature of intrinsic ship design which persisted up to, and indeed well after, that disastrous day in July 1545 when King Henry VIII of England stood and looked on as his pride and joy, the great ship *Mary Rose,* turned turtle and sank with her guns never fired in the smooth calm waters of Portsmouth harbour.

The early seafarers of Spain and Portugal were intrepid adventurers and explorers, but when it came to fighting at sea they were rather less efficient. The French were hardly much better, and the roost was ruled throughout the sailing ships era by the English and the Dutch. There is an interesting historical corollary: Adolf Hitler lamented in 1941 that if only England and Germany had fought together, none could have prevailed against the alliance. In the 17th century, this would certainly have been true of England and the Netherlands. Then, it took three separate wars to convince these protagonists that they were so evenly matched as to make any further struggle a non-productive waste of time.

In 16th century England, Henry VIII instigated changes of tactics unparalleled since those of Alfred the Great. At a time when other nations still relied heavily on the Venetian-inspired galleas, Henry was building the first of his great ships, huge 1,000-ton seagoing fortresses capable of mounting a massive range of artillery. There were some costly disasters, not least that of the *Mary Rose,* but important lessons were learned and as Tudor shipwrights drew further away from the stubby, top-

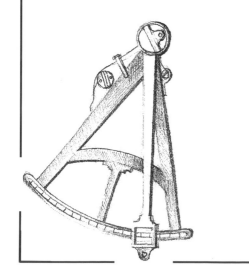

heavy basic carrack mode and began to design ships with a higher ratio of length to beam, the fast and weatherly English fighting ship began to emerge. With the qualified exception of its Dutch counterpart, it evolved ahead of all others, but it did so at no small cost. Unlike its predecessors, this was a ship with only one function, that of making war. It was in no way suitable for easy conversion to use as a merchantman and so, in the periods between hostilities, must be laid up and maintained. In this respect, Henry VIII was the first English monarch to keep a permanent *royal navy,* a fleet of ships not commandeered but which actually belonged to the crown. When he died in 1547 only one small galleas remained in his service; the rest of his ships were big, all-sail men-o'-war. Inevitably, these huge floating gun platforms were cluttered to excess with every available manner of ordnance, an illogical proliferation which persisted well into the Elizabethan period. Cannon, demi-cannon, light and heavy culverins, falcons and falconettes, and a range of smaller pivot-guns all called for different stores, so that in any protracted engagement many gun crews were made idle when their own size of shot ran out. Henry very properly mounted his heaviest guns on the lower deck, but these were often less of a danger to the enemy than to the men who fired them. The barrels of early Tudor bar-guns were wrought, as the name suggests, from long thick bars of iron sweated together edge to edge to form a hollow tube, the whole then strengthened at intervals by heavy iron hoops. They were breech-loaders, a separate powder chamber of similar construction being slotted into the barrel and held in place against backfire by a solid oaken block wedged against the end of the wheel-less carriage. It was fortunate that the gunpowder of those days was of such poor quality, or the whole contraption might have burst asunder. It must in any event have blasted clouds of smoke and fire from all around the ill-fitting breech block, and from every leaky seam along the barrel's length.

Later, when improved smelting techniques allowed for the casting of barrels not only of bronze but also of iron, breech-loading was rapidly phased out and succeeded entirely by loading at the muzzle. This put the gunners at greater risk than ever before, because whereas the softer iron of the old bar-guns and the malleable alloy of the bronze muzzle-loaders would often give notice of danger by bulging or splitting, a worn or flawed cast-iron gun could and sometimes did explode without warning into a maelstrom of red-hot fragments.

When the reign of the Tudors ended with the death in 1603 of Elizabeth I, English rulers were on their way to becoming sovereigns of all the seas. They were to be severely hampered in this course by the Dutch, but the reign of the Virgin Queen had seen an enormous flowering of master mariners: Drake, Hawkins, Raleigh, Essex, Frobisher, Grenville and many others. The mighty Spanish Armada of 1588 was defeated (albeit thanks in no small part to the weather) and three years later, in 1591, a

solitary English galleon – Drake's old flagship *Revenge,* commanded then by Sir Richard Grenville – took on a large Spanish force and held it off for over fifteen hours of constant fierce battle, including three attempts at boarding by ships of more than twice her size. Accounts differ, but the Spanish fleet certainly numbered no fewer than thirty ships, and might have numbered fifty. *Revenge* sank either two or three, and so badly damaged a further 16 that all went down to the bottom in the storm which blew up towards the end of the engagement. *Revenge* was battered into submission when her powder and shot were exhausted, and Grenville mortally wounded. She too sank in the storm.

The end of the Elizabethan period coincided neatly with the dawn of a new (17th) century, and the start of a rapid evolution in the design of fighting ships. It was a world phenomenon confined to Europe. Development in England, Holland and France ran along similar lines, but with recognisable characteristics. The Dutch came to favour a two-decker, full-bellied ship with fore- and stern-castles, the very high stern having a flat tuck. French ships were somewhat less broad in the beam but they too had fore- and stern-castles, and again a high stern with flat tuck. The English mode, largely inspired by Hawkins, featured three full decks with a greater margin of length to breadth, and an overall lower profile. Spanish shipwrights went traditionally on to build men-o'-war made cumbersome and unweatherly by excessive top-hamper; formidable in ideal conditions of wind and wave, but woefully inadequate in the vital aspect of fast and variable sailing.

Most great sea battles of the 17th century were those fought by England and Holland, between 1652 and 1674, for control of the English Channel. Both sides scored victories, but neither might decisively be said to have won either of the three Anglo-Dutch wars. Holland was never quite strong enough and England, weakened by the Civil War of 1642–49 and ravaged in 1666 by the Great Fire of London and the fearsome plague which followed, was also involved in 1655 in a war with an older enemy, Spain. In 1672 England and France joined forces against Holland; in 1689 England and Holland were allies in a war against France. English Protestants, at loggerheads with their Catholic monarch James II, had invited the Dutch Stadholder William of Orange to become King William III of England, and 1689 saw the outbreak of war with the exiled James II and his host King Louis XIV of France. A French fleet won the minor battle of Bantry Bay on 10 May 1689, and was again victorious in an encounter with the Allied fleets in June 1690 at the battle of Beachy Head. However, the French never did go on to press home their advantage and were severely beaten by the Allies at and after the 1692 battles of Barfleur, Cherbourg, and Le Hogue, when a great many of their ships were sunk or burned and destroyed.

It is a general truism that the machines of war undergo accelerated development during times of international conflict, but it must be noted that England in the 17th century was worn down by both external and internal strife. The seeds of the world's greatest sailing navy, sown by the Elizabethans, had fallen sadly among the thorns of social and political dissent. The treasury was impoverished by successive wars, and many of the country's fighting men perished in the internecine struggle between Royalist and Roundhead. Charles II was interested in his

navy, and would doubtless have liked to allocate funds, but his administrators lacked unity or strength of purpose. A few honest crusaders such as Samuel Pepys fought valiantly for proper funds, but the fight was long and arduous and that native genius which should have been directed into creative channels was wasted instead upon the maintenance of a reasonable *status quo.* Only in civilian yards, most notably those of the Honourable East India Company, did ship design and construction continue to improve. The company's Blackwall frigates were far superior to any then built in royal yards and among those built to royal commission between 1651 and 1680 were *Dreadnaught, Essex, York, Suffolk* and *Kent.*

In the meantime, and onwards into the 18th century, France was usurping Holland as foremost and only real challenger to England's dominance of the oceans. The strength and numbers of her fighting ships appeared to increase as those of Holland declined, and this burgeoning shift of sea power had a marked effect on the English attitude. The fighting with Holland had been about trade and commerce; this now with France was about the preservation of national identity. The Channel was no longer just a disputed sea lane, it was a narrow stretch of water across which came the threat of invasion.

The course of world history during the 18th and 19th centuries was largely dictated, mainly in Europe but later in America, by the design and deployment of warships. French shipwrights had become masters of innovation but, with several notable exceptions, France's record of war at sea was not illustrious. Napoleon Bonaparte (1769–1821) concentrated his military genius and the bulk of his country's resources upon his land armies, to the inevitable neglect of his navy. The English copied all that was best in French design, and proceeded to build up the world's largest fleet – by 1715 a total of some 250 vessels, no fewer than 130 of which were ships of the line. By 1750 the grand total had risen to 340 and by 1783, which saw an end to the American War of Independence and a lull in the almost-constant wars with France and Spain, Britain had a fighting navy of over 600 ships. However, numerous damages at sea coupled with massive corruption and inefficiency among admiralty officials and civilian contractors alike, had resulted in many of these being in poor condition, and the final quarter of the 18th century saw an effort by the government to put its fleet in good order. Old vessels were scrapped, new ones were built and in 1790 two-thirds of a total 150 great ships of the line were at sea and in first class state. At and around the turn of the century more English adult males were employed in ship building and allied trades than in any other industry, including agriculture, and the British naval and merchant fleets assumed enormous proportions.

It was during the 17th century that European warships were first classified by size and type, and in England's fighting navy these divisions were known as rates. There was some confusion in early years, but this was largely resolved in the middle of the 18th century when Lord Anson ordered that the rates were to be defined according to numbers of guns. There were six such rates, vessels of the first three being classed as ships of the line – ships, that is, which were assigned to a regular formation in the fighting of big, pitched, sea battles. The lower rates were by no means precluded from taking part in these major engagements, but they formed no part of that line of battle station which was firmly established by Admiralty decree. The smallest of the lower rates were used, often singly but sometimes in squadrons, for merchant convoy escort duties and for wide-ranging cruises in search of intelligence as to the whereabouts of enemy fleets. But the various rates were by no means the whole of royal ships; there was a multitude of others including brigs, sloops, gun-boats, schooners, cutters, transports, fire- and bomb-ships, receiving ships, hospital ships, store-ships, etc and etc. At the start of the 19th century England's Royal Navy had almost one thousand ships under sail: 175 ships of the line, over 200 in the lesser rates, and around 600 others many of which were well-armed fighting ships.

In the days of Nelson, the division of rates was as follows:

The first rate: a mighty three-decker mounting at least 100 guns, 200 feet on the gun deck, and having a crew of 850 men. Each of these great ships, which were always few in number and which always wore the flag of an admiral, was distinguished by its own unique features, not least being its own figurehead.

The second rate: a big three-decker of no fewer than 90 guns, around 175 feet on the gun deck, and again with special characteristics including a distinctive figurehead. A crew of 750.

The third rate: a sort of mongrel rate. Some had three full decks and were only slightly smaller than ships of the second rate, others had only two full decks but carried batteries of between eight and 16 guns under the round-house or the fore-castle. They were ships of between 80 and 60 guns, their crew numbers varying between 650 and 420.

The fourth rate: a ship of fewer than 60 guns, usually carried on two full decks; 24 on the 144-foot gun deck, remainder on the upper. Again, however, there was no absolute set pattern. Some of the fourth rates mounted guns under the round-house or quarter-deck. A crew of around 350.

The fifth rate: no more than two decks, about 130 feet on the gun deck, and crewed by a complement of some 260. Normally of 40 guns.

The sixth rate: a small two-decker of 24 guns, all of which were mounted on the one and only gun deck.

This definition of the separate Royal Navy rates is just about as accurate as any now available. It takes notice of many contemporary and later accounts, and arrives at an objective conclusion. But exception, as ever, will always prove the rule.

Although of much the same pattern, the guns of 'rated' ships differed not only in number, but also in size. There was some variation among European navies, but English first rates of the mid-18th century carried 42-pounders on the lower (main) gun deck, whilst second rates mounted 32-pounders. And so on, more or less, down the scale. It should not be assumed, however, that ships not included in the six RN rates were incapable of giving fight. Those known as sloops by the British and as corvettes by the French carried an average of 16 guns, and often in skirmishes gave extremely good account of themselves.

Fire-ships were costly to use and often, except on those rare occasions when deployed in fortuitous wind and weather conditions against enemy fleets lying at anchor, wasteful and ineffective. An old two-decker was laden with combustible and explosive materials, and sailed by a skeleton crew onto a collision course with the enemy vessels. The small crew then took to the longboat, leaving the blazing fireship to sail on into the anchored

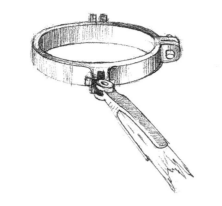

fleet, hopefully to wreak havoc and destruction. It was a chancy and hazardous exercise and one which, saving just a few memorable exceptions, had a disappointing rate of success.

Unlike fire-ships, bomb vessels were purpose-built. Of very stout construction, they were designed for the bombardment with (usually) a pair of huge mortars of harbour and shore installations. HMS *Fury*, built at Rochester in 1814, was a typical example. Of 377 tons, she was ship-rigged on three masts, 105 feet on the gun deck and 86 feet on the keel. She was 28 feet on the beam, and had a depth of 14 feet. Her armament consisted of one 13-inch and one 10-inch mortar, and ten 24-pounder carronades. She also carried a couple of six-pounders. Smaller bomb vessels were called ketches, but in the archaic use of the word. They were ship-rigged on two masts, and were very much like their larger counterparts but with the foremast removed. The extra-heavy scantling of these vessels – necessary to absorb the mortars' tremendous recoil – rendered them ideal for withstanding the crushing pressures of pack ice, and several were used for Arctic exploration. British naval officer and Arctic explorer Sir William Parry (1790–1855) used the bomb vessels *Hecla*, *Fury* and *Griper* in his early attempts to find a north-west passage, and it is interesting to note that at one time in his career, Horatio Nelson served in the bomb vessel *Carcass*.

After about 1650, there was very little difference in the ordinance used by the major European powers. Once the foundries had mastered the art of casting iron a basic gun design became common to all, and remained very much the same for the better part of two hundred years, until sail gave way to steam. A bronze gun was fine and handsome and lent itself readily to beautiful embellishment, but it cost several times more than its iron counterpart and so was gradually, except for prestige or decorative purposes, phased out. Cannon were cast in various sizes, but they differed only in weight, and following the demise in the 18th century of the cumbersome 42-pounder, most of the pieces mounted on main gun decks fired a ball of 32 pounds. Figures are approximate according to nationality but the principle heavy gun, cast all of one piece with its trunnions, was just under ten feet long and weighed upwards of three English tons. It had a bore of six and a half inches and the full charge of powder, at about 11 pounds, was near enough one-third of the weight of the shot. With two degrees of elevation, a 32-pounder had an effective range of over 1,000 yards. The charge was ignited by a large, fixed flint-lock triggered off by a lanyard, but a

burning torch was always kept handy against the event of a failure. The gun was mounted on a solid carriage of oak or elm, called a truck, which ran on four, thick, wooden wheels. The barrel was elevated or depressed by means of a large, oaken chock levered under, or out from under, the breech. It could be trained sideways when necessary by similar iron-bar leverage, much to the detriment of the gun-deck planking. In order to allow for unhampered operation after recoil, port and starboard guns were staggered so that room was left for the re-loading of opposite numbers. (The term 'oppo', short for 'opposite number', is still used in the Royal Navy to denote shipmates whose duties are complimentary.) After loading, the muzzle of the gun was run out of its port by means of ropes and tackle attached to the ship's side, and recoil was halted by other stout ropes reeved through ringbolts set low on the truck.

Although round-shot was much the most commonly used, dressed stone in the early days and later rough-finished iron, it was by no means the only missile fired from ships' cannon. There were several types of chain-shot, perhaps the most effective of which was two halves of a round shot joined together by a heavy chain. On firing, the two halves flew apart to the extent of the chain, very useful for tearing away spars and rigging. The various kinds of bar shot also served this purpose. Again, they were usually two halves of a round-shot, or sometimes two solid iron cylinders, joined together by a solid bar rather like a weight-lifter's dumb-bells. Grape-shot was that which we now call anti-personnel; many small pieces of round shot closely packed together in a container designed to burst open and scatter widely. But the most ingenious type of projectile was the fagot-shot, five or six pieces of iron which slotted together and fitted into each other to form a perfect cylinder about ten inches long. The cylinder, which exactly fitted the bore of the gun, burst after firing into its separate jagged pieces. Finally, the gun decks of some ships were equipped with furnaces for the provision of red-hot shot, but as might well be imagined this was extremely dangerous and the practice never gained much favour.

It now seems odd that throughout two hundred years of use, the iron gun was never developed beyond its original simple form, and gunnery lagged behind other naval techniques for some considerable time. Despite their having been constructed mainly by rule of thumb (our archives contain not one single shipwrights' drawing) Elizabethan galleons were said to be '. . . so nimble and of such good steerage that they did with them whatever was desired.' Not so the gunners. In 1588 master gunner William Thomas reported to Elizabeth's royal treasurer Lord Burghley: '. . . and so much powder and shot were spent so long time in the fighting, and in comparison so little harm done.' Real improvement was very slow and, mortars aside, it was not until 1774 that a new kind of gun appeared. This was the carronade, so called because it was first made in the town of Carron, in Scotland. Less than half the length of a 32-pounder, and very much lighter, it could throw a ball of the same size and weight albeit only half so far. The powder chamber was a good deal smaller in bore than the barrel, and a 32-pounder carronade needed a charge of only three pounds, or only about one quarter of that required by a 32-pounder cannon. It was a mere four feet long overall against the cannon's nine and a half feet, and weighed only 18 hundredweight against the cannon's massive three tons. The carronade could be handled quite efficiently by two men, or even a man and a boy, whereas the cannon needed a skilfull crew of at least a dozen brawny men. Having little recoil from its relatively small charge, the carronade needed no truck. It was mounted without trunnions on a solid baulk of timber which slid in turn on a timber frame, and elevation was by means of a large screw passing through the cascabel from an iron-plate base on the slide. Although never more than a second-string weapon, the carronade was extremely effective in close combat situations and for the pounding of shore installations, and the navies of foreign nations were not slow to adopt the design.

However, the striking powers of both cannon and carronade depended entirely upon the skills of seamanship, and the speed with which the decks of a man-o'-war could be cleared for action. Gun decks served also as living quarters for gunners and top-men alike, with mess tables placed between the guns and hammocks slung above. Came the call to Action Stations, whether during the hours of daylight or at night with the watch below turned in, mess tables were collapsed and stacked away and hammocks were lashed and stowed, and amazing though it might seem, the captain of a big three-decker would expect this very complex exercise to be performed in fifteen minutes. As to that rapid rate of fire essential to the firing of successive broadsides, the complex operation of fire, recoil, swab, re-charge, reload, run out, and fire again was commonly accomplished in under one minute. When one considers the enormous physical effort involved, the painfully cramped conditions under deckheads so low that a moderately tall man was unable to stand upright, and the constant pitching and rolling of the ship, it is small wonder that naval gunnery was not always absolutely accurate.

It was for this very reason that there evolved in the 17th century the tactic known as line of battle. This, a manœuvre which became standard to all, involved the commanders of opposing fleets vying for position of their most powerful vessels ie their ships of the line, sailing in close-hauled line astern as near as possible to the direction of the prevailing wind. Thus, having every advantage by way of swift and ready ship handling, they could deliver a succession of broadsides to optimum dispatch. After its introduction by Britain, the concept of the line was made statutory by the Admiralty, and any commander who failed or neglected to adopt the formation could be severely disciplined. Nelson flouted the rule with impunity because his alternative strategies, known as The Nelson Touch, were brilliantly successful. In fact, Nelson had borrowed his 'new' ideas from Prince Rupert, whose far-seeing battle tactics had then been not only ignored but actually forbidden for over a hundred years. There is no doubt, though, that Nelson was the first-ever admiral to insist that all of his ships be painted alike with the hulls banded yellow and black, the gun ports black against the yellow streaks giving a chequerboard effect, and yellow masts

with black hoops. As a further aid to instant recognition by friend and foe alike, the mast-hoops of his flag-ship were always painted white. The Dutch and French and other navies held to no such uniformity and this, in the enormous density of fire and smoke attendant on any fierce battle, helped to preclude the mistaken firing of one British ship on another.

Were it not for the sober records kept by Nelson's and other navies, the speed of sail-handling during those times would now seem unbelievable. Such efficiency, however, was no small thanks to the manner in which ships' companies were made familiar with every rope, sail and spar. When a captain was given a new vessel, all he got was a bare hull with only the lower masts stepped in. He was responsible for the rounding-up of a crew (although not for the appointment of officers) then using it to perform the enormously complex exercise of fitting out his ship. Masts and spars had to be raised, and acres of canvas used for the shaping and stitching of two full suits of sails. A vast amount of running gear had to be cut from the coils and spliced, whipped, served, reeved, wormed, etc, etc, and before the introduction of iron wire in about 1850, all of the standing rigging needed to be raised and adjusted again and again until the hempen rope could stretch no more. There was good sound sense behind this routine: every man involved knew that his life was going to depend upon himself and his shipmates having done a first-class job. All of this, with a full crew working normal daytime hours and including the hoisting inboard of guns, ammunition and stores, would take about two months. There were, however, some astonishing exceptions. In 1815 the first rate HMS *Royal Sovereign* was fitted out and made ready for sea in 18 days, and an article in the *Mariner's Mirror* of July 1911 records the staggering fact that in 1850 two line-of-battle ships were masted, rigged, armed, stored and provisioned in 37 working hours.

After her fitting out, a ship was 'proved' by a programme of gruelling exercises in which men were sometimes killed. The end result, though, was that in men-o'-war of most nationalities the tossing aloft of spars and sails was well nigh incredible. The seasoned crew of a ship of the line could set all square canvas, including studding sails, in something like five minutes, and reef the topsails of a 40 gun frigate in a minute and a half. The British first rate HMS *Queen* once sent up lower yards and top-masts and crossed topgallant yards in 4 minutes 45 seconds, the total weight of spars and sail hoist aloft being well over 18 tons. On another occasion, totally unprepared, the *Queen* struck topmasts and lower yards in under 10 minutes. Her usual time for the reefing of all three topsails was about one minute, but she is known to have performed the drill in under 50 seconds. Captain David Millar of the frigate HMS *Sirius* set a record whilst serving on the West Indies station which was never even challenged. Starting from scratch, with lower yards down and topmasts down, he made all plain sail in under five minutes. Some other navies were not far behind the British, if indeed at all. From the middle of the 19th century, French line of battle ships were expected to weigh anchor, with 90 fathoms of cable chain out, and make all plain sail in not more than nine or ten minutes. Captains of all nations commonly sent down yards and upper masts to ease the ship in bad weather, and promptly hauled them aloft again in around the same time it took to hoist or lower a boat.

These evolutions demanded skills and team-work of such ex-

traordinary high order it is difficult to imagine how they came to be performed by men who were grossly underpaid, abused and ill-fed. Certainly, so far as the British navy was concerned, only commissioned officers had any security of tenure, and the days when it was virtually impossible for a man to rise from the lower deck to the quarter deck remain very well within living memory. In the days of sail, crews were either taken on or pressed into service for the duration of current hostilities, and afterwards just dumped ashore to make a living as best they could. There were no set terms of service, and aside from the occasional small share of prize-money, no paying-off gratuities. Conditions at sea were extremely poor to say the least. Men ate, lived and slept between and over the guns, the space between their head-to-toe hammock hooks (up to and including the writer's own service 1944–52) being a standard 16 inches. Not every 18th and 19th century captain pocketed up to one-third of his ships' victualling allowance, but far too many did, and food on the lower decks of most warships was scant, and had often gone bad. In some ships making long voyages men died as much from diseases of malnutrition as from wounds sustained in battle. Flogging, most often for insubordination (and again as recently as during the writer's own service, 'dumb insolence' by facial expression was a punishable offence) could be harsh and even barbaric. The captain of a man-o'-war was to all intents and purposes, God. He held absolute power over the life or death of every man on board, and his judgements allowed for no appeal. Almost any form of rebellion could be construed as mutiny, and the penalty for mutiny was death. Men were flogged for trifling offences, and anyone foolish enough to strike an officer was usually made dire example of by a flogging around the fleet; ie clapped in irons on bread and water until such times as the fleet returned to harbour, then bound to a hatch cover set up in the longboat and rowed around the ships at anchor whilst receiving 200 lashes. There appears to be no hard evidence of such, but stories of men having died from the whipping cannot be ignored.

With seamen's messes on the gun decks, junior and noncommissioned officers were usually quartered on the orlop deck together with the surgeon and the surgeon's mate, the purser, the chaplain and the lieutenants of marines. The cabins were to port and starboard, half of them placed well forward and the rest situated down aft. The remaining deck space was used to accommodate the captain's stores, the wardroom stores and two large cable tiers. The space between the after cabins was left clear for the carrying below of men wounded in battle and for the surgeon's operating table. The orlop, mostly below the water-line, was only dimly lit by means of scuttles angled down from the gun deck, and as there was no forced ventilation the fetid atmosphere might well be imagined. Midshipmen messed then as now in quarters known as the gun room, situated aboard most sailing ships in the after part of the gun deck. Senior officers enjoyed comparative luxury. The captain occupied the entire coach under the poop deck, usually comprising a dining room, sitting room, one large or two lesser bedrooms, office, and steward's pantry. Directly beneath the coach was the ward-room, or officer's mess, also the cabins of the master, the captain of marines, the first, second and third lieutenants, and the captain's personal steward.

Among the very last of British wooden warships was the frigate HMS *Newcastle* built in 1874. Steam power had then been slowly encroaching for over thirty years, first with the clumsy and briefly-transitional paddle-steamers and later with the screw-driven vessels which finally put paid to the era of sail. That the final chapters of this short history deals primarily with the ex-ploits of Royal Navy ships is due much less to chauvinism than to a careful regard of various archive material. The French were masters of innovatory hull design and their efforts were regularly adopted by the British, but their materials and skills were, com-paratively, very poor, as were their standards of seamanship and gunnery. British naval warfare had progressed beyond the tra-ditional fair-weather fighting as early as 1759, when Hawke des-troyed the French fleet in November of that year at the Battle of Quiberon Bay. British squadrons were capable then of remain-ing on station in summer and winter alike and the facts, generally acknowledged by all sides, speak for themselves. In the 127 years (1688–1815) during which Britain was more or less continually at war, mainly with France and Spain, the Royal Navy lost only 27 ships of the line. Over that same period, France lost 178, Spain lost 78, Holland lost 33, Denmark lost 23, and Russia and Turkey lost one each. It is significant, however, that throughout all of these years 26 of the 27 British ships of the line were lost to the French, the odd one out having blown herself up in 1747 during an action with the ships of Spain. Perhaps the most stri-king example of that yawning gulf between France's brilliance of design and her inability to follow up with the construction it deserved was the taking at Toulon in 1793 of the 120-guns *Commerce de Marseilles*. Of beautiful design, and then the biggest warship in the world, her build was of such poor quality that the British took out her guns and used her as a troopship before breaking her up after only two voyages.

1793 remains the most memorable year in all of the long his-tory of sailing ships at war. It saw the start of the longest and most fiercely-contested series of battles ever fought at sea. It was the year in which Nelson was appointed to the command of HMS *Agamemnon* and one which heralded the start of almost a quarter of a century of wars between Britain on the one hand, and Spain, France and America on the other. During the whole of this time not one British ship of the line was sunk in action. Four were captured between 1794 and 1801, but none was ever demolished. Conversely, France and Spain lost a total of 160 ships of the line, including 131 taken as prizes and a further 29 destroyed. This same period embraced a senseless war with America (1812–14), but fighting between American and British ships was confined almost entirely to skirmishes between indiv-idual vessels. There were no big pitched battles, for the simple reason that America had no ships of the line and therefore no battle fleet. Thanks, however, to the genius of designer and builder Joshua Humphreys, they did have some half-dozen most excellent frigates, including the famous *Constitution* and the ill-fated *Chesapeake*. Originally conceived as ships of 76 guns, it was decided during construction to fit them out as a revolutionary breed of super 44's; fast and weatherly sailers, very roomy be-tween decks, able to stand well off and deliver heavy punishment upon any other ship of comparable armament.

The last great battle between sailing ships of war was fought in the Bay of Navarino on 20 October 1827, when an allied fleet of just 27 French, Russian, and British ships engaged what was numerically a vastly-superior force of Turks and Egyptians. The latter fleet was severely beaten with the total loss of 51 ships and 4,000 men, whilst casualties in the very much smaller allied fleet were comparatively minimal. The historical *Pax Britanicca*, al-ready well on its way, might be said to have well and truly arrived with the Battle of Navarino Bay.

Glossary

ABACK — The situation of the sails when the wind presses their surfaces against the mast, and tends to force the vessel astern.

ABAFT — Towards the stern of the vessel.

ALOFT — Above decks, or up in the rigging.

A-HULL — The situation of a vessel when she lies with all sails furled and her helm lashed a-lee.

A-LEE — Opposite direction from that which the wind blows.

ATHWART — Across.

BALLAST — Weight carried in ship's bottom to improve stability.

BARE POLES — A ship with no sails set has *bare poles*.

BARK, BARQUE — A three-masted vessel having square sails on fore and main masts, and a spanker on the mizzen.

BEAMS — Heavy timbers stretching across the vessel to support her decks.

BEAT — To sail obliquely to windward.

BEND — To make fast, eg to bend a sail onto a yard. A knot used to bend one rope onto another.

BILGES — The bottom of a ship's hold, in which waste water tends to collect.

BINNACLE — A short pillar near the helm on which is mounted the ship's compass.

BLOCK — A wood or metal pulley with sheaves or wheels through which the ropes are rove.

BOATSWAIN — (Pronounced *bo-s'n*) A non-commissioned officer who has charge of rigging, and who calls the crew to duty.

BOBSTAYS — Stays or chains used to steady the bowsprit down to the stem or cutwater.

BOLTS — Iron fastenings used to unite different parts of a vessel.

BOOM — A spar used to extend the foot of a fore-and-aft or studding sail.

BOWSPRIT — A large, strong spar standing out from the bows of a vessel, used to support parts of the rigging.

BRACE — A rope by which a spar or yard is manipulated.

BREAM — To clean a ship's bottom by burning off weed.

BRIGANTINE — A two-masted square-rigged vessel – a *brig*.

BULKHEAD — A vertical partition below decks.

BULWARKS — The waist-high 'walls' around a vessel, above her deck.

BUNTLINES — Ropes used for hauling up the body of a sail.

BY THE HEAD — Said of a vessel when her bows are lower in the water than her stern. Opposite to *by the stern*.

CABLE — A heavy rope or chain used to anchor or secure a vessel.

CABLE TIER — That part of a vessel where anchor cables are stowed.

CAREEN — To haul a vessel onto her side in shallow water or on a beach in order to clean or repair her hull.

CASCABEL — The heavy, round knob at the rear end of a cannon.

CAT HEAD — Large timbers projecting from a vessels side to which the anchor is raised and secured.

CAULK — To seal the seams of a vessel with oakum and tar.

CHAIN PLATES — Plates of iron bolted to the sides of a vessel to carry the chains and dead-eyes of the lower standing rigging.

CLAW OFF — To beat off a (usually dangerous) lee shore.

CLEW — The lower corner of a square sail, and the after corner of a fore-and-aft sail.

CLOSE-HAULED — A vessel which is sailing with her yard braces up so as to get as much as possible to windward.

COUNTER — That part of a vessel between the bottom of her stern and the wing transom and buttock.

CRANK — A vessel is *crank* when inclined to lean over, so that she cannot carry much sail.

CROSS-JACK — (Pronounced *cro-jack*) the crossjack yard is the lower yard on the mizzen.

CUT-WATER — The foremost part of a vessel's prow.

DAVITS — Curved supports projecting over a vessel's sides, fitted with blocks and tackle for the hoisting-up of boats.

DECKHEAD — The underside of the deck above.

DEAD-RISE — The difference in height, if any, between those parts of a vessel's floor which rest on the futtock.

DRAUGHT — That depth of water which a vessel requires to float her.

DROP — The depth of a sail, from head to foot, amidships.

EASTING — That part of her voyage when a vessel, having rounded the Cape of Good Hope, begins her Eastwards passage to the Orient.

FALSE-KEEL — Timbers fixed beneath the main keel.

FATHOM — Six feet (of rope, or depth of water).

FLOOR — The bottom of a vessel on each side of her keelson.

FOOT-ROPE — The rope stretched under a yard on which men stand when reefing or furling a sail.

FORE — Used to indicate the forward part of a vessel.

FORE-AND-AFT — Lengthwise with the vessel, opposite to *athwart*.

FORECASTLE — A short deck built over the main deck forward of the foremast.

FORE MAST — The forward mast of all vessels.

FOUNDER — A vessel *founders* when she fills with water and sinks.

FULL-AND-BY — Sailing close-hauled to the wind.

GAFF — A spar to which the head of a fore-and-aft sail is bent.

GRATING — Heavy, open lattice work of wood, used mainly for covering hatches in fine weather.

GUNWALE — (Pronounced *gun-nel*) the upper rail of a boat.

HAWSE-HOLES — Round openings in the bows of a vessel through which her cables run.

HEAD-SAILS — All sails set forward of the fore-mast, and usually secured to the bowsprit.

HEAVE DOWN — To careen.

HEAVE-TO — To stop the progress of a vessel at sea by either counter-bracing the yards or taking off sail.

HEAVER — A short, hardwood bar, tapering at each end, used for the levering of taut ropes or cables.

HEEL — The after part of the keel, also the lower end of a mast or boom, also the bottom of the stern-post.

HELM — The devices by which a vessel is steered, including the wheel, rudder, tiller, etc.

HULL — The body of a vessel.

JIB — A triangular sail set on a stay and secured between fore-mast and bowsprit.

JURY-MAST — A temporary mast, rigged at sea, to replace one broken or lost. (Likewise *jury-rudder*, etc.)

KNEES — Curved or angled arms of iron or timber used to connect the beams of a vessel to her timbers.

LABOUR — A vessel is said to be labouring when she rolls and pitches in heavy seas.

LARBOARD — The left side of the vessel looking forward. (Obsolete, now *port*.)

LEACH — The border or edge of a sail, at the sides.

LEE — The side opposite to that from which the wind blows.

LEE SHORE — A shore to the leeward of a vessel, one towards which the wind is blowing her.

LIE-TO — Same as *heave-to*.

LIGHTER — A large boat used in loading and unloading vessels lying in the roads.

LIST — The inclination of a vessel when it leans to either port or starboard.

LOG — The ship's record, kept by her captain.

LOG-LINE — A line made fast to a batten, knotted at

LONGBOAT fixed intervals, so that when the batten was thrown overboard astern and the line permitted to run out, the number of knots expended in a given period provided an indication of the ship's speed.

LONGBOAT Normally, the largest boat carried on a vessel.

MAINYARD The lowest yard on the main mast, the yard which carried the mainsail.

MARLINGSPIKE A heavy iron pin, pointed at one end, used primarily for the splicing of ropes and cables.

MESS Any number of men who live and eat together.

MIZZEN MAST (Or, equally, *mizen* mast), that mast which is furthest aft.

MOON-SAIL A small sail sometimes carried in very light winds, above the sky-sail.

ORLOP The lowermost deck of any vessel. In warships, the deck on which the surgeon lived and worked.

PAY The process of coating with pitch or tar.

PITCH A ship is said to *pitch* when she plunges alternately head and stern into head-on or following seas.

POOP A short deck raised over the after-end of the quarter deck.

PRICKER A small kind of marlingspike, like an ice-pick, used for splicing light ropes and for sail-making.

PRIVATEER An armed merchant ship licensed by the Crown to attack and plunder enemy vessels in time of war.

PUT ABOUT To veer the vessel onto another tack.

QUARTER That part of a vessel's sides between the main chains and the stern. Her aftermost sides.

QUARTER-DECK That part of the upper deck abaft the main-mast, occupied in warships by their commissioned officers.

RATLINES (Pronounced *rat-lins*), rope lines running horizontally across the shrouds, like the rungs of a ladder.

REEF To reduce the area of a sail by bundling it up upon its head or, in the case of a fore-and-aft sail, upon its foot.

REEVE To *reeve* a rope is to pass it through a block.

RIBS A figurative term for a vessel's timbers.

RIGGING Applies to all ropes, shrouds, stays, halyards etc, attached to masts or yards.

RIGHT To *right* the helm is to put the rudder amidships.

ROADS Anchorages in the *stream*, outside a harbour.

ROYAL The first square sail above the topgallants.

RUN The after part of a vessel's hull which rises and narrows as it approaches the stern-post.

RUNNING RIGGING All ropes which are reeved through blocks, and hauled or let go in the handling of sails.

SCANTLING The heavy timbers (or iron) of a ship's hull.

SCARF The joint between two pieces of timber, overlapping and pegged or morticed.

SCHOONER A vessel with only fore-and-aft sails.

SHIP Properly used, a vessel square-rigged on three masts.

SHROUDS An arrangement of ropes reaching from the mast-heads down to the ship's sides to support the masts and also to provide access (via the ratlines) for work aloft.

SKYSAIL A small sail set next above the royal, but underneath the moon-sail.

SLOOP A small vessel with only one mast.

SNUB The means by which a rope is suddenly checked.

SPANKER The aftermost sail of a ship or barque, always set fore-and-aft, and always with a boom and a gaff.

SPAR Describes all masts, yards, booms, gaffs, etc.

STARBOARD The right-hand side of a vessel looking forward.

STEM That heavy timber at the forward part of a vessel to which is scarfed both keel and bowsprit and to which is united the sides of her hull.

STERN GALLERY An open gallery running the width of the stern.

STERN POST The aftermost timber of a ship, reaching from the after end of the keel to the deck.

STREAM A current, or that part of an anchorage in which a tide flows.

STRIKE To lower a sail, or lower the ship's colours.

STUDDING SAILS Additional or supplementary sails set on booms outside of square sails, used in moderate weather.

TACK To put a ship about so that from having the wind on one side, she has it on the other.

TAFFRAIL The rail around a ship's stern.

TOP A platform built around the head of a mast.

TOPHAMPER All structure above the upper deck of a vessel which might tend to be an encumbrage in heavy wind and weather.

TOPGALLANT Referring to the topmost of the three separate spars which go to make up a complete mast, and its yard(s), sail(s) and rigging.

TOPMAN A sailor who works aloft.

TOPMAST That part of the mast second above the deck, above the *lower mast*.

TOP-ROPES The ropes used for sending topmasts up and down.

TRIM To stabilise a vessel by shifting cargo or ballast. Also to re-arrange sails with reference to the wind.

TRUCK A circular piece of wood atop the highest mast of a vessel, with small holes or sheaves for the reeving-through of signal halyards. Also, the wheel of a gun-carriage.

TRUNNIONS The arms on each side of a cannon by which it rests on its carriage and on which, as an axis, it is elevated or depressed.

TRYING-OUT A whaling term. The process by which blubber is stripped from the animal and turned, by boiling, into oil.

TRY-WORKS Large metal cauldrons in which blubber is rendered.

TRYSAIL A fore-and-aft sail with both boom and gaff, set on a small mast abaft the lower mast, called a *try-sail mast*. Usually applied to a sail so set on the foremast of a full-rigged brig. Commonly called a *spencer* when carried on the foremast or mainmast of a ship or barque, and a *spanker* when carried on the mizzen.

TUMBLE-HOME Said of a ship's sides when they curve inwards above the bends.

WAIST That part of the upper deck between the quarter-deck and the forecastle.

WALL-SIDED A vessel is wall-sided when her sides from bends to bulwarks are perpendicular.

WARDROOM The quarters in a warship occupied by her commissioned officers, usually in the quarter-deck.

WARP To move a vessel from one position to another by means of a cable made fast to some fixed object, sometimes a kedge-anchor.

WARPS The cable or cables used in *warping*.

WATCH A division of time on board ship. Also, that part of a ship's crew currently on duty.

WEATHER The *weather-side* of a ship is that towards which the wind is blowing.

WEATHERLY A *weatherly* ship is one which sails well to windward.

WEIGH To lift up, as in to *weigh* anchor.

WINDWARD The direction from which the wind is blowing.

YACHT A vessel used for pleasure, or for state occasions.

YARDS The spars on which square sails are bent.

YARD-ARM The extreme outer end of a yard.

YAW The motion of a vessel when forced by wind or water to veer or sway off her course.

CLASSIC
Sailing Ships

Great Harry

IT WOULD BE very difficult indeed to write about famous sailing ships without the use of superlatives such as 'then the biggest in the world' but the *Great Harry*, known more properly as the *Henri Grace à Dieu* or else the *Henri Grace de Dieu*, was a real phenomenon. Built in 1514 to the order of King Henry VIII of England, she was a giant of over 1,000 tons at a time when a ship of only half that size was regarded as something special, and she was patently intended by Henry to confirm and reinforce his claim to the title of Sovereign of All the Seas. The *Great Harry* cost a literal kings' ransom, and must, when fitted out, have presented a stunning spectacle of pomp and majesty. Modern economists might find it impossible to believe that there ever was a time when a ruling monarch had the power and gall to squander most of one whole year's national income on the building of a single ship, but this is exactly what Henry did. It is not easy, either, for us now to visualise the result. Contemporary depictions of all such great ships seem so excessively gaudy and colourful as to suggest wild flights of artistic licence, but in fact they were nothing of the kind. The ancient Britons daubed themselves with woad before doing battle, and the process of decoration became more and more sophisticated over the centuries until it reached an extravagant peak in the flamboyant heraldic devices of the Age of Chivalry. And when it became conceivable that decisive battles might be fought at sea, all of the trappings and emblazonry were embodied in the design of ships. Hulls and superstructures were carved, painted and gilded; sails were painted with intricate motifs, and the ships dressed overall with a riot of huge woven banners and enormously long streaming pennants. All of this cumbersome peacock display must seriously have impeded any practical deployment of the vessel as a fighting machine, so we must assume that it was probably intended to dismay and intimidate.

In any event, there is plenty of archive material to evidence King Henry's lavish expenditure on his pride and joy, and there is no reason to believe that a painting of her by the artist Volpe, made on the occasion of Henry's embarcation at Dover on his way to the field of the cloth of gold, is anything but reasonably accurate. Volpe has the ship wearing four huge royal standards, one on each angle of the fore-castle, and four equally large banners bearing the cross of St George placed in like positions on the stern-castle. In vast addition to these she was caparisoned from mastheads to topsides with numerous other embellishments just one of which, the 50-yard-long pennant streaming from her main mast, having cost three pounds – the equivalent then of 30 compasses or 180 boat-hooks. Just one glance at this over-exuberance of adornment prompts the startling thought that it might actually have exceeded the ship's total sail area; and all of this, together with her enormous piles of fore- and stern-castles, makes her seem ridiculously overburdened with useless top-hamper. Small wonder, then, that in 1536–39 she was extensively cut down and re-built.

The original design of the *Great Harry* indicates an enthusiasm for the 'bigger and better' carried to the point of madness; a ship to be complemented by an unprecedented 700 men and no fewer than 184 guns. All three of her principle masts embodied topmasts for the wearing of topgallants, as indeed did her small bonadventure, or mizzen. Aft of the mainmast she was decked in six tiers. A bottom or orlop deck running from stem to stern provided area for stowage, then came the lower and main decks which housed the heaviest guns. Much lighter cannonades and railing pieces were carried on both quarter-deck proper and on the deck above, with the upper deck manned by musketeers and bowmen. A ponderous four-pronged iron grappling hook swung from the end of her huge bowsprit, and others dangled on the ends of her yards. She appears, to the modern eye, as a comic monstrosity.

But in her day she was an object of marvel. Henry went on to develop some sound ideas in ship design, and did more towards the establishment of a permanent standing navy than any other English king since Alfred, his predecessor by some seven hundred years. The *Great Harry* represented a giant step forward in naval architecture, being one of the first, if not the very first, European ship to embody the concept of heavy artillery as a principle force at sea. He took the big heavy guns previously confined almost entirely to use on shore and mounted them behind closed gunports on the lower decks. This afforded greater ship stability and endowed the *Great Harry* with a tremendous new power: the ability to rake an opponent with shattering broadsides of fire. The days when battles at sea were won or lost by boarding parties fighting hand-to-hand with the ships grappled hard alongside were soon to be relics of the past.

It was the early blossoming of a whole new era, one which Henry VIII did much to hasten in. He built a considerable number of smaller ships in the meantime and then, in 1536, he had the *Great Harry* brought completely up to date. The extensive re-building went on over more than three years, many of the ideas for improvement being suggested by Henry himself. She was given new armament: 19 heavy bronze cannon and 103 big iron guns from the Sussex foundries, all of them mounted in gunports on the two complete main decks. She was re-rigged on her mizzen with a (more useful) lateen sail and although still retaining the huge grappling irons on bowsprit and main- and foremast yards, she was obviously intended to be much more effective as a powerful floating battery and this emerges clearly from a drawing of her, executed after the refit, by an artillery officer named Anthony Anthony. The big guns had arrived, and they had come to stay.

However, despite her real importance in the development of the fighting ship this re-born *Great Harry* marked the beginning of transition, and not its end. She still remained a mongrel, a brave but unfortunate cross between the flat-sterned galleon, caravel and carrack, with an unwieldy forecastle projecting too far out over her too-heavy bows, and it is difficult to imagine that she might have been weatherly safe in any but favourable seas. There is no record of her ever having triumphed in action, so it might now fancifully be said that she acted, in her day and throughout her long life, as the ultimate deterrent.

GREAT HARRY

Revenge

AS WITH SOME OTHER 15th and 16th century ships, there is no authentic contemporary painting of *Revenge*. She was, however, among the first of a much-described breed of warship, so we know near-enough exactly what she looked like. King Henry VIII of England believed in a future for the Great Ship, and so built his famous *Henri Grace à Dieu* of a massive 1,000 tons. His daughter Elizabeth very wisely took advice for the design and building of her ships from those best fitted to the task, master mariners such as Drake and Raleigh. These were men who knew from practical experience exactly what they wanted, and what they wanted was a ship of '... marvellous charge and fearful cumber'. Raleigh built one such ship, the *Ark Royal,* at his own expense (although he later sold it to the Crown), but always admitted that *Revenge* was better in every way. The new English galleon was designed not for sheer size, but for speed and manœuvrability. It was to the slow and top-heavy Great Ship as a race horse is to a lumbering Shire, only half the size but twice as fast. In an age when England's principal enemy, Spain, still clung to the Great Ship principle the revolutionary Elizabethan galleon, with its far superior sailing qualities, proved a formidable adversary. A small host of Davids against a larger host of Goliaths.

Revenge was not merely typical of her kind, she was the best; flagship in turn of three great English sea commanders and all-time favourite of her first one, none other than Sir Francis Drake. Laid down and built in 1574–75 she was a vessel of between 450 and 500 tons; 120 feet from beak head to taffrail, 92 feet on her gun deck, and a rather bluff 32 feet on the beam. She was rigged, as were all capital ships of that time, on four masts, with two large square sails on the fore and main, and with lateen sails on the mizzen and bonaventure. She might or might not have sometimes bent a tops'l on the main; no-one can positively know.

With two full decks and long half- and quarter-decks her weight was kept low as possible by a stepping-down of the main gun deck to accommodate her four sternmost guns and this, because it allowed also for the stepping-down of successive decks, gave considerably more head-room to the officers' quarters up above. Which, incidentally, were grossly disproportionate to that remaining part of the ship left to the rest of the crew. *Revenge* carried a complement of 250, comprised approximately of 140 officers and sailors, 40 gunners, and 70 'soldiers' or fighting men. There was nothing arbitrary about these categories. The Spanish did not arm their seamen, or instruct their 'infantry' in the rudiments of ship-handling; but flexibility

was expected of every man on board an English galleon with each, in emergency, able to take the place of any other. This sort of versatility made for maximum fighting power under all conditions of loss or damage, a facility which – and most remarkably in *Revenge* – was to teach all adversaries a lesson they never forgot.

If these Elizabethan race-built galleons did have a fault, it was in the matter of armament, and *Revenge,* like all of her contemporaries, was cursed with too great an assortment of ordnance. Burdened with almost every type and size available, from cannon, demi-cannon and culverin down to minion, falcon and small bronze pivot-guns, adequate supplies of every different size and type of shot were difficult to maintain. So, any protracted engagement was liable to see some guns standing useless for want of proper stores. *Revenge*'s main battery of 18 truck-mounted 18-pounders were carried on the lower or main deck and the rest of her heavy pieces, culverins firing a ball of about 10 pounds, were mounted on the deck above. The remaining wide variety was ranged topsides, here, there and everywhere. It was a sorry sort of mish-mash but, somehow, it worked.

When in 1588 Philip of Spain was known to have organised an invasion of England, Queen Elizabeth's lord admiral, Lord Howard of Effingham, appointed Sir Francis Drake as his second-in-command and invited Drake to choose any of the queen's ships in which to hoist his flag. Drake, who knew as much about ships as any man in England, elected to sail in *Revenge.* Howard himself was in Raleigh's old ship, the 600 tons *Ark Royal,* and his two other admirals, the veteran John Hawkins and Martin Frobisher were in *Victory,* of 800 tons and *Triumph,* a Great Ship of 1,100 tons, respectively. The latter was by far the biggest ship in a fleet of 100 sail. Of this number 16 belonged to the queen, the rest being privateers and requisitioned merchantmen. The Spanish Armada, a force of 27,000 fighting men in 130 Great Ships, commanded by the Duke of Sidonia in the mighty *San Martin,* was sighted off the Lizard on Friday, 19 July 1588 by a relative of Hawkins', Captain Thomas Flemyng. The news reached Plymouth late that afternoon, and the following morning saw most of the English ships up anchor and out at sea. Howard led half of the fleet to the leeward of Eddystone Rocks so that, by sailing to windward, he could double back on the enemy. Drake's half of the force, which included the squadrons of both Hawkins and Frobisher, prepared to attack from the rear.

The first encounter between Howard and Sidonia, on 21 July,

was something of an anti-climax. Sidonia's people were dismayed by the speed and manoeuvrability of their opponents. One of the Spanish captains afterwards wrote: 'The worst of them, even without main course or topsail, can beat the best sailers we have.' On the other hand, Howard was taken aback by the range and power of the Spaniards' ordnance, and wisely forebore from pressing on into certain headlong disaster. Much shot was exchanged, but no great damage done. None, that is, as a result of direct action. But the English tactic of hit and run threw one of the Spanish flagships, the *San Juan de Portugal,* into collision with her sister ship the *Nuestra Senora del Rosario* commanded by Don Pedro de Valdes, and the *Rosario* in turn clashed so violently with a third big galleon that she lost her bowsprit and foremast. Crippled, she fell astern of the Armada and was spotted by Drake just before darkness fell.

What happened next became the subject of fierce controversy. *Revenge* was only half the size of *Rosario* but Drake, with his mind set on taking the big galleon as a prize, extinguished his stern lantern in order to steal up on her in the night. After one false alarm when Drake drew close to, and was about to fire upon, a neutral German merchantman, he finally overhauled *Rosario* and forced her captain to surrender. He took de Valdes and his officers on board *Revenge* as prisoners, and put a prize crew in *Rosario* with orders to take her into Tor Bay. When he returned then to station at the head of his squadron he sailed into a storm of criticism, mainly from Frobisher. The fiery Yorkshireman accused Drake of putting the squadrons at risk by deserting his command in the interest of personal gain, a charge supported by John Hawkins. Lord Howard, however – who was later to go off himself in pursuit of a prize – completely exonerated Drake and there was further action against the Armada just two days later on 23 July. Again, neither side inflicted serious damage on the other. The lighter English ships continued to harrass the Spaniards, and on Wednesday the 31st during an attack on Sidonia's huge flagship the *San Martin,* Drake showed himself perhaps a little too daring. *Revenge* took a severe battering from '... every size and manner of shotte', and Drake's own cabin was almost wrecked.

The fate of the Armada is well known. Harrassed by the English, but even more so by appalling adverse weather, the Spanish ships were driven up to and all the way around the north coast of Scotland, a long and terrible passage home which only about half survived.

The next time Drake hoisted his flag in *Revenge* it was to lead

REVENGE

REVENGE

an expedition almost equal in both size and disaster to the ill-fated Armada of Spain. He set sail in May 1589 in joint command with Sir John Norreys of 130 ships, 1,500 officers and gentlemen, 17,000 soldiers, and 4,000 seamen. The force had three objectives: one, to destroy those remnants of the Armada then sheltering in ports on the Atlantic coast of Spain; two, to free Portugal of Spanish occupation and set the claimant Don Antonio (then in exile in England) firmly on the Portuguese throne; three, for Drake to sail on then to the Azores, there to secure rich prizes from the Spanish treasure fleet. The grandiose plan was a failure. Norreys found no support for his soldiers in Portugal because the native population did not want Don Antonio, and that same cruel fate of weather which had so bedevilled Philip's great Armada now bedevilled Drake's. Some of his ships were wrecked by gales, others were driven far off course, and *Revenge* sprang a leak so unmanageable that Drake was forced to limp home. A furious Elizabeth condemned him to disgrace and kept him ashore for the next seven years, adding insult to injury by giving *Revenge* to his bitter rival Frobisher.

Frobisher, now Sir Martin, wore his flag in *Revenge* for only a year before handing her over to another of Drake's detractors, Sir Richard Grenville. Elizabeth, determined to recoup the losses incurred by Drake's abortive expedition, had ordered a

Watch on the Azores, a move designed to relieve Spanish treasure ships of their loot from South America. The small fleet which made up the Watch of 1591 was commanded by Thomas Howard, a cousin in family and name of the Lord High Admiral of England.

Came the first confrontation, Thomas Howard acted with that same prudence as shown by his illustrious namesake. The homeward-bound treasure fleet of 1591 was escorted by a force of warships so formidable as to make attack quite hopeless. Howard's ships had the wind, and he made good use of it to sheer off and leave well alone. All, that is, except *Revenge*. It is difficult now to understand why Grenville chose to stand and fight alone against such overwhelming odds, but he stayed to take *Revenge* into single-handed combat against no fewer than 53 enemy ships, several of which were more than double her size. But, hero or fool, he fought a battle at sea the like of which must forever remain unique.

The grotesquely uneven contest off Flores in the Azores began in the early morning of 31 August and went on unabated for 15 hours. The Spanish fleet commanded by Alonzo de Bezan included 30 big galleons, six of which were newly built to the latest design. As *Revenge* had been at sea for almost four months, sickness and death had reduced her able-bodied complement to 120

men. Ranged against them were over 5,000. *Revenge* was twice grappled hard alongside very much larger enemy ships, but boarders were repelled both times. Finally, with his powder and shot completely exhausted, his ship part-dismasted and riddled from stem to stern, himself mortally wounded and only 20 others left alive, Grenville surrendered. In the fighting, the little *Revenge* had destroyed most certainly two and possibly four big galleons and so badly damaged a further 16 that all were lost in the storm which followed next day. Inevitably, the stricken *Revenge* sank also, robbing the Spaniards of their hard-won prize and doubtless permitting Grenville to die happy. His last words had been 'Split me the ship, master gunner!', but the gunner had no powder left with which to carry out the order.

Richard Grenville died of his wounds on board the Spanish admiral's flagship, but some of *Revenge*'s survivors were eventually returned to England and one of them told Sir Walter Raleigh that during the course of the 15-hour engagement, *Revenge* was hit many more than 500 times. The erudite Raleigh wrote a studied account of the battle and in 1880, almost 300 years later, Alfred Lord Tennyson immortalized the epic struggle in his poem *A Ballad of the Fleet*.

BRITISH

Golden Hind

WERE THE *Golden Hind* preserved today as is the *Cutty Sark,* and were the two docked alongside each other, the most amazing feature of the juxtaposition would certainly be seen in their relative size. The clipper, by no means a big ship at only 921 tons and 212 feet long, would make the older vessel look very small indeed.

Probably built at Deptford to a design first developed by the French, the *Pelican* (as she was named at her launching) was a ship of around 130 tons, not more than 100 feet long, with a beam of something like 18 feet. Drawing a mere 13 feet, she could sail with impunity in a sounding of less than three fathoms. Curiously, however, and in spite of the fact that she was then and will always remain the best-known ship in English history, details of her exact dimensions were never committed to paper. But we do know from various contemporary illustrations, including several aspects of the ship inlaid on the underside of the lid of Drake's big, leather-bound sea-chest, exactly what she looked like; and there also remains a beautiful model wrought in silver. Both of these historical treasures may still be seen, together with Drake's famous drum and many other of his personal effects, at Buckland Abbey, the house in which he lived. There also survives a graphic description written by Nuño da Silva, the pilot of a Portuguese ship captured by Drake off the Cape Verde Islands in February 1578. Pressed into service by Drake, da Silva spent the next fifteen months on board the *Pelican* and marvelled at the wide variety of her stores and standing equipment. She might have been a galleon quite small even by the standards of her day, but there seems no doubt that *Pelican,* with her double-sheathed hull, was extremely well constructed, although by whom, we do not know.

Looking now at the *Pelican,* first impressions of her would seem to belie da Silva's glowing account. Equally, though, we must assume that a superlative mariner such as Drake would examine every possible option before choosing his flagship for the enormous enterprise, and that he would settle for only the best. She was square-rigged on her fore and main masts with topsails, spritsails and top-gallants, and she carried a lateen sail on her mizzen; a total canvas area of approximately 1,400 square yards. Her after-castle was considerably higher than her fore-castle, lending her an appearance of forbidding unstability. She was well armed for her size with 16 heavy guns, two of which were in the poop with the others being mounted under hatches seven on each side. These were supplemented by a number of lesser cannon. She was manned by a complement of some 90

fighting seamen, nine of whom were 'gentlemen' – the younger sons of merchants and landowners who were probably Drake's personal friends. This is not to suggest that they were permitted to regard themselves as supercargo. Drake, himself of humble origins, allowed no man to sail with him who could not pull his weight, and the highest-born among them was required to work alongside of, and as hard as, the lowliest member of the crew. 'I must have the gentleman to haul and draw with the mariner, and the mariner with the gentleman, and would know him that would refuse to set his hand to a rope . . .'.

Nevertheless, Drake regarded himself – or, rather, in the person of his office – as being representative of Queen Elizabeth's pre-eminence among the world's most powerful sovereigns, a sort of roving ambassador. His ship's great cabin was lined with carved oak panels, and furnished in lavish style, '. . . whereby the civility and magnificence of his native country might amongst all nations, whithersoever he might come, be the more admired.' His officers ate with him in this great cabin, and were berthed in much less splendid quarters down aft. The fore-castle could not have accommodated more than a few of the seamen, so the majority must have messed on the gun deck.

When the miniature flotilla sailed out of Plymouth harbour in November 1577 only one man, the admiral himself, knew that it was embarked upon an undertaking so perilous as to make the small force seem woefully inadequate. Drake's command was made up of just five ships, largest by far of which was the little *Pelican.* The other four, in order of size, were: the *Elizabeth* of 80 tons under the command of his vice-admiral John Wynter, the *Swan* of 50 tons under John Chester, the *Marigold,* a bark of 30 tons, under John Thomas, and the *Christopher,* a tiny pinnace of 15 tons commanded by Thomas Moore. So, with a total company in all five ships of fewer than 170 stalwarts, Drake set out over oceans beset with every possible privation to round Cape Horn by the fearsome strait discovered by Magellan in 1520, and then to harrass the Spanish settlements on the New World's Pacific coast. Every man on board was an eager volunteer, but had they known what Drake knew, it is doubtful if more than a handful would have agreed to sail with him. All of them, from John Wynter down to the humblest seaman, believed themselves to be committed to nothing more than a routine voyage of licensed piracy along the Spanish Main, with every good prospect of taking rich prizes in safe and familiar seas. But this was the age in which Queen Elizabeth's loyal servant Sir Francis Walsingham initiated the world's first secret service, and the

fleet's real mission was a clandestine one. Had Drake been allowed to confide in his captains, much of the strife which ensued might well have been averted.

As it was, the venture seemed doomed from the outset. The ships had not even cleared the Lizard when all were damaged by violent storms, and Drake was forced to seek refuge in Falmouth harbour before putting back to Plymouth for repairs. On 13 December, four weeks after his first departure, he set sail again and this time made a fair passage to the island of Mogador, arriving on Christmas day. Further south at Cape Blanco Drake paused for a week to clean his ships and take on fresh water, and decided here that the *Christopher* was in no fit state to continue the voyage. He replaced her with one of the two Spanish caravels he had captured en route to the Cape. The next ship which fell to Drake, a Portuguese trader which he re-named the *Mary,* brought him the most valuable prize of all – a most experienced pilot together with all of his charts and other aids to navigation, the aforementioned Nuño da Silva. Drake placed Thomas Doughty, one of Elizabeth's courtiers, in command of the *Mary,* and the little fleet sailed on.

After nine, long weeks at sea the sight of a shoreline near the mouth of the River Plate must have heralded the welcome prospect of fresh food and water and a chance to careen the ships, but before the fleet could make a landfall it was battered by the most gigantic tempest any man on board had ever seen. But for the skill of the Portuguese pilot, the *Pelican* would certainly have been hurled upon a lee shore and wrecked. Having weathered the storm, Drake looked for his scattered ships up and down the coast of Brazil, refusing to abandon the search until all were accounted for. The *Swan* was deemed beyond repair, and after transferring her stores and armaments to *Pelican,* Drake scuttled her in Seal Bay in Patagonia. He made a similar decision with regard to *Christopher II,* and when the last missing ship, the *Mary,* was found off Port St Julian near the Strait of Magellan, she too was retired from the fleet.

This was in June 1578 and it was here, with Drake's men ashore at St Julian, that history repeated itself. By this time, Drake had revealed his intention to traverse the Cape and rumbles of dissent, stirred up by Doughty, burgeoned close on mutiny. Drake reacted with characteristic boldness. Doughty was put on trial, found guilty, and put to death, 58 years on, in the very place where Magellan had executed his own mutineers. Afterwards, Drake addressed the assembled ships' companies, acquainting them frankly with the dangers which lay ahead and

BRITISH

GOLDEN HIND

adding that if any man should wish now to turn back, he was free to do so. None did, and they left St Julian on 17 August refreshed and in good spirits.

As the ships – now reduced to *Pelican, Elizabeth,* and *Marigold* – rounded Cape Virgins on the approaches to the strait, Drake ordered them to strike topsails in homage to their queen and he also, as a mark of esteem for his friend and patron Sir Christopher Hatton, changed the name of his ship from *Pelican* to *Golden Hind,* the heraldic beast which surmounts the Hatton family coat of arms. Incredible as it now may seem, Drake led his ships through what is still the world's most dangerous strait in a traverse of only 16 days. Magellan took 38 days and over the next 300 years very many sailing ships simply failed to make the passage at all, forced to turn back by the constant howling gales. Ironically, it was with the strait safely astern that Drake's ships sailed into a tempest far worse, even, than that which they had encountered off Brazil. In an enormous towering storm which raged unabated for one whole month, the three ships were thrown many leagues apart, never to join forces again. The *Marigold* was lost with all hands, and *Golden Hind* was driven far south towards Antarctica. In *Elizabeth,* John Wynter assumed that his ship was the only survivor and decided, under pressure from his officers and crew, to put back through that terrible strait and set a course for home.

But with superhuman perseverance, Drake rallied his men to press doggedly on. After regaining the west coast of South America, and after seeking out a landfall at which he could stop to repair his ship, he sailed north up the coast of Chile. From then on, his depredations against the Spaniards might only be described as staggering. In the tiny *Golden Hind,* he attacked and plundered numerous Spanish vessels, including the heavily-laden treasure ships *San Cristobel* and *Nuestra Señora de la Concepción,* both mighty galleons many times the size of his own. He slipped one dark night into the harbour at Calleo, largest in Peru, and in the panic which ensued when dawn's early light revealed his identity, calmly boarded the most promising of thirty ships anchored there, and looted and burned her before sailing out with all guns booming. Further north, he seized and temporarily occupied the town of Guatulco, where he left his friend da Silva among friendly fellow Catholics.

Drake sailed out of Guatulco on 13 April and remained at sea until 17 June when he landed at a place which he named Nova Albion, and which we now know as Drake's Bay, very close to the modern city of San Francisco. Here he off-loaded his huge cargo of gold and silver and precious stones in order to careen and repair his leaking ship and to rest his weary crew. Five weeks later, he sailed to the west and fetched Ladrones Island, north of the Moluccas or Spice Islands, on 30 September. Drake lingered in the lush islands long enough to buy six tons of cloves but although the local sultan begged him to stay, and although the

Golden Hind was badly in need of careening and overhaul, Drake sailed on in search of an isolated shore on which he could beach his ship far away from hostile eyes. He finally came upon an uninhabited island south of Celebes, which he named Crab Island, and made it his base for four weeks. Afterwards, and having been the first of his nation's voyagers ever to sail the Pacific, Drake became the first Englishman to sail the Indian Ocean. On 12 December 1579, one day short of exactly two years since leaving home, Drake left Crab Island. Less than a month later, during the night of 9 January the *Golden Hind* was driven aground on one of Indonesia's many reefs and with the single exception of Drake himself, every man on board gave himself up as lost. 'Of all the dangers that in our whole voyage we met with,' wrote the chaplain, 'this was the greatest.' But Drake had no time for such faint-hearted resignation. He bullied the men unmercifully until his ship was refloated and could be laboured on to a haven in Java, which they reached on 12 March. Sailing again, *Golden Hind* rounded the Cape of Good Hope on 14 June and five weeks later, with both water and provisions run desperately low, they fetched Sierra Leone. With the end in sight, Drake came to anchor in Plymouth Sound on 26 September 1580 and so became (as Magellan died before he completed his voyage) the first fleet commander in history to circumnavigate the world.

GOLDEN HIND

BRITISH

Royal Prince

CERTAINLY ONE of the most interesting ever built in England, this great man-o'-war was launched in 1610 as the *Prince Royal,* and ended her very long life in 1666 with the name of *Royal Prince.* Few vessels could ever have been the subject of more controversy. In the first place, she was the brain-child of a young Phineas Pett, a fact which of itself gives rise to speculation.

Between 1560 and 1660 the Pett family produced four generations of shipwrights, and as most of the male offspring were christened either Phineas or Peter, the result was often confusing. As, indeed, were the Petts themselves. Contemporary aspersions as to their professional abilities varied between the darkest of hints and the most violent of accusations. Competence aside, they certainly fell short on integrity. In an age when bribery and corruption had become an accepted way of life, they were masters of survival. Design of their ships, all of which were built to a secret rule-of-thumb, were inevitably subject to hit-or-miss, and many other shipwrights hotly disputed their worth.

It was against this background that, in 1607, the current Phineas Pett conceived the notion of building a warship bigger and better than any then afloat in the northern hemisphere. There is little doubt that his primary concern was to make a lot of money but he produced, although thanks in large measure to his partner and co-designer William Bright, a ship which remains almost unparalleled in terms of longevity. Built, re-built, and modified yet again, she was destined to sail and fight over a span of 56 years.

During the reign of Elizabeth the First (1558–1603), England's greatest queen, the island's sea power became virtually undisputed. Her unworthy successor, James I, was made of lesser stuff. A man of strong homosexual tendencies (in spite of having fathered six children) James was largely consumed by his personal pleasures, and he permitted the navy to drift into a backwater of neglect. In 1607, only four years after he ascended the throne, the number of royal ships had dwindled to a mere 27, and many of these were rotting and useless. So, with the ship-building business deep in the doldrums, Phineas set his plot in motion by presenting Prince Henry, James's younger son, with the beautiful model of a mighty warship called – and what else? – the *Prince Royal.* The ploy was blatantly sycophantic, but it worked. The young prince was delighted with the model and King James, in spite of knowing for a fact that the man had swindled him on more than one occasion, issued Pett with an order to build the full-scale article. There was loud and bitter

protest from Parliament but the Lord High Admiral, Lord Howard, Earl of Nottingham, was a crony of the Petts, and Phineas got the job.

It really was the most astonishing example of corruption in high places because although the Pett family had been building ships for 50 years or more, Phineas himself had very little experience. He had in fact, only ever designed two ships, and one of these was a small 25-foot replica of *Ark Royal* presented to James's eldest son Edward in order to curry royal favour; the other, a ship he built for himself using materials misappropriated from the king's own yards. This one he loaded with stores and cannon, also stolen, and sold to England's arch enemy, Spain. However, he was permitted to go ahead with the ambitious project, and *Prince Royal* was laid down at Woolwich in 1608. She was to have a length at keel of 115 feet, be 135 feet on her main deck, 43 feet on the beam, and have a hull depth of 18 feet. The largest ship ever built in England, she was the first to have a hull double-planked overall and her bulkheads double-bolted with iron. Her 55 guns, weighing a total of over 80 tons, were to be mounted on three decks, whereas previously there had never been more than two. She was not, however, a true three-decker, as the upper tier was mounted under a half-deck and the fo'c'sle deck. Her gross weight burthen was said to be 1,330 tons, but measured by modern standards was probably closer to 1,200. She was rigged at first with four masts, having lateen sails on both mizzen and bonaventure-mizzen. Although the several excellent paintings of *Prince Royal* depict her in various guises, there is no reason to doubt that each is an accurate portrayal of her as she appeared at the relevant time. The two most famous canvases were painted by the celebrated Dutch marine artist Hendrik Cornelisz Vroom, one in 1613 when she first visited Flushing and the other in 1623, some time after her first big refit, when she visited Holland again.

Prince Royal was of course conceived as a showpiece and a status symbol, a mighty galleon superior in size and firepower to any other in Europe, and she did in fact go on to acquit herself reasonably well. Nevertheless, she was built in a storm of dissent and criticism, subject to inquiries by no fewer than three royal commisions, the final one being chaired by the king himself. Just one enormous blunder by Pett – and not, one suspects by William Bright – was his calculation that the ship would require 775 cartloads of timber. In the end, she used up more than double this number, a massive 1,627. Even so, experts sitting on the commissions pointed variously to serious faults in design, and

Pett was accused of using cheap and inferior materials. After an inspection by independent shipwrights whilst she was still in frame at Woolwich, it was said that her construction embodied 'gross errors and absurdities', not least being that her frames were sawn out of straight timbers and so, being cross-grained, were dangerously weak. It was also claimed that her scarfs were too short, and that while some of her planks were green and unseasoned, others were rotten with age. Some naval architects warned that the upper tier of guns, together with excessive top-hamper, would render the ship crank and unweatherly. Pett blandly refuted all of these criticisms, but subsequent events proved beyond all doubt that some were quite well-founded.

There cannot ever have been a ship more plagued during her construction than King James's *Prince Royal.* The king's casual acceptance of her ever-increasing cost became something of a national scandal. The sums involved were staggering. Those extra 775 loads of timber added £5,908 to Pett's original estimate, and he had the gall in the end to present the king with a bill for £20,000. To offer some idea of the enormity of this sum, a good sound ship, the *Merhonour,* launched shortly before *Prince Royal* and of almost the same size, had been built and delivered under contract for £3,600. It is true that *Merhonour* had none of the *Prince*'s elaborate decoration but the cost of this, though relatively huge, accounted for only a fraction of the difference. Examination of documents in the Public Records Office in London show that one Sebastian Vicars, was paid £441 for wood carvings, and that £868 was paid to the craftsmen responsible for painting and gilding.

Pett seems to have been impervious to the raging controversy. He could do no wrong in the eyes of Nottingham and the king, and was strongly supported by the young Prince Henry whose opinions, although completely bereft of any expertise, carried a lot of weight. Work on the ship went on, and she was ready for launching in 1610. Came the great day, what was to have been a joyous occasion turned out to be a disaster. Built in the Woolwich dry dock, it was discovered at the last moment that *Royal Prince* could not be floated for the simple reason that she was too wide to pass through the dock gates; yet more expense when they had to be widened.

It is apparent from accounts of her fitting-out that much more care was lavished on *Prince Royal*'s embellishments than was put into her basic construction. Ships of war had long been richly decorated, but this one set a whole new standard both within and without. Her figurehead was a great carving of St George

ROYAL PRINCE

ROYAL PRINCE

slaying the dragon and above this, on top of the fore-rail, a large knight's helmet surmounted by a crown. The great profusion of wood sculptures on her three huge stern galleries included intricate carvings of the Prince of Wales' feathers, to glorify Henry, and the lion and unicorn for the glory of his father King James. More than £1,300 was expended on sumptuous but worthless adornment, yet not one penny on sheathing. Pett excused himself in this respect by pointing to the then-well-known fact that sea water created in sheet lead a galvanic action which corroded and weakened the iron pintles securing the rudder. It was a specious argument. Years earlier, Hawkins and other of the great Elizabethans had effectively protected their ships against the ravages of the toredo worm by a double-planking of hulls beneath the water line and packing the cavity with a mixture of horse-hair and tar. Pett could easily and cheaply have implemented this measure because *Prince Royal* was double-planked throughout, and it seems amazing that he neglected to do so. Even more amazing, though, is the fact that copper – discovered and used in the late Stone Age by Neolithic man – was not employed for the sheathing of ships' bottoms until HMS *Alarm* became the first in 1761.

In any event, this and other of Pett's oversights, deliberate and/or otherwise, were soon to prove expensive. As the experts had predicted, serious faults soon made themselves manifest, and barely 10 years after her launching *Prince Royal* was back in dock at Woolwich for a refit so extensive it cost over £6,000. Not much less than the price, in those days, of *two* first-class merchantmen. It was after this first of her major refits that Hendrik Vroom made his second painting, and this shows significant modification of her superstructure; also, a switch from lateen to square rig on both mizzen and bonaventure.

Prince Royal never really distinguished herself in battle, serving instead as a powerful emblem and deterrent. Almost 30 years were to elapse before the building in England of her superior in size or majesty, and they were years of relative peace. Only once in her very long life was the *Prince* seen outside of her northern home waters, on a peaceful visit to Spain. Her end, when at last it came, was sadly inglorious. It happened on 3 June 1666, in the second year of the Second Dutch War, during a battle which became known as the Four Days Fight.

The English fleet under joint command of Monck and Prince Rupert was ranged against the allied forces of Holland and France, and expecting attack from both sources the ships were deployed on two fronts. Rupert sailed west to engage the French, and Monck sailed east to take on de Ruyter. It was a most disastrous mistake. The French never appeared and de Ruyter, faced by only half of the English fleet, achieved a momentous victory. This is not to disparage that great seaman de Ruyter, who said: 'If we can but defeat the English divided, how can we hope to defeat them united?' The answer came seven weeks later on 25 July in a battle off the North Foreland. Monck and Rupert, now together, visited a terrible vengeance upon de Ruyter, and drove the Dutch off the seas.

In the meantime, however, the English had suffered heavy losses. During the third day of the Four Days Fight, *Royal Prince* was driven aground on the Galloper Sands 20 miles off the coast of East Anglia, and forced to surrender. The crew, including her flag-commander Sir George Ayscue, were taken prisoner, and their ship was set alight and burned.

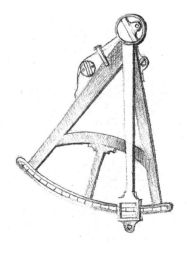

Sovereign of the Seas

So far as ships under sail are concerned, the *Sovereign of the Seas* was certainly the most revolutionary man-o'-war ever built in England, and probably in the world. Not only yet another biggest and best, she was so marvellously innovative as to set a basic pattern for the construction of large warships which endured for well over 200 years, until the end of the age of sail. The first-ever real, full three-decker, her hull was triple-planked and she was rigged so tall, in conservative ship building opinion, as to cause very serious alarm. It was said at the time that the sail plan for her three masts, which included the unheard-of addition of royals on the fore and main, was impractical and rash to the point of madness. She was the only ship in the entire English fleet to carry royals, and they did not become a general feature of warships until 150 years later, in the final quarter of the 18th century. Another item of the *Sovereign*'s rig which remained unique to her over very many years was a topgallant sail on her mizzen. Adjunctive to her spritsail, she carried a further small, square sail on a precarious-looking sprit topmast (which also bore the jackstaff) and this, before the introduction of the foremast stay-sail, would be used to bring the head about during manoeuvring and tacking.

So much for her rig. When it came to hull design, the *Sovereign of the Seas* set a pattern and a standard for every English capital ship which followed her launching in 1637 and the gradual introduction, around 250 years later, of steam. With her first-ever, rounded stern, and bereft of her long beak and sprit topmast, she would not have looked out of place fighting alongside HMS *Victory* at Trafalgar in 1805 or even, 50 years later, with the ships which did battle at the Crimea. All were mighty war machines carrying 100 guns on three full flush decks, and their profiles would not have been too dissimilar. The *Sovereign* was laid down with a keel measuring 127 feet, but this was lengthened when she was 14 years old to 136. Her main gun deck was 168 feet long, and her total length from beak head to taffrail was 234. She had a beam of 48 feet, and towered 63 feet from the bottom of her keel to the top of her lantern – a lantern so enormous it could comfortably accommodate 12 men standing inside. Reckoned originally to be a ship of 1,637 tons burthen, a figure which coincided perhaps a shade too precisely with the year of her launching, an Admiralty list of 1652 has her down as being of 1,141 tons and with a crew of 600 men. This last statistic would appear to support a school of thought which proposes that *Sovereign* was cut

down at her major refit the previous year from three decks to two; but another group of naval historians remains quite convinced that although she lost some of her superstructure, the *Sovereign* remained a full three-decker right to the end of her days.

No matter, she still represented a tremendous leap forward in size, design and fire-power, features made all the more remarkable for having been conceived by that same Phineas Pett who 25 years earlier had created such a furore in the land by his terrible work on *Prince Royal*. Now, aided and abetted by his son Peter, he appeared to be at his mischief again, and it was doubtless in the light of this that his proposals for the *Sovereign* were met by a similar storm of protest. Pett had persuaded James I to invest in *Prince Royal* by first beguiling him with a beautiful model of the ship he proposed to build. This time, with King Charles I, he went one step further. He created another fine model, but this one all the more ingenious for having parts of the hull cut away in order to show all forms of the structure within. Charles was mightily intrigued, but those around him, whose duty it was to advise him, roundly condemned Pett's design. Foremost among the critics were the powerful Elder Brethren of Trinity House which was a highly-respected body, founded by Henry VIII for the training of pilots and ships' officers and later made responsible by Elizabeth for lighthouses, beacons, and seamarks. Its judgment of plans for the *Sovereign* was expressed in a letter, still extant, to the king's principal secretary:

'The art and wit of man can not build a ship well conditioned and fit for service with three tier of ordnance . . .' The Brethren went on to assert that no port in the kingdom, except perhaps the Isle of Wight, was big enough to harbour so large a ship, and '. . . it followeth, if she be not in port then she is in continual danger, exposed to all tempests and storms that time shall bring. In a desperate estate she rides in every storm; in peril she must ride, when all the rest of her companions (His Majesty's ships) enjoys peace, rides quiet and safe in port . . . Yet anchors and cables must hold proportion, and being made, they will not be manageable, the strength of man can not wield nor work them, but could they do it, yet the ship little bettered in point of safety, for we are doubtful whether cables and anchors can hold a ship of this bulk in a great storm.'

Events were to prove that the Brethren were quite wrong in their somewhat excessive condemnation, because the king turned a blind eye to it. Charles I took a great interest in his navy,

and was prepared to spend huge sums on its maintenance and expansion. So much so, in fact, that his raising of special taxes to provide what he called his Ship Money was a major one of the many grievances which gave rise to the Civil War. It was an irony of fate that once the internecine struggle broke out, almost all of his splendid ships and their crews remained under the control of Parliament.

However, Charles contrived during his reign to build more and better royal ships than any monarch preceding him. He reigned from 1625–49, and the *Sovereign of the Seas* being his crowning achievement, he had her adorned in so riotous an exuberance of decoration as to make even *Henri Grace à Dieu* and *Prince Royal* pale into insignificance. The only part of her freeboard left plain was her main or lower gun deck, and that part of the middle gun deck for'ard of the side galleries. All the rest, from beak head to taffrail, was one vast intertwining of carving and so much of it covered with glittering gold leaf that the Dutch, who had good cause to know and fear her, called her 'The Golden Devil'.

There stood at her beak head, beneath the bowsprit, a huge equestrian statue of King Edgar trampling under his horse's hooves the bodies of seven kings, and behind and above this the stem head was crowned with a gilded figure of Cupid riding upon a pouncing lion. Her fore-rails and fo'c'sle head presented a solid mass of heraldic devices, and a carved frieze running along the entire length of the upper gun deck was composed of stands of arms and the accoutrements of war. Her stern and galleries were embellished overall with a vast profusion of crests and figures; gods and godesses twice as large as life, caryatids and mermaids, dolphins and satyrs. Lions, unicorns, dragons and greyhounds chased each other through an endless flowing of swags and garlands which included the roses of England, the thistles of Scotland, and the fluer-de-lys of France. No such lavish display of majesty had ever been seen before, or was ever seen again, and the cost was astrononomical.

When King James paid Phineas Pett £20,000 for his earlier great ship the *Prince Royal*, there ran through the corridors of Parliament a wave of shock and horror. The final bill for the *Sovereign of the Seas* was in the sum of £65,586. 16s. 9½d. Of this, no less than £6,981 was spent on decoration. Fifteen years later an extensive refit cost well over £6,000 bringing her total cost – apart from the ongoing expense of manning and maintenance –

SOVEREIGN OF THE SEAS

to around £72,000. A hard-working farmhand or labouring man of that time would be lucky to earn £3 *a year*.

But the *Sovereign* was not merely a ship, she was the visible symbol of a nation's wealth and power. Further, her name was deliberately intended to suggest a maritime dominance by England which in fact was not to come until the passing of more than a century, and in the meantime her neighbours across the Channel were not only able but perfectly willing to dispute the arrogant boast. The Dutch were masters in the art of building ships, and her seamen were second to none, and a growing rivalry between the two countries made a clash inevitable. This became manifest in three separate conflicts; the First Dutch War of 1652–54, the Second of 1665–67, and the Third of 1672–73. *Sovereign of the Seas* saw action in all three. Battle honours in the first two of these wars were divided, with both sides sustaining heavy losses, but in hindsight the final outcome was entirely predictable. Holland was a relatively small country with few natural resources and not nearly so large a population, and when after a disastrous period of unrest and two Civil Wars (1642–60) England was firmly re-united, the contest became plainly uneven.

There can be no doubt that, whether or not engaged in any particular battle, *Sovereign of the Seas* played a major role in all of the wars which took place during the course of her extremely long life. Just like the mighty 20th-century German battleships lurking in unknown fjords and harbours, she represented a constant threat without which there could be no reckoning. Her armament was unprecedented. She was the first ship in the world to carry 100 truck-mounted guns, and their deployment was brilliantly conceived. All three of her gun decks were flush without falls, a facility of enormous advantage in the discharging of broadsides. She was powerful also in attack and defence both astern and up for'ard with guns known as fore- and stern-chasers. Each of her gun decks was equipped to maximise firepower; on the main, 28 heavy cannon; on the middle, 24 broadside cannon and six light chasers; on the upper, 24 broadside cannon and four lighter chasers, all of the latter mounted up front. The remaining 12 guns were mounted in the waist under heavy gratings, giving *Sovereign* the appearance at first glance of a four-decker.

This was the ship with which Phineas Pett, aided by his son, vindicated himself for all of the errors he had made in the building of *Prince Royal*. It might reasonably be argued that the *Sovereign of the Seas* represented the point at which England began a hundred-years progress towards the historic *pax Britannica*. Meanwhile, the great ship survived five wars and underwent two changes of name. Under Cromwell she became, quite simply, the *Sovereign*. After the Restoration, she was re-named the *Royal Sovereign*. It was during the interim that Cromwell had her stripped of all those trappings of royalty which had made her so glorious a spectacle. In 1651, a commissioners' report suggested:

'... that as to the *Soveraigne* wee conceive that to make her more serviceable .. the gratings and upper-decke in the mid-shippe bee taken down .. the upper state room to bee taken away, the forecastle to be lored to six foote high and the works abaft to be taken down proportionably to the waist .. the half decke to be shortened .. alsoe the head to be made shorter .. and the galleryes to bee altered as may be comely and most convenient for service.' – an archive which lends strong support to those who now believe that, in spite of a heavy cutting-down, she never did lose her top deck.

After an active life even longer than that of *Prince Royal,* the end of this marvellous man-o'-war was made premature by accident. Due to a candle left burning in his cabin, a nameless cook was the cause of a disastrous fire, and she was burned at the age of 60 whilst lying at anchor in the Medway, in 1697.

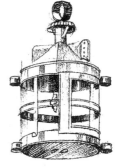

SOVEREIGN OF THE SEAS

HMS *Victory*

NELSON'S *Victory* was not the first of His Majesty's Ships to bear that name. It had been passed on, as was and is the custom, and the first-rate laid down at Chatham on 23 July 1750 was the fifth in line. Her construction was oddly spasmodic over a period of almost exactly 15 years, and she was not launched until 7 May 1765. Of 2,162 tons, her gun deck was 186 feet long, 34 feet longer than her keel. She had a beam of 52 feet, and depth to hold of $21\frac{1}{2}$ feet. The armament she mounted varied considerably over the span of her active life, but consisted at Trafalgar of 108 guns: on her lower deck, 30, 32-pounders; middle deck, 28, 24-pounders; main deck, 30, 12-pounders; quarter deck, 12, 12-pounders; forecastle, six 12-pounders, and two 68-pound carronades. Before an extensive refit carried out in 1803, the guns on her lower deck were heavier, all of them 42-pounders. A first-rate of this size would normally ship a crew of 837 men.

The *Victory* saw no action until 1778, when she was the flagship of Admiral Keppel in his indecisive battle with D'Orvilliers off Ushant on 27 July. She saw action again in 1781, and again off Ushant, this time wearing the flag of Admiral Kempenfelt, having taken part the previous year in the Relief of Gibraltar under Lord Howe. Lord Hood commanded *Victory* during the evacuation of Toulon in 1793, but it was under the flag of Admiral Sir John Jervis that she first really lived up to her name in the Battle of Cape St Vincent in 1797. She was given to Admiral Lord Nelson upon his appointment to Commander-in-Chief, Mediterranean in 1803, and apart from one or two very brief periods he spent the rest of his life on board.

That *Victory* was a splendid three-decker under sail is witnessed by the succession of illustrious flags she wore, and although her name is forever linked with that of Nelson, this is her story and not primarily his. Sir John Jervis was another redoubtable seaman, and when in 1797 he commanded the English fleet at the Battle of Cape St Vincent, he rose to the occasion with distinction.

Apparently forgetful of the crushing defeats inflicted by Drake in 1588 and by Tromp in 1639, Spain signed a treaty with France in 1795 and declared itself at war with England in October of 1796. In February 1797 Jervis was patrolling England's long-time favourite hunting ground, the waters off that rocky headland at the south-western tip of Portugal known as Cape St Vincent. The Spaniards, hitherto reluctant to engage the English at sea, had ventured out of port to escort a convoy of merchantmen with 27 ships of the line, including the *Santissima Trinidad* of 136 guns, by far the biggest man-of-war in the world. Jervis in *Victory* attacked this great fleet with just 15 sail of the line one of which, HMS *Captain*, flew the pendent of Commodore H Nelson. It was a battle reminiscent of David and Goliath, with Jervis outnumbered two to one. The action began around noon, and all was over in two or three hours with the Spaniards soundly defeated. Nelson in *Captain* had taken two Spanish ships, the *San Joseph* of 112 guns and the *San Nicholas* of 80 guns, and the *Santissima Trinidad* struck her colours in surrender. She thus avoided possible sinking, and afterwards escaped being taken as a prize. In recognition of his great St Valentine's Day victory his grateful monarch elevated Jervis to the peerage with the title Earl of St Vincent.

Nelson hoisted his flag in *Victory* in 1803, and smart and clean after her refit, she sailed from Spithead on 20 May. Her gun decks would have been given a fresh coat of red paint (to minimise the psychological effect on her gunners when the footing became awash with blood) and the yellow bands along her hull doubtless bright as gold. But the blood which was shed in the heat of battle was only a part of it, and Nelson's devotion to his flag-captain Hardy reveals a curious anomaly of character not easily excused. It is quite evident from *Victory*'s log, and not a little from contemporary portraits, that Hardy was a harsh and cruel man. In the eighteen months between July 1803 and December 1804 he ordered a staggering 380 punishments by the lash, including three of 'flogging around the fleet'. The men, William Brown, John Marshall, and Richard Collins, were each sentenced to 200 lashes, 50 alongside *Victory*, and 50 alongside each of three other ships. Whilst it is true that the captain of a flagship remains in entire command of all administration it is equally true that Nelson, never an excessive flogger himself, could easily have intervened. Flogging in the navy was not fully suspended until 1879.

But whereas the men on *Victory*'s lower deck lived lives no better than those of some animals, the admiral's 'family' on the quarterdeck lived in considerable style. They rose at six o'clock and took a gentle stroll up top before sitting down to a lavish breakfast of tea, hot rolls, cold meats and preserves. Dinner served promptly on the stroke of six bells (three o'clock) consisted of three main courses and a dessert of choice fruits, each course accompanied by a different vintage wine. The 'family' went to bed when Nelson went to bed, not later than nine o'clock.

In 1804, when she was persuaded by Napoleon to renew her war against England, Spain can only be described as a veritable glutton for punishment. Nelson regarded the Spaniards with contempt, and had little more respect for the French. He was exasperated by their practice of running away from a fight, and ached to get to grips with them. After several abortive attempts to do so, he returned to England arriving on 18 August, 1805. There he spent just over three weeks on shore and it was during his final day in London that he met, for the first and only time, the future Duke of Wellington.

Back on board *Victory*, Nelson hoist his flag and sailed out of Portsmouth on Sunday 15 September. The combined fleets under overall command of the French admiral Villeneuve in *Bucentaure*, a total of 35 sail of the line, were safe in harbour at Cadiz, and Nelson took up station off the Costa de la Luz. Villeneuve ventured out of his sanctuary on 19 October, bound for a passage through the Straits of Gibraltar into the Mediterranean. Nelson gave hot chase. Villeneuve's nerve failed him on the approaches to the straits, and he ordered a return to Cadiz. It was a fatal error. On that morning of the 21st, Nelson had the wind in his favour, and the Spanish commodore in his ship the *San Juan Nepomuceno* is on record as having said – 'our fleet is doomed'.

He was right. The English men-of-war, inferior both in size and number but far superior in experience, fighting spirit, seamanship and gunnery, fought a battle off Cabo Trafalgar which, so far as the combined fleets were concerned, ended in disaster. First in magnitude among their ships destroyed and sunk was the mighty *Santissima Trinidad* (*Trinidada*), lucky escaper after her previous surrender to the English at the Battle of Cape St Vincent. After being engaged by *Victory*, Villeneuve surrendered *Bucentaure*, and both he and his ship were taken.

But the English, too, suffered a disaster. At about a quarter past one in the afternoon, with the battle only two hours old and not yet won, *Victory* was disengaged from the *Bucentaure* and fighting hard almost scuppers-on with the French ship *Redoubtable*. Nelson, with his customary and some say foolhardy disregard for personal safety was directing the conflict from an exposed position up on the quarterdeck and must, in a uniform bedecked with all the trappings of his rank, have presented a fine, prime target. An unknown and forever unsung musketeer took aim from one of *Redoubtable*'s fighting-tops, and Nelson fell mortally wounded with a leaden ball in his breast.

Victory's last fighting action took place in the Baltic in October 1812, and after being paid off in Portsmouth before the end of that year, she never went to sea again. She was docked for repair in 1814 and emerged two years later with a built-up bow and, among many other alterations, the bands along her gunports painted white instead of yellow. Used then as a floating utility for over a hundred years on, she was moved to dry dock in 1922, when work began to restore her to the condition and appearance she had at Trafalgar. Flagship in her time of half a dozen famous admirals, including the most famous of all, HMS *Victory* is preserved today at Portsmouth, more than two hundred years after her launching, viewed and admired by visitors from many parts of the world.

HMS VICTORY

HMS *Bounty*

OF ALL THE numerous mutinies at sea, that which took place in HMS *Bounty* on 28 April 1789 is probably the most widely known. Unfortunately, the actual details have been obscured by a welter of foolish romanticism in poetry (such as Byron's *The Island*), in stories and in films and even as recently as 1985, in a musical play on stage. But the proper truth of the matter has long been sadly neglected, and, as may be seen from a sober examination of Navy records, fact and fiction are worlds apart; the line between hero and villain is not easily drawn.

Until she was chosen for the mission which made her famous, HMS *Bounty* was a small and unimportant merchantman of only 220 tons with a length from stem to stern of 90 feet and a beam of 24. Built privately and launched as the *Bethia*, she was sold to the Royal Navy by none other than the uncle of her future captain, and re-named HMS *Bounty* when first she was commissioned. Although she cost the Navy more to rebuild and refit than the price originally paid for her, she remained a three-masted transport square-rigged on the fore and the main, and with a lateen sail on her mizzen.

When she sailed out of Bristol under Royal Navy colours in the wintry December of 1787, her commander William Bligh was thirty-three years old and already well embarked upon a distinguished naval career. He had been sailing master under Captain Cook of HMS *Resolution* during the celebrated explorer's second voyage of discovery 1772–74, and it was indeed this same experience with Cook which prompted his appointment three years later as commander of the ill-fated voyage which made his name, and that of his ship, a byword of seafaring history. In his official 1874 report to the Admiralty, Cook had described the staple diet of the Otaheite islanders as '. . . a natural "bread-fruit", growing abundantly, simple to prepare, and extremely nourishing.' To the sugar planters of the newly-founded West Indies, this sounded like a veritable gift from heaven; a very cheap and easy means by which to feed their growing numbers of African slaves. So, Captain Bligh's orders could hardly have been more straightforward: he was to sail directly to Otaheite (Tahiti), take on board several hundreds of pot-planted breadfruit saplings, transport the healthy young trees to Jamaica, and then return to home port.

All apparently quite simple, but trouble developed fast. Heavy storms south-west of the Canary Islands battered *Bounty* off course, and a subversive element in the crew of 44 officers and men was responsible for endless mischief. Food lockers were broken into and reserve supplies wantonly pillaged, and Bligh, a strict though not unduly harsh disciplinarian, was moved to dole out punishment. Then having brought his ship safely to a landfall at Tenerife, where she lay for five days, Bligh was determined to make up for lost time by heading direct for the Pacific islands via the perilous Cape Horn route. His men wanted a longer stay at Tenerife, and to go on then via the much longer but infinitely safer and more comfortable passage around the Cape of Good Hope, but Bligh, a master seaman of the highest order, knew that if *Bounty* was to avoid the worst of the South Atlantic storm season he must press on without delay. He set a course for South America and after crossing the Line on 10 February 1788 he promoted the 25-year-old Fletcher Christian, who had sailed with him on two previous voyages, to the rank of lieutenant. This act might now be seen as an attempt to pre-empt his junior officer's loyalty, but such would be taking advantage of hindsight. Fletcher Christian greatly admired his captain's masterly knowledge of ships and the sea, but being himself of a free and easy disposition, he was resentful of Bligh's rigid adherence to the rules of navy conduct.

Their differences of opinion constituted a recipe for a disaster which first began to manifest itself when *Bounty*, beaten off from Cape Horn by gales and mountainous seas, was forced to put up helm and turn back east to make the long and weary passage by the Cape of Good Hope. But the map-maker Bligh, knowing exactly where he was and so being aware of all the hazards ahead, ordered every man on board (not excluding himself) to go on short rations. As he beat eastwards, the storms continued and conditions on board grew worse. In brief periods of calm, the crew fished for any and everything they could catch, and even went so far as to trap and eat that bird of ill omen, the albatross. It was a stormy passage in more ways than one, but Bligh eventually brought his ship to anchor under Table Mountain in the third week of May, 1788. Knowing full well that his crew was in ferment, he stayed at the cape until all were refreshed and his small ship completely reprovisioned before setting sail yet again for Tahiti, still almost three thousand miles away across the Indian Ocean. With no shortage this time of essential victuals, he fetched Tasmania (then known as Van Dieman's Land) on 13 August. He rested there for two weeks, and finally sighted Tahiti towards the end of October, ten months after leaving England.

Having at last reached her first destination, *Bounty* lay at anchor off the idyllic island for almost six months whilst Mr Nelson, the botanist, collected several hundred breadfruit saplings and established their growth in small wooden casks. In the long meantime, the seamen were permitted to desport themselves ashore with the free-loving female natives, and looking back over a distance of time it seems obvious that this, more than any other factor, brought about the mutiny which followed. The puritanical Bligh did not permit himself that licence which he gave to his crew – a licence indulged especially by Christian Fletcher – and wanted only to fulfill his assignment: to take on the saplings and proceed with all dispatch to Jamaica. It must, for the conscientious Bligh, have been a period of extreme frustration. The native islanders, knowing nothing of property or theft, stole any and every item of chandlery left lying around by the careless crew, and Bligh was driven almost to distraction. The last straw came when the boatswain, Mr Cole, heedlessly 'lost' a gudgeon. Bligh had Cole flogged, and ordered that he be kept in irons for the rest of *Bounty*'s stay in Tahiti which, unfortunately for the bosun, turned out to be a further three months. The ship's surgeon, a fat and lazy drunken profligate named Huggan died in Tahiti from his excesses and some of the crew, beginning now to show symptoms of social disease, vented their frustrations in endless brawling. Some of them, wanting to stay forever in Tahiti, cut *Bounty*'s anchor cable during a storm, hoping that the ship would be wrecked. Bligh foiled the plot, and sailed out of Tahiti on 4 April, 1789.

Three weeks later, Bligh put in at the Friendly Islands in order to top up his extra-large, fresh water facility with which *Bounty* had been specially fitted out, and to build up maximum supplies of fresh food. So laden, *Bounty* left the islands on 27 April, and as the mutiny took place when she was barely one day out, the facts make a nonsense of the widely-believed myth that it was sparked off by men driven mad by thirst. The truth is, Christian seized the ship following a trivial incident involving the theft of a few coconuts. He and three accomplices, Charles Churchill, Alex Smith and Thomas Burkitt, burst into Bligh's cabin shortly before sunrise on the 28th and dragged the captain up top. The other twelve active mutineers had raided the arms locker and taken possession of the ship's weapons. After clearing the lower deck, Christian announced to the ship's company that he was taking over command. The launch was hoist out and provisioned with 150 pounds of bread, a little pork, 28 gallons of water, a compass and a quadrant, and several cutlasses. When Bligh was forced to step down into the launch, far too many of the crew than the boat could possibly accommodate opted to take their slim chances with the captain rather than stay in *Bounty*

HMS BOUNTY

HMS BOUNTY

with the mutineers. Most significantly, Mr Cole the boatswain. Those permitted to throw in their lots with Bligh included Cole, the ship's chief carpenter, Mr Nelson the botanist, assistant surgeon Fryer Ledward, and two midshipmen, Hayward and Hallet. 18 people cast adrift in a 23 foot open boat intended for no more than 12. It must have seemed to Christian that none could possibly survive, but he reckoned without the superhuman grit and determination of Captain William Bligh.

Bligh had the boat's small sail hoisted and set a course for the volcanic island of Tofoa, thirty miles away. As they were gathering coconuts there, his men were attacked by natives and one of them was killed. This incident decided Bligh to head directly for the Dutch settlement on Timor, over 3,000 miles away. They had normal rations for seven days, and in order to make them last seven weeks, each man was allocated one ounce of bread, one tiny piece of pork, and a quarter of a pint of water per day. So provisioned, Bligh set out on 2 May 1789 to cross a vast expanse of ocean equivalent in distance to that of the North Atlantic. With little or no shelter from a blazing tropical sun, the men suffered agonies of thirst, but even when violent rainstorms permitted a gathering in sailcloth of sweet fresh water, Bligh insisted upon maintaining strict rations. Attempts to catch fish resulted in total failure, although four seabirds were caught and

eaten on 22 and 23 May, two of them with fish in their stomachs. Then, after almost a month on storm-lashed open sea, they came upon salvation in the form of a tiny uncharted islet.

They explored the three-miles wide strip of land which Bligh named Resolution Island, finding fruits, berries, oysters and fresh water. There were native huts, but no inhabitants. Bligh forbade his men to eat from any unfamiliar tree or bush, but three of them defied the order and became violently ill. And it was here, with food of sorts in fair abundance, Bligh was furious to find that someone was stealing from their tiny reserve of pork. He made a stew of that which remained and, dividing it equally, said: 'Better that we eat it now than the despicable thief amongst us steal it all.' Then, fearful that those who had built the huts might return, he ordered a departure from the island. The men were reluctant to leave their haven, but Bligh insisted and it was as well that he did. On embarking, they narrowly escaped a sudden attack by a fleet of native canoes and on 3 June, and thanks to Bligh's superb navigation, made a landfall at Cape York on the northern tip of Australia.

But there was still another 1,200 miles to go, and this huge remaining expanse of ocean proved the roughest of all to cross. Miraculously, the survivors endured a further seven weeks of near-constant bailing before finally reaching the Dutch settle-

ment at Coupang in Timor after sailing their tiny open boat a total of more than 3,600 miles. The 17 living skeletons who staggered ashore at Coupang towards the end of July, all skin and bone and covered in sores, were treated by the Dutch with the utmost kindness, but Mr Nelson the botanist succumbed and died. All were suffering from exposure and extreme malnutrition, but the indomitable Bligh would allow only a minimum of rest. The Dutch lent him a ship, and he and his remaining men set sail on 20 August bound at first for Java. Here, Bligh himself fell seriously ill, and two more of his men died from the aftereffects of their terrible deprivations. Still, however, Bligh would not properly rest. He and those who were left with him took passage on 2 October in a Dutch ship bound for Europe. Yet another two of the original eighteen castaways died on the voyage home, but Bligh returned to a hero's welcome in England, still enormously determined to see Fletcher Christian and the *Bounty* mutineers sought out and brought to justice.

That which actually happened to Fletcher Christian and his fellow conspirators is a separate and far from happy story, but William Bligh went on to pursue a highly-successful career during which he became Captain General and Governor of New South Wales and which culminated, in 1814, with his appointment to the rank of Vice Admiral.

HMS *Endeavour*

THE SHIP WHICH became famous as HMS *Endeavour* was launched at Whitby in Yorkshire, one of that breed known as Geordie Brigs, sturdy little coal-ships or colliers built to withstand the buffeting seas up and down the east coast of England. Of 368 tons, she was flat-bottomed with very stout scantling, 106 feet long and about 30 feet on the beam. When purchased or 'bought in' by the Royal Navy at Deptford on 28 March 1768, she was given a major refit which included the laying on of another deck to provide for cabin accommodation. As the *Earl of Pembroke* she had been rigged as a bark, but when the navy re-launched her under her new name she was square-rigged overall. The aim of the Admiralty was to provide a vessel for a twofold mission: first to observe from a position off Tahiti the transit of Venus, part of a large, scientific exercise to try and determine the distance of the earth from the sun; and second, to carry out an ambitious voyage of discovery. The man chosen to command this expedition was James Cook, a brilliant, natural genius and quite possibly the most remarkable figure in the whole of British naval history.

Son of a humble farm worker, Cook first went to sea in 1746 when he was 18 years old, serving before the mast in just such a collier as was later to become his first command. He joined the Royal Navy as an able seaman in 1755 and in 1757, *only two years later*, was sailing master of a 60-gun ship. In 1758 his accurate charting of the St Lawrence river made possible the naval assault on Quebec, and he went on in 1763 to make a wonderfully detailed survey of Newfoundland. In 1767 the Royal Society published an account of his various scientific, astronomic and geographic observations, all of which they accepted as being astonishingly accurate.

So it was that when the Lords of the Admiralty began to look around for someone to take command of *Endeavour*, James Cook stood head and shoulders above every other possible candidate. Nevertheless, there was a big problem. Any commander of the expedition must obviously be a commissioned officer and this, in spite of his outstanding brilliance, Cook was not. Sailing master was a warrant rank, and one which did not entitle him to a place in the wardroom. In those days, and indeed over the next 200 years, it was virtually impossible for any seaman ever to become an officer. But Cook was made the exception. He was commissioned in the rank of lieutenant, and sailed out of Plymouth in command of *Endeavour*, with a complement of 70, on 25 August 1768. He carried with him Charles Green of the Royal Society, Joseph Banks, wealthy young man interested in botany, and Banks' friend from Sweden, Daniel Solander.

It is important to record that Cook's scientific genius was matched by many other exemplary qualities. He was a fair if stern humanitarian, and his many years of sailing before the mast had given him a profound understanding of, and sympathy for, men on the lower deck. His caring for and about them won their unswerving loyalty, a not-unimportant element in the ongoing success of his voyages in command. He was greatly concerned in the health of his crews and had far-seeing theories about diet, insisting always that they be provided not only with full and proper rations, but that these be amply supplemented by such unheard-of exotics as malt extract, pickled cabbage, carrot marmalade, and preserves of oranges and lemons. Those ordinary seamen who found this strange fare difficult to stomach were *made* to eat it, and results were staggering. Cook was the first navy captain, Royal or Merchant, ever to eliminate – completely – the dreadful curse of scurvy. Other of his innovative health disciplines included regular bathing, the wearing of clean shirts, and the immediate changing into dry clothes after those worn on watch became wet. Cook also provided between-decks heating by means of charcoal stoves and, whenever possible, a three-watch system designed to ensure that every man on board got sufficient, undisturbed sleep.

Thus began the first of his three great voyages.

Endeavour set sail out of Portsmouth with her course, at first, set south-west. Pausing en route at the Azores and Cape Verde Islands to take on fresh fruits and vegetables, he crossed the South Atlantic to traverse Cape Horn and enter the vast Pacific. There, he charted the Tuamotu Islands, afterwards coming to anchor at Tahiti on 13 April 1769. He stayed there exactly two months and the botanists made important finds, but unfortunately the planet Venus behaved so erratically that year as to make scientific observation difficult and unreliable. Insofar as this part of his brief was concerned the voyage had been a waste of time, but Cook did succeed in setting up such friendly relations with the native Tahitians that the experience would later prove invaluable. He left Tahiti on 13 July, and discovered and named the Society Islands before heading further south into unknown seas. He sighted New Zealand on 7 October, his landfall being near that part of the coast known now as Poverty Bay. Then, forever charting his progress, he sailed completely around both North and South Islands in a brilliantly conceived figure of eight. His masterly survey of the islands occupied the best part of 18 months, during which time he made very good friends of the natives, putting boats ashore at frequent intervals to forage for health-giving fresh foods.

After leaving New Zealand on 1 April 1771, Cook determined to sail north up the unexplored coast of Australia and to chart that huge eastern shore. Then unknown, these were perilous waters, and on more than one occasion during the making of Cook's masterly running survey *Endeavour* came dangerously close to foundering on the 1,250-mile-long Great Barrier Reef. But soon came real tragedy. After re-discovering and passing through the Torres Strait, Cook put in at Batavia for his customary replenishing of stores, and the consequences were devastating. Having enjoyed perfect health for almost three years at sea – unheard of in those days – *Endeavour*'s seamen fell prey to an epidemic of tropical diseases then raging in the Dutch colony, and many died of malaria and/or dysentry. In spite of this depletion of his crew, Cook went on to make a good fast passage home, reaching England on 12 July after an absence of nearly three years. In almost every respect, the voyage had been a tremendous success, and Cook was promoted to the rank of commander.

James Cook went on to make two further great voyages of discovery, but although he never again sailed in *Endeavour*, he chose for his second voyage exactly the same kind of ship. This time the Admiralty bought in, not only one, but two small colliers which, after extensive refit, were launched again as *Resolution* and *Adventure*. However, the expedition was not without its teething troubles. The rich and influential civilian Joseph Banks, who was again to have accompanied Cook, had insisted upon the addition of cabin-space superstructure which, in Cook's opinion, made *Resolution* dangerously unwieldy. He demanded that this excessive top-hamper be taken off, and there followed a battle of wills. Cook won, and when at last *Resolution* sailed it was without the extra deck and without the disgruntled Mr Banks. So, with *Adventure* captained by Tobias Furneaux, and with Cook in overall command, the two ships set sail from England on 13 July 1772, exactly one year and one day after HMS *Endeavour*'s return.

Innovative oceanographer that he was, Cook was interested now in a circumnavigation of the globe making good advantage of the westerly winds always prevalent in extreme southern latitudes. He was aided in his objective by the Admiralty's provision of not just one but *four* ships' chronometers. Cook had hitherto relied for the fixing of longitude on his expert observations of the stars but now, nine years after a final acceptance by the Admiralty's tardy Board of Longitude of Mr Harrison's wonderful clock, he need no longer trust completely in the position of heavenly bodies. Nevertheless, he had already surveyed the

HMS ENDEAVOUR

coasts of New Zealand and Eastern Australia with amazing accuracy by his method of calculating lunars, and he continued in this manner using the chronometers as a sort of double check. In fact, the timepieces – made variously by the English craftsmen Kendall and Arnold – were a mixed blessing. Those three made by Arnold proved themselves unreliable; that one made by Kendall stayed marvellously accurate. In his journal, Cook referred to Kendall's masterpiece as 'our trusty friend', and 'our never-failing guide', and came towards the end of his long voyage utterly to rely on it. In this, as in every other aspect of global navigation, Cook was many years ahead of his time. With the aid of Kendall's fine chronometer he solved, once and for ever, the age-old problem of fixing absolutely the position of longitude. Inevitably, though, there was a serious drawback; Mr Kendall's 'time machine' cost what in those days was the staggering sum of £450.

Cook's second voyage was even more successful than the first. Out of Plymouth on 13 July, his ships fetched the Cape before the end of November. After the traverse, and using Tahiti and New Zealand as winter bases for the rest and refreshment of his crews, he planned to chart the whole of the Antarctic Continent by means of three separate cruises. He made the first of these between December 1772 and March 1773, charting the Atlantic and Indian Ocean sector. He explored and charted the Pacific sector between November '73 and February '74, and completed the circumnavigation by charting the main Atlantic sector in January and February 1775. In accomplishing this momentous feat, his most southerly position was at latitude 71° 10′ south, longitude 106° 54′ west, and the long-held continental theory was banished once and for all.

As though this were not enough, Cook used the time in between these cruises to make an astonishing series of new discoveries. In one of his great sweeps, February to October 1774, he took in Easter Island, the Marquesas, the Society Islands, Niue, Tonga, the New Hebrides, New Caledonia, and a large number of smaller islands. On the last part of the voyage he discovered South Georgia and the South Sandwich Islands, and was home again on 30 July 1775 having carried out the most enormous work of Antarctic navigation, hydrographic work of inestimable value, and having proved absolutely the value of the chronometer in finding longitude. Amazing in a somewhat different way is the fact that in a voyage of three years and one week, only one man had been lost through sickness, and this one from tuberculosis most probably contracted before the voyage began.

For his third and last great voyage Cook sailed again in *Resolution*, leaving England on 12 July 1776. His main objective this time was to make a careful scrutiny of the most northerly Pacific coast of America, looking for a north-west passage. Once again he traversed the Cape and called in at Van Dieman's Land, New Zealand, Tonga, and the Society Islands. He left the latter on 8 December 1777 and, sailing north, discovered the Hawaiian group on 18 January 1778. Then, he made the American west coast and sailed up it, around the Aleutian Islands, and on through the Bering Strait until pack ice drove him back at latitude 70° 44′ north. He decided to return to Hawaii, do some coastal surveys, and winter there in order to rest and replenish. He anchored first in beautiful Kealakekua Bay and spent over two weeks there, from 17 January to 4 February 1779. Shortly after leaving Kealakekua, *Resolution* sprang a topmast, and Cook put back into the bay in order to effect a repair. On 14 February, there occurred one of the most tragic events in naval history. A trivial incident involving the theft of a boat resulted in a scuffle with the natives, and Cook received wounds from which he died.

It was a terrible and wasteful end to the life of a man whose massive contribution to nautical science had never before, and has never since, been equalled. Cook was a man of giant enterprise and virtually unlimited resource. When he was killed, a seaman on board *Resolution* unwittingly penned what might be regarded as a fitting epitaph:

'He was our leading star, which at its setting left us involved in darkness and despair.'

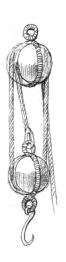

HMS ENDEAVOUR

BRITISH

Tweed

A BRIEF HISTORY of the Blackwall frigates appears elsewhere in this book, but even in such a vast and illustrious company one ship was in a class by herself. For speed, grace and beauty the equal of any clipper, the *Tweed* was one of those rare examples of man's genius as a craftsman, a ship divinely inspired.

In 1852 the last pair of frigates built in the East India Company's Bombay shipyard by that prolific and industrious Parsee shipbuilding heirarchy, the Wadia family, were laid down as sister ships *Punjaub* and *Assaye*. Never excelled for skill and integrity, the Wadias were superb shipwrights and they used only the very finest of materials. First among these was the costly Malabar teak, well known by virtue of its great strength and natural oils as easily the most durable of timbers ever used in the construction of ships.

Originally designed as a paddle steamer, the *Punjaub* was a vessel of 1,745 net tons with an overall length of 250 feet, a beam of 39.6 feet, and a depth to keel of 25 feet. Her engines were of 700 horse power, and her armament consisted of ten 8 inch, 68 pound guns. Launched on 21 April 1854, it was during her fitting-out period that *Punjaub* first demonstrated what was later to become her legendary capacity for survival. On 1 November, Bombay was hit by an enormous cyclone which wrecked or severely damaged no fewer than 142 ships. Five square-rigged ships and three large steamers were hurled ashore and dismasted, and *Assaye* smashed her bowsprit against the castle walls, only narrowly escaping total destruction. But *Punjaub* virtually alone among all of the ships in the harbour that day emerged completely unscathed, and she was ready on 9 January 1855 to embark in a small convoy upon her maiden voyage.

Hastily fitted out with stalls for 250 horses, she took on the colonel and half of his 10th Hussars, bound for Suez and then overland to the Crimea, where troops were urgently needed for the approaching Battle of Sebastopol. It was during this passage to Suez that *Punjaub* revealed her remarkable sailing powers. *Assaye* was damaged and forced into port, and whilst other ships in the troop-carrying convoy struggled along in foul weather under a full head of steam and a press of sail, *Punjaub* shut down her engines, lowered her topsails on the cap, and in spite of the impediment of her cumbersome paddle boxes, ran them all hull down.

In November of that same year, *Punjaub* sailed again from Bombay, this time as a warship in an expeditionary force sent to fight into the Persian war. Orders and circumstances precluded her from any distinction in this campaign, but back in Bombay

on 22 May 1857, she was just in time to play her part in the Indian Mutiny. Space does not permit any detailed account, but *Punjaub* and her crew acquitted themselves most brilliantly throughout this grizzly struggle, not least in the shore action which saved Decca from the mutineers. Four seamen were killed and 21 wounded, but Lt Lewis and his detail from *Punjaub* received the highest possible commendation and one member of the crew, a young midshipman called Arthur Mayo, was awarded the Victoria Cross.

In 1862, after the old Indian Navy was merged with the Royal Navy, *Punjaub* and *Assaye* were sent to England for conversion to screw steamers. Upon their arrival in the Thames, however, both were sold to John Willis, a wily north-country shipowner with a canny eye for a fine vessel. 'Old John' promptly resold *Assaye* for almost as much as he had paid for both ships, and set about stripping *Punjaub* of her engines and paddle boxes. He re-launched her as an honest-to-goodness sailing ship, the *Tweed*, after the beautiful river on which he was born; but she quickly became known as 'Willis' Wonder' and mightily famous in ports all over the world.

First master of the *Tweed*, Captain William Stuart, was famous in his own right. A Scotsman of Viking descent (the family name was originally Skigvard), Stuart was far beyond doubt one of the finest captains ever to set foot on deck. In all of the years he commanded the *Tweed* he never lost a man or damaged so much as a spar, a record unsurpassed or even approached by any other master of any seafaring nation. Stuart made a huge fortune for Old John Willis and also, justifiably, for himself.

On her very first run under the Willis house flag, the *Tweed* carried the India-European cable out to Bombay in a passage of just 77 days. On her return she was re-fitted yet again, this time as a first-class passenger ship, a role for which her 66-foot long poop made her eminently suitable. And so it was that, ironically, the government which had irresponsibly sold her took her up on charter year after year during the 1860s for the safe, swift and comfortable passage home from India of sick or wounded troops. Her outward-bound passages were made via Sydney or Calcutta, often with an anncilliary run up the China coast. Extremely fast in light winds, the *Tweed* ran some of these China passages at such incredible speeds that she was periodically boarded by sceptical naval officers bent on examining her log, taking details of her sail plan, and the placing of her masts. But any lingering doubts as to her true capabilities were finally dispelled when she easily outran the Royal Mail steamer between Hongkong and Singapore.

By this time, the *Tweed* was a living legend, spoken of in tones of awe wherever seamen gathered. On her first voyage to Melbourne she left Lizard Point North at noon on 6 September 1873 and came to anchor inside the Heads at Cape Otway at 6 pm on 17 November, a passage of 72 days. She made the difficult return passage under adverse conditions, Melbourne to London 3 February to 27 April 1874, in a remarkable 83 days. She was taken up then for the carrying of emigrants to New Zealand, and showed her stern to St Catherine's Point on 17 June. She crossed the equator on 8 July, 21 days out, and in a strong north breeze on the 19th of that month she ran 324 miles in 24 hours. She ran 320 miles on 5 August, and 316 miles on the 15th, to arrive at Otago in New Zealand on 3 September, 78 days out.

The *Tweed* left England bound for Sydney in June 1875 loaded very deep with passengers and cargo, including eight valuable stallions in stalls on the main deck. Hampered as he was, Captain Stuart was unable to drive so hard as he would have liked, and he was twice forced to heave to whilst running her easting down. Yet, and in spite of having been becalmed off Montagu Island for one whole day, he still arrived at Sydney only 82 days out. On her homeward passage, the *Tweed* left Sydney on 10 December 1875 and took up her pilot off Dungeness on 17 February 1876, having made the truly astounding passage in exactly 69 days.

In 1877, when Stuart relinquished command of the *Tweed* to Captain Byce, the old Viking seemed to take away with him some part of the magic of his ship. She continued to race and most often beat her rivals for almost a further decade, but when in 1885 Captain Moore left *Cutty Sark* to take over as master of the *Tweed*, her record-breaking days were over. It now seems strange that coming as he did straight off that most famous of English clippers, Moore was no great sail-carrier, and under his command passages regularly made by the *Tweed* in 70 or 80 days began at once to take 80 or 90.

The *Tweed*'s sad end came in July 1888, just 36 years after her launching. Laden with a cargo out of China for New York, she was dismasted in a gale on the approaches to the Cape of Good Hope, and was towed into Algoa Bay by the steamship *Venice*. So severe had been her battering she was damaged beyond repair, and it was reluctantly decided to break her up. But no finer teakbuilt ship ever sailed the oceans, and even after her dismemberment, the magnificent old lady was very far from done. Her hull frames and timbers were as sound as when the Wadias first fashioned them and the *Tweed* lives on, still in great splendour, as the beautiful vaulted roof of a Port Elizabeth church.

TWEED

Thermopylae

IF EVER THERE WAS a British tea clipper seriously to challenge the speed and beauty of *Cutty Sark*, that ship was the *Thermopylae*. Built by Walter Hood in his Aberdeen yard and completed one year before her great rival, she must have presented a stunning spectacle in her Aberdeen White Star Line livery of verdant green hull with a wide gold stripe and gilded scrollwork, her all-white blocks, bowsprit, lower masts and all yardarms, much enhanced by her gleaming proliferation of polished brasswork. She was described by one who sailed in her as 'More beautiful than the most beautiful woman, fairest of all the fair.' Such praise by an old sea-dog is not lightly given, so it must be assumed that *Thermopylae* in all her finery was a very handsome vessel indeed.

Until she was launched up there on the north-east coast of Scotland in August 1868, it might fairly be said that the two major west-coast shipbuilders over on the Clyde – Steele, and Connel – had a virtual monopoly in the design and construction of crack British clippers. Steele's *Taeping*, *Ariel*, *Sir Lancelot*, and *Serica*, and Connel's *Taitsing*, *Spindrift*, and *Windhover* together with their respective sister ships were the ocean queens of the tea trade, vessels absolutely without peer. But George Thompson of the Aberdeen White Star Line was determined to alter all that with his *Thermopylae* which, unlike almost every other clipper, was not designed by those who built her. Instead, Thompson engaged an outsider, Bernard Waymouth, who was the Secretary of Lloyds Register. Waymouth drew her hull with the usual long, hollow entrance and very fine lines, but he also gave her more bearing and less counter to help stop her scooping up seas over her stern, and a rocker false keel hopefully to assist her when sailing to windward. But the most significant difference between *Thermopylae* and other clippers lay in her rigging and sail plans. She was not nearly so tall from truck to deck, but although she wore nothing above her royal yards, she carried her canvas on tremendous spars. Her huge main sail, with its drop of 40 feet was carried on a yard fully 80 feet long. Waymouth's faith in far fewer, but much wider and bigger, sails was fully vindicated, and there are many who still argue that his somewhat daring creation was the all-round fastest medium clipper ever to sail the seas. All of her basic measurements are detailed elsewhere in this book (see comparisons with those of *Cutty Sark*) so I will concentrate here on her qualities of handling and sailing.

Cutty Sark could and did leave her hull down in strong favourable winds, but *Thermopylae* was arguably the most versatile sailer. She could maintain a smooth seven knots in airs so gentle that a lighted candle might be carried about on deck, and go 13 knots in quarterly breezes with helm amidships and all sails set. She went to windward like a flying fish, and very few ships of any size or description could match her when she was running

her easting down. She excited the envy and praise of all who saw her at work and on one occasion when she left Port Phillip Heads along with HMS *Charybdis*, the warship's captain tried to make a match of the course. Both ships crowded on sail, but *Thermopylae* drew so rapidly away that the Royal Navy captain was moved to hoist the following signal: 'Goodbye. You are too much for me. You are the finest model of a ship I ever saw. It does my heart good to look at you.'

Thermopylae was lucky to have as her first master the renowned Captain Kemball, late of another famous Aberdeen clipper, the *Yangtze*. Kemball was destined to stay with his new ship until he relinquished command to Captain Matheson in 1874, and his six round voyages between London and Foochow or Shanghai included a succession of passages which made the shipping world sit up and marvel. *Thermopylae*'s maiden voyage, which she made from Gravesend, began on 19 August 1868 and she managed on that first outward run to break all previous records for both of the two main passages. On the first leg, London–Melbourne, she made no fewer than nine 24-hour runs of over 300 miles including one, in a strong quarterly breeze, of 330. She came to anchor at Port Phillip on 9 January, having made the pilot to pilot passage in an unprecedented 60 days. She capped this feat by crossing the Pacific from Newcastle, New South Wales, to Shanghai in a pilot to pilot passage of only 28 days, so creating another new record. When she sailed then into Foochow in order to take on tea for the passage home, excitement among shippers, captains and crews became intense.

Although *Thermopylae* was first ship home in the Tea Race of 1869, beating by a full ten days all three ships which had sailed before her, it must be remembered that loading and departures from Foochow were made over a period of several weeks, and that vessels engaged in the race were subject to various imponderables not least being that of weather. Of the 23 ships taking part that year, and every one a crack China clipper, only three made a passage home of under 100 days. *Thermopylae*, with a passage of 91 days, was narrowly beaten by the great *Sir Lancelot* with a passage of 89 days. Had the pair of them left Foochow on the same tide, the result might well have been reversed. *Thermopylae* sailed on 3 July and due to unfavourable squalls did not pass Anjer until she was 24 days out: *Sir Lancelot* sailed two weeks later, had better sailing weather, and so passed Anjer only 21 days out.

Speculation over what might have been has long been the subject of controversy, but it is a curious fact that the next and last of the great races, that of 1870, produced an uncannily similar result. Once again *Thermopylae* left Foochow ahead of *Sir Lancelot*, once again had her passage bettered, and once again by exactly two days. It must be recorded however that the pair of

them were well beaten by no fewer than six others, which serves again to underline the imponderables besetting these China runs. The 27 ships which took part left Foochow over a period of three months, 25 July to 3 November, and the two best passages (of an equal 98 days) were made by *Leander* and *Lahloe*, both of which left very late in the season and on the same day, 12 October. *Thermopylae* and *Sir Lancelot* left on 29 July and 2 August respectively.

But as has been shown, the measure of a great sailing ship is not to be judged by the result of a single passage, and the qualities which set *Thermopylae* high amongst the greatest of all time were made manifest in her performances throughout the span of a long working life. Although beaten by *Sir Lancelot* in the 1869 race back home from Foochow, *Thermopylae* set a record time for the whole round voyage which was never equalled. Over her first ten passages out to Melbourne she averaged 69 days, and on her passages home with tea from China she averaged 106½ days, times never attained by many a fine clipper on an individual run. She made the fastest runs home in 1874, 1875, and 1877, coming second only to *Cutty Sark* in 1876. She continued to demonstrate this wonderful consistency well beyond that stage at which most ships begin to slow down with age and it was indeed on 31 December 1888, when she was just over 21 years old, that Captain Jenkins logged her biggest-ever one-day run of 358 miles. In all of her years under the Aberdeen White Star house flag she made only one poor passage, and that was out to Sydney in the winter of 1882–83. She was severely battered by heavy storms all the way down to the equator, which she crossed after 45 days out. Compare this with her previous voyage, when she left Lizard Point to cross the line after 16 days at sea. In almost a quarter of a century of ocean racing only one ship ever left her hull down, that one ship being the *Cutty Sark*.

In 1890, George Thompson sold *Thermopylae* to the Canadian shipowner Mr Meford, and she was put into the rice trade to ply between Vancouver and Rangoon. She went on in that work to make many more remarkable passages, the most notable of which being one from Shanghai to Victoria, British Columbia, in the record time of 28 days. After employing her for five years, her Canadian owner made the disastrous mistake of selling her to the Portuguese government, who re-named her the *Pedro Nunes* and turned her into a training ship. Her end came 12 years later. Although she was still sound and seaworthy, the wonderful little beauty was callously destroyed. On 13 December 1907 she was towed out of Tagus harbour, her poles and spars all bare, and set up as a floating target. Using torpedoes, Portuguese warships blasted her asunder, a terrible and ignominious end for a fine, proud ship whose marvellous achievements will be told and retold so long as men love the sea.

THERMOPYLAE

BRITISH

Cutty Sark

Who can define that ethereal quality which sets one particular work of man above all others of its kind. The *Cutty Sark* was not unique; she was rivalled in speed, grace and beauty by many of her contemporaries, including her great competitor *Thermopylae* and not a few of the marvellous yankee clippers such as Webb's *Young America* and Mackay's famous *Lightning*. Nevertheless, she has come to represent the epitome of all that is awe-inspiring in a tall ship under sail, and this splendid painting of her by Cornelis de Vries prompts yet another account of her remarkable history.

Cutty Sark was designed by Hercules Linton to a specific order by 'Old John' Willis, who gave instructions that she was to be modelled along the lines of his favourite ship, the wonderful, legendary *Tweed*. She was built in 1869 at Scott & Linton's yard in Dumbarton but the firm went bankrupt before completing the order and she was finished off, somewhat too hastily, in the nearby yard of Denby Brothers. It is widely held that the latter's work topsides was inferior to that of Scott & Linton's beautiful hull, which might well account for the fact that she was plagued on her maiden voyage by numerous failures aloft of slings, trusses and yards. Once refitted however, she went on magnificently to fulfill her destiny.

Although Old Willis had his new ship built especially to beat the *Thermopylae*, the two vessels were remarkably similar in details of Register. Those of *Cutty Sark* are followed in brackets by those of *Thermopylae*: length 212 feet 5 inches (212 feet), beam 36 feet (36 feet), depth 21 feet (21 feet), depth moulded 22 feet 5 inches (23 feet 2 inches), gross tonnage 963 (991), net tonnage 921 (948), tonnage under deck 892 (927), raised quarter deck 46 feet (61 feet). The essential though not particularly striking differences lay in hull design (*Cutty Sark* had a much sharper entrance), in masting (*Cutty Sark*'s had more rake and the fore was stepped further aft), and in sail plan (*Cutty Sark*'s sail area was tremendous). For the rest, and so far as performance was concerned, this depended, as always, on two vital imponderables; the ability or otherwise of the men in command, and the enormously variable conditions of weather. But handled well in strong breezes, and especially when running her easting down, *Cutty Sark* was capable of overdrawing and leaving hull down astern any ship of whatever rig that ever sailed the seas. She was equally fast with a good blow on beam or quarter, and she made astonishing headway when ploughing to windward in short and ugly seas. But her debut was less than impressive, although for the valid reason already stated.

Despite the fact that her first three voyages in the tea trade for which she was built were made under the excellent and hard-sailing Captain Moodie, her overall performances were not spectacular. Actual extracts from the log of her first race home with the new season's teas include such notes by Moodie as: 'In all my sailing of the China Sea, I have never experienced such weather … the principle complaint has been want of wind … not enough wind to give her steerage way … the ship rearing nearly end over with this North West swell …' But like the little girl with the little curl, when the *Sark* was good, she was very, very good. On many different occasions during those first voyages Moodie measured her speed through the water by the common and patent log and found her to be maintaining an incredible 17½ knots. Moodie logged her best 24 hours work under his command at 363 miles, and she once made two consecutive days of 363 and 362, the biggest runs ever made by any clipper engaged in the China trade. Indeed, it was only by a gross misfortune that Captain Moodie's third and final voyage in *Cutty Sark* failed to end in a most spectacular triumph.

She was competing against the mighty *Thermopylae* in the Tea Race of 1872. The ships left Shanghai within an hour of each other, but both were hampered by squalls, fogs and calms and not least by the north-east monsoon. These early bad conditions bode ill for a record passage and the race might be said really to have started on 26 June, one week out, when the two ships sighted each other at latitude 20° 27' north, longitude 114° 43' east. They hove into view again on the 28th, but sail-splitting gales beat them apart and the next sighting came on their approach to the Gaspar Straits. As they crossed the equator on 15 July, *Cutty Sark* was about eight miles ahead and the two ships remained in frequent sight of each other until, as they approached Keeling Cocos Island on the 26th, a strong wind came up from the east-south-east. This was the sort of blow in which *Cutty Sark* excelled. Out came the stunsails, some booms of which snapped like celery sticks, and away she went. She flew before the trades until 7 August, building up what must have seemed to Moodie like an unassailable lead. But then his good wind went away, and 11 August found him struggling against a fierce westerly gale during which, after four days of constant battering, *Cutty Sark* lost her Denby Bros. rudder. Even the awning stanchions which connected the steering chains were carried away in the tempest, as were the eye-bolts holding the rudder to the stern-post.

It was a disaster. To anyone who has ever seen a ship's rudder,

the actual making and fixing at sea of a jury substitute, and under such apalling weather conditions, must seem a hopeless task and it is likely that such a feat of seamanship would be regarded these days as quite impossible. But Moodie and his crew did construct a replacement rudder and they did carry out the enormously difficult operation of fitting it to the ship. Working night and day they did it in just under a week whilst all the time hove-to in furious head gales. What is more, she ran a creditable 194 miles on her first full day, 23 August, and in spite of being hampered and having lost so much time, when she rounded Cape Agulhas her rival *Thermopylae* was only 490 miles ahead.

But with her makeshift steering gear giving endless trouble in the continuing heavy head storms, *Cutty Sark* was at a crushing disadvantage. Any attempt by Captain Moodie to 'carry on' resulted in more serious damage, and after effecting a further succession of time-consuming repairs he was forced to trim his ship and keep her speed down to something around eight knots, less than half that of which she was capable. She fetched St Helena on 9 September, and crossed the line on the 15th, making daily runs of between 207 and 227 miles. Which, for a ship so severely restricted, was little short of miraculous. Then, on 20 September, the jury rudder broke its fastenings and this time the entire massive contrivance needed to be hoist inboard for repairs to be carried out on deck. The ingenious means by which Captain Moodie managed in only one day to lower and refit the rudder to the stern-post is a fascinating story in itself, but manage he did and ironically – because he dared not press *Cutty Sark* beyond runs of 300 miles a day – he was favoured then by splendid north-east trades. However, good fortune was followed by ill, and when on 12 October *Thermopylae* had gained the Downs, *Cutty Sark* was struggling against a north-north-east gale which smashed at her all the rest of the way home. Nevertheless, the great race ended with *Thermopylae* only six days ahead, and seafaring men the world over awarded victory to the *Cutty Sark*. The two ships continued to race each other for many years and with honours roughly even, but there can be no doubt that had *Cutty Sark* not lost her rudder in the Tea Race of '72 she might have crushed the spirit of her rival once and for ever more.

Insofar as the great tea races were concerned the following year, 1873, heralded the last one. Steam plus the Suez Canal had finally triumphed, and the great racing clipper ships were reduced to making trips between China and Australia in order to fill their holds for a viable passage home. *Cutty Sark* was among the very first to be taken out of the China trade, and it was when

CUTTY SARK

CUTTY SARK

she was embarked upon her 20 glorious years of runs between London and Australia that she really came into her own. Properly refitted after her disastrous rudder troubles, she startled the seafaring world with an initial passage under Captain Moore, running from London to Melbourne, in an unprecedented 69 days. She was never to better or even equal this time again, yet all except one of her passages between London and Sydney during the years 1873–1893 were made between 75 and 80 days. By comparison, *Thermopylae* made only one out of nine outward passages to Sydney in fewer than 80 days, the rest being passages of between 80 and 109 days. *Cutty Sark*'s longest-ever time to Sydney was in 1893, when she made the passage in 82 days. And so it was that over these 20 years, she became a living legend. Once, when running her easting down she ran 2,163 miles in six days, a feat of which almost a hundred years later some modern steamers might feel proud.

One of the *Sark*'s famous masters, Captain Wallace, was a great sail-carrier. At Manila, he took on a cargo for New York, then made the crossing from New York to London in 10 days, one of which was spent hove-to whilst the hands bent on new sails! Then, in 1880, her owner shocked all who knew his marvellous record-breaker by having her sail plan cut down and loading her with coal out of Cardiff for American naval steamships in the Far East. As though to repay Old Willis for the dreadful insult, the voyage was a catalogue of disasters from beginning to end. The first mate, a brutal Yankee Bucko, killed a seaman with a marlin spike, and when Wallace allowed the murderer to escape at Anjer to an American ship, the angry crew promptly mutinied. Wallace and the apprentices got *Cutty Sark* out to sea, where she lay for 48 hours in a dead flat calm. Wallace himself was not a harsh man. Made sleepless by conscience and worn out by worry over the killing, he jumped over the side and was taken by sharks before the crew could put out a boat. The second mate took *Cutty Sark* back into Anjer and thence to Singapore, where an inquiry was held and the entire crew dismissed. The man sent down from Hong Kong to take over command, a Captain Bruce, was the worst possible choice. He turned the beautiful little *Cutty Sark* into an absolute hell ship in which everything went wrong, and conditions on board went rapidly from bad to worse until, in the spring of 1882, Old Willis replaced Bruce with the fine and reliable Captain Moore. The old man relinquished command in 1885, and *Cutty Sark* began a whole new decade of glory under the famous sail-carrying Captain Woodget. Spruced up and seemingly infused with temendous fresh spirit, she flew again over the southern oceans making passages which put many a new 'fast' rival to shame.

After a quarter of a century of extraordinary service, *Cutty Sark* was sold in 1895 to a Lisbon firm, and re-named the *Ferriera*. The Portuguese made hard use of her over yet another 25 years, at the end of which she was barely recognisable. In 1922 she was purchased from the Portuguese by Captain Dowman, a retired tall ships skipper from Trevissome in Devon, who paid £3,750 for the grand old lady. The captain re-rigged her from her original sail and spar plans, and set about restoring her former beauty. Sadly, the old man died before he could fulfill his dream of sailing her out again to Port Jackson in a passage equal to her best. His widow made the splendid gesture of giving *Cutty Sark* to the Thames Nautical Training College and she now stands tall and proud, for all to admire and visit, in a dry dock at Greenwich in London near the National Maritime Museum.

DUTCH

Nova Zembla

THIS IS THE extraordinary story of a small 16th century vessel which, although widely known in her native Holland as the *Nova Zembla*, never actually had a name. Her captain and crew alike called her quite simple *de Boot*, which means the Boat, or the Ship. In order properly to appreciate the magnitude of her one and only voyage, it is necessary first to understand the background against which it was made.

England's wild seafarer Martin Frobisher had been eager to attempt a north-west passage to India and Cathay since 1650, and when in 1671 he finally achieved his ambition, he started a series of efforts which for some years remained largely English. But, eighty years earlier, to find a north-*east* passage to the Orient had been the lifelong dream of a Flemish merchant named De Moucheron, who fled Antwerp to live in Zeeland following the 1587 siege of his native city by the forces of Parma. In 1592, aided by the celebrated Dutch cartographers D S Plancius and Jan Huygen van Linschoten, and with financial backing from merchant companies in Zeeland, Amsterdam, and the Isjelmeer (then the Zuider Zee) port of Enkhuizen, he put his plans into action. Three ships were prepared, none of more than 150 tons; the *Zwaan* in Zeeland, the *Mercurius* in Enkhuizen, and a nameless vessel in Amsterdam. Significantly, the latter was commanded by one, Willem Barents.

At first all went well. The ships sailed out of Texel on 5 June 1594, and had rounded North Cape by the 23rd. There, the little fleet became separated by fog and storm, and on encountering much pack ice off Novaya Zemlya at 77° north, Barents was forced to turn back. The other ships had returned before him, having learned much less by their experience. When De Moucheron began almost at once to organise a second and larger expedition, Barents was the obvious choice for command. As before, the enterprise was funded by Zeeland, Enkhuizen and Amsterdam, each of which provided one 170 ton ship and an accompanying 80 ton yacht. We know the names of the ships; they were *De Griffieon*, *De Hoop*, and *De Windhond*. This second attempt at a north-east passage was marginally more successful than the first; the only ostensible benefit being that it represented something of a trial run for men whose names are now writ large in history. Barents commanded Amsterdam's *Windhond* with, serving under him as captain of her consort yacht, a young man by the name of Jan Cornelis Rijp. With Barents in *Windhond* was another young man, Jacob van Heemskerck, the 28-year-old son of a noted sailmaker. Jan Huygen van Linschoten sailed with the fleet, as did Plancius, and the ships left Holland on 2 July 1595.

This, really, was much too late in the season, and the ships were dogged from the start by ill omen. Nineteen days out, one of the ships narrowly avoided what might easily have been a disastrous encounter with a sleeping whale, and on 5 August another of the ships was lucky to be spared a broken hull when she struck a submerged rock. On the following day, 6 August, two of the ships were unaccountably involved in a collision so heavy that both sustained much damage. Delayed by the need to make repairs, the fleet did not reach Novaya Zemlya until 19 August, and the sea all about them was beginning to freeze solid. The ships turned around, and were back home in Holland on 26 October.

The third, final, and truly epic voyage in search of a north-east passage began on 18 May 1596. De Moucheron and van Linschoten having abandoned the idea, the project was organised entirely by the wealthy Plancius, who provided two 150 ton ships. Willem Barents was placed in nominal command of the expedition, sailing in the nameless ship with Jacob van Heemskerck as her captain. Jan Cornelis Rijp was chosen to skipper the second ship which, like the first, carried a total of 17 men. Both had two good longboats, and were very well provisioned, but in fact the overall operation was curiously ill-conceived. Barents and Plancius had always disagreed; the former remaining convinced that the way to the East lay through a strait south of Novaya Zemlya, the latter equally certain that a northern traverse was essential. The brave but headstrong young Jan Rijp agreed with Plancius, and so were sown the seeds of discord.

Only 17 days out, on 4 June, Rijp began to challenge Barents' authority. The ships were at about 70° north, and when Barents ordered a change of course, Rijp produced written orders from Plancius that the ships must continue sailing north before seeking their eastern passage over an open polar sea. Barents could only comply, and on 8 June the ships discovered the small island now called Bjornoya. After resting for five days they set sail again. On 19 June they made another landfall and were amazed to find (thanks as we now know to the Gulf Stream) grass, animals and birds, including geese and deer. Thinking at first that they must somehow have reached Greenland, they later realised their mistake and named the place Spitsbergen. But the quarrels between them grew daily worse, and on the 1st day of July, Barents and Rijp decided to go their separate ways. That occasion was to prove momentous. Pursuing his own belief, and that of Plancius, Rijp was soon forced by ice to abandon the quest and return, unsuccessful, to Holland.

Barents, whose name is now immortalised by the sea to which he gave his name, was made of sterner stuff. He set sail south east, and sighting Cape Kanin about two weeks later, was soon beset by icy fogs and blizzards. With visibility at zero, he was often forced to make fast for days against the ice field, and to send out scouts in search of wide open water. These went in constant fear of polar bears, whose natural camouflage, especially in fog, made them practically invisible until actually stumbled upon. It seems most probable that during most of this very slow progress, Barents did not know where he was. On 15 August, however, he calculated his position as 77° north, off the north-western coast of Novaya Zemlya. Here, a scouting party sent to the top of a high hill returned with the glad news that there was nothing to the south east but a huge expanse of open water. Vastly encouraged, Barents sailed on, and by 18 August he had rounded the northern cape and was sailing south east into what is now the Kara Sea. Within only a few days, however, the ship came up against an endless wall of ice and Barents was forced to head back inshore and into a bay, which he hopefully named Ijshaven, at about 75° north.

After further attempts to force a way through the swiftly-encroaching ice, Barents knew before the end of August that there would be no getting away from Ijshaven until the following spring brought a thaw. More, the relentless massive pressure of ice had cracked the ship's hull, and she had begun to leak very badly. Barents and his men hauled the longboats up onto snow-covered ground, and worked like beavers to empty the ship of her stores and of anything else which might be of use – tools, weapons, ropes etc, and enough of her braces and superstructure to build a shelter for themselves. They were very fortunate in this to have on board a master carpenter from the town of Purmerend, and working to his instruction they built a hut roughly 30 feet long by 14 feet wide, and 8 feet high. This simple but solid structure was so beautifully put together that much of it was still intact after 274 years. Sadly, the man from Purmerend died just before it was completed.

In the meantime, the men had the extreme good fortune to find great quantities of driftwood, but the terrible hardship of that long winter, the howling Arctic blizzards in a seemingly endless dark night, might readily be imagined. Always afraid to venture outside for fear of attack by the ferocious white bears, they suffered also from inadequate food supplies and inevitably began to fall sick. It seems a miracle that every one of the 16 men confined in the hut from mid-October 1596 to the end of April

NOVA ZEMBLA

1597 survived to see the spring. Then, with a dawning at last of the six-months-long Arctic day, and the meagre rations of salted meat now exhausted, the men began to press their leader for a start on the long voyage home.

By this time, Barents was too ill to command, and the burden of responsibility fell on the shoulders of van Heemskerck. He knew that if he abandoned the hut too soon, there would still be great problems with pack-ice and icebergs; if he left it too late, scurvy and starvation would render the men too weak to perform the work of making ready. With the ship damaged beyond repair, they must pin their faith in the longboats. This required the making of spars and sails, and a heightening of the freeboards, using materials scavenged from the ship. All of the remaining food and everything else of use or value was packed into small kegs, for ease of handling when the boats must needs be hauled across icefields to the next stretch of unfrozen sea, and all was ready by 13 June. Before leaving Ijshaven, Barents wrote his famous *Cedelken*, a record of their privations on the voyage from Amsterdam, the building of the hut (the *Behouden Huys*), and that awful six-months hibernation. The *Cedelken*, stuffed into an empty powder horn and hung in the chimney of the *Behouden Huys*, was found by Elling Carlsen, a Norwegian whaling skipper, in 1871. Carlsen sold it and other souveniers he had found to an Englishman, Ellis C Lister, who passed them on for the price

they had cost him to Holland's national museum, the Rijks Museum in Amsterdam. Today, almost 400 years later, Barents' handwriting and van Heemskerck's witnessing signature are still quite perfectly clear.

The longboats sailed out on 14 June 1597, but the constant rub and pressure of ice forced a stop after only three days. They were hauled up onto a floe for re-caulking, and it was during the five days of this labour that Willem Barents, together with first mate Claes Andriesz, died. Young van Heemskerck and his remaining men pressed on, hugging the coast of Novaya Zemlya and stopping often to hunt for birds' eggs and any other kind of food they could find. Progress was tortuously slow. Much of the Kara Sea was still frozen, and during their long portages over ice fields the weakened men were often forced to fight off the huge Arctic bears. On the 1st of July, they suffered a near-disaster. An ice-floe on which they had stopped for the night suddenly broke up in pieces, and they lost about half of their remaining small stock of food. They struggled on and four weeks later, on 28 July 1597, made their first human contact in almost 13 months when they met up with two Russian ships. Remarkably, some of the Russian sailors remembered once having met van Heemskerck, and gave him all the food they could spare. Still following the coast, the two boats met with other Russian ships on the 4th and again on the 12th of August, and sighted Cape Kanin on

the 18th. On the 25th they reached a small inhabited island at some point east of Murmansk and were told by the people there that at Kola, only 60 miles away, there were two Dutch ships. Van Heemskerck dispatched one of his men overland, together with a Laplander guide, and the guide returned alone on the 29th carrying a letter from one of the Dutch captains.

Incredibly, this was none other than Jan Cornelis Rijp, and after abandoning the longboats at Kola, the survivors were taken on board Rijp's vessel for the final passage home. Rijp left Kola on 15 September, but with business in Varhüs and other ports of call, did not reach harbour at Amsterdam until 11 November.

Everyone in Holland thought them dead, but of the 17 men who sailed out on the ship, no fewer than 13 came back. One of these, a young man named Gerrit de Veer who had kept a rather inaccurate diary of his travails, never fully recovered from the ordeal and died within a year. Jacob van Heemskerck went on before his death in 1607 to attain the rank of admiral and become famous for a voyage to the East Indies in 1601 during which he made the prize capture of a big, richly-laden Portuguese merchantman. De Moucheron, one of the first partners in the Dutch East India Company when it was founded in 1602, made a fortune from that enterprise. But not, as had been his original vision, from ships sailing out via an icy north-east passage.

NOVA ZEMBLA

De Eendracht

THE STORY OF *De Eendracht* is bound up with that of Isaac Le Maire (1558–1624), a wealthy Dutch merchant of vision and stature. Arriving in Amsterdam after the Fall of Antwerp in 1585, he founded the Nieuwe Brabantse shipping firm and so, upon its merger in 1602 with the newly-formed East India Company, became one of the *Heeren Zeventein*.* However, his term of office with the 'Seventeen Gentlemen' did not last long. Furious at being accused of fraud, he resigned in 1605 and set himself up to challenge the rights of *de VOC* in the manner of its charter. All aside from this staggering act of defiance, his energies included the siring of no fewer than 22 children one of whom, Jacob (1585–1616), he sent abroad on voyages of exploration. Inevitably, both father and son were plagued at every turn by the immense power of *de VOC*, and their perseverance in the face of such opposition is a tribute to their pride and stamina. Alienated from *de VOC*, and thus denied any right of passage around the Cape of Good Hope or through the Straits of Magellan, Le Maire adopted the theory first expressed by England's Sir Francis Drake that there existed a vast southern continent as yet undiscovered. It was to find this continent, and an alternative sea route to the East, that Le Maire despatched his son Jacob. In 1615 he organised and privately financed an expedition of two ships, the *Eendracht* and the *Hoorn*. There is no contemporary depiction of either of these vessels, but we know from descriptive accounts that each was typical of its time. The *Eendracht*, well-armed with 41 assorted guns, carried a crew of 65; the *Hoorn* was a much smaller vessel, with no guns at all, and a crew of only 22. Jacob was in overall command of the enterprise, but its ultimate success depended primarily on the *Eendracht*'s captain and navigator, Willem Cornelisz Schouten (1580–1625). Although his navigation was not of the very best, Schouten was an intrepid sailor and a man of boundless courage.

The two ships sailed out of Hoorn's small harbour – which, over 350 years later, looks very much now as it did then – on 14 June 1615. Le Maire had a four-years charter from Prins Maurits to explore, discover and hopefully make treaties with that great unknown south land of which, it was believed, Tierra del Fuego was only the northern tip. At first, the expedition seemed doomed to failure. The ships took a severe battering on the first leg of their voyage down the coast of Africa, and it was almost three months before they reached a latitude at which Schouten was ready to head due west. There was more heavy weather in the South Atlantic, and the crossing was a difficult one which took almost a further three months. But the ships did manage to

stay together, and they sighted the east coast of South America on 7 December. Schouten then steered a southerly course, hugging the shoreline to look for a suitable strand on which to beach the ships for cleaning, and to forage for fresh food and water. They quickly sighted a likely place, probably near Deseado, and set about the arduous task. It was an exercise which ended in disaster.

There is no record of how, or even whether or not, the ships' hulls were sheathed below the water-line, but one method certainly then in use was that of *paying*. Ships' bottoms were thickly layered with a poisonous (to the voracious toredo, or shipworm) mixture of sulphur and pitch and sometimes powdered glass, then covered with a sheathing of softwood planking which was itself then *payed*. The theory was that those worms which survived the first dose of poison would eat the softwood but perish on the second dose before chewing their way into the oak of the hull proper. Sheathing with lead came later, in about 1680, but no one hit upon the final and lasting solution of copper plates fastened with copper nails until 1758, when copper served a dual purpose; not only did it foil the worm, it greatly reduced fouling by weed.

In any event, after six months at sea the bottoms of both *Hoorn* and *Eendracht* were festooned by great masses of marine growth and someone, either Schouten or young Jacob Le Maire, decided upon a drastic tactic by means of which they could quickly be rid of the nuisance. When the vessels had been hauled up onto the beach, and after the weed was dried by the sun, the crews were sent to gather tons of withered reeds. This highly inflamable material was piled up against the hulls and set on fire, the object being to burn off the weed and kill the worm all at one fell swoop. The expedition doubtless felt itself well behind schedule and pressed for time, but having regard to the fact that the ships had not been completely off-loaded as was the usual practise, it was an incredibly foolhardy act. The *Hoorn* very quickly became a blazing inferno, the fire beyond any control. And, in addition to a large hoard of silver coin, she was carrying all the reserves of gunpowder for *Eendracht*'s range of guns. By the time the flames reached the magazine, the coins had melted down into one huge solid block of silver, and came the inevitable tremendous explosion, the fused lump of bullion was hurled into the sea. It was later recovered, but the *Hoorn* was reduced quite literally to splinters of burning matchwood.

Eendracht was saved and re-floated, and set out again on 16 January 1616 in search of the southern continent. Forbidden by *de VOC*'s sole right of passage through the Straits of Magellan, they sailed on south and eventually came upon another channel,

which they named the Strait of Le Mare. They were of course quite correct in their assumption that the land mass on their starboard side was the real southern tip of South America, but totally wrong in their belief that the land out to port (which they called Statenland) was a cape of the fabled southern continent. Nevertheless, they were the first Europeans ever to reach that latitude, and they named the northern landfall Cape Hoorn, in honour of the little port in Holland from which they had set sail. Now, sadly and improperly, 'Hoorn' has been forgotten and corrupted into 'Horn'.

Having traversed that grim southern cape, Schouten took *Eendracht* north-west into the Pacific, still in search of the elusive continent. Good luck rather than good navigation brought the explorers to various fortuitous landfalls such as the Cocos Islands south of Fiji, and the Hoornse Islands farther to the west. In the course of what was to become a circumnavigation of the globe, Schouten is credited with having discovered that group of islands to the north of New Guinea which today bears his name.

During the course of their momentous voyage, the masters and crew of the *Eendracht* suffered grim privations. For want of food and water they put in at many small islands, some of which were inhabited by warlike, hostile natives who drove the shore parties off with their water casks unfilled. Ironically, they encountered even greater trouble when at last – thanks entirely to Schouten having made an error of navigation – they fetched Jacatra and came, ill and half-starved, among their own people. Jan Peterszoon Coen, all-powerful representative of *de VOC* and virtual governor of the settlement there, seized the *Eendracht* as a ship having violated his company's charter. Young Jacob Le Maire protested in vain that his ship had *not* sailed through the Straits of Magellan, and he and Schouten were thrown into prison together with all of the remaining crew. Those of the sailors who falsely admitted to having transgressed were permitted to take passage home in one of *de VOC*'s merchantmen, but Le Maire and Schouten were sent back to Holland as prisoners on board the *Amsterdam*. The vessel arrived in Zeeland on 2 July 1617, two years and eighteen days after *Eendracht* and *Hoorn* had first set sail.

Sadly, Jacob died on the voyage home, and Schouten was left to face the charges alone. Old Isaac raised a lawsuit against *de VOC*, and finally won substantial damages for the illegal restraint of his ship, but this was small compensation for the loss of his favourite son. In retrospect, and although of small comfort to Isaac in his lifetime, the voyage of the *Eendracht* ranks high amongst the most important of the early 17th century.

* See the History – Merchant Adventurers, *page 13*.

DE EENDRACHT

DUTCH

Aemilia

THERE ARE SOME ships whose real, intrinsic qualities are far eclipsed by the fame of their commanders, and as with Nelson's *Victory*, *Aemilia* is a classic case in point. A fine man-o'-war of about 600 tons, she was built in 1639. She carried 46 guns and a crew of 200, and though a good deal smaller, might fairly be classed as the Dutch equivalent of an English first rate. No Dutch ship of that period was built with more than two decks, and other differences in design made them readily distinguishable. The hulls were full-bellied to restrict draught in their shallow coastal waters, and also to provide for greater stowage. English warships had an endurance at sea of around 10 weeks only, whilst the Dutch were able to provision for four months. Also, the sterns of Dutch ships were much higher than those of either the English or the French, and invariably had a square tuck as against the English rounded one.

Aemilia was the flagship of Maerten Harpertszoon Tromp, whose name ranks with that of de Ruyter as one of the two most famous in Dutch naval history. Born at Brielle in the south of Holland in 1597, Tromp first went to sea in 1605 when he was only eight years old. The East Indiaman in which he sailed was taken by an English frigate, and several years passed before he was able to escape and make his way back home. There are conflicting accounts of his teenage years, but Admiral Barjot in his *Histoire Mondiale de la Marine* asserts that Tromp entered the navy with the rank of lieutenant in 1622. Other sources put the year as 1624. In any event, his rise to lieutenant-admiral was rapid to say the least and in 1637, at the age of 40, he was appointed Commander-in-Chief of the Dutch fleet. Not unnaturally, Dutch, English and French histories offer somewhat differing versions of Tromp's achievements at sea, and what follows is a distillation of all three.

Although there was no officially declared conflict between the English and the Dutch until 1652, the world's two seafaring giants had been waging a fierce commercial war over very many years, and it was a war which the English were losing. On 27 February 1623 the small English colony at Amboyna in the East Indies was massacred by the Dutch and driven off the island. England took no action, and two years later even joined forces with the Dutch to fight the Portuguese for a foot-hold in India. But relations continued uneasy and in 1639, when Tromp chose to fight a Spanish fleet in English waters, England's neutrality was severely strained. Years later, Tromp cocked another snook at Holland's rivals by refusing to dip his flag in salute as he sailed past Dover Castle, an insult upon which pretext open war was

finally declared. In the meantime, Tromp won his famous victory in the Battle of the Downs.

Holland was at war with Spain, and that summer of 1639 saw the assembly at Corunna (*La Coruna*) of a huge combined Spanish and Portuguese fleet, by far the biggest armada since that of 1588. Tromp had intelligence of this muster, and decided that his only chance of beating such a vastly superior force was to engage it in waters so confined as to prevent its optimum deployment. To a lesser man, the odds would have seemed terrifying. The Spanish and Portuguese admirals commanded a fleet of 75 sail, including the great ship *S Teresa*, a mighty carrack of 2,400 tons, 68 guns, and a crew of 1,000 – four times the size of Tromp's *Aemilia* – and several others almost as big. Altogether, a force of 21,000 fighting men. Tromp had his *Aemilia* and 16 other ships whose complements, in total, numbered fewer than 2,000 men.

Nevertheless, the Dutch admiral sailed out to meet the enemy in accordance with his bold plan. The first engagement took place off Beachy Head on 16 September and most ironically, Tromp paid tribute to his future adversaries by adopting the tactics employed by Drake and Howard in their defeat of the previous Armada. Eschewing any strict line of battle formation, each of his captains harried the enemy at will, and in the smoke and confusion of such close encounters the firing of Spanish and Portuguese ships was often directed against each other. The Dutch emerged as decisive victors, and the combined fleets withdrew to the Downs. Tromp pursued them and ordered his own small fleet to anchor slightly to the south. He was confident that, trapped in the neck of the channel and hampered by unfavourable winds, his battered enemy would make no attempt to beat north. So he lay at anchor and sent an urgent request home for more ships, including fireships. His grateful government was quick to respond, and Tromp struck again on 21 October. He let his ships drift north with the tide, and attacked from the luff with great ferocity. The Spanish and Portuguese were utterly routed and almost entirely destroyed. The *S Teresa* was set on fire and blown to pieces in an enormous explosion, and the rest of the combined fleet suffered hardly less drastically. Only nine ships escaped. Tromp captured 16, and the others were either sent to the bottom or damaged beyond repair. Tromp lost 100 men killed. The Spanish and Portuguese lost 7,000. So far as the Iberian peninsula was concerned, the Battle of the Downs marked a definite end to its years of glory at sea. So final and decisive a defeat of the English became a somewhat different matter.

In the 14 years which immediately followed the Battle of the Downs, Tromp enjoyed the well-earned adulation of his fellow countrymen. He was worshipped by his men, who spoke of him always as *Bestevaer* – our good father. But they looked to him when war with England was at last and inevitably declared, for perhaps a little too much. He sailed again for the Downs, scene of his former glory, and in May 1652 he anchored his ships off Dover. The oft-repeated story that he fixed a broom to his masthead as a sign of his intent to sweep the channel clean seems oddly out of character and is probably a myth. In the event, he was subsequently engaged and defeated by a much inferior English fleet commanded by Admiral Blake, and was forced to withdraw with the loss of two ships. He was back again in November, this time with a far stronger fleet of 80 men-o'-war acting as escort to a convoy of 300 merchant ships bent on passing through the Straits of Dover. He successfully fought off an attack by Blake and then, with all of the merchantmen safely away, came to anchor off Boulogne.

A few months later, in February 1653, Tromp attempted to repeat his triumph by escorting another large convoy. This time, though, his opponents were ready. A combined English fleet under Blake, Penn and Monk engaged him in a running battle from Portland to Calais Sands, and defeated him by sinking nine of his warships and 40 merchantmen. In his next encounter with the English in June of that year, he lost 17 of his ships and the Dutch government sent a message to Oliver Cromwell asking for peace to be restored. Cromwell spurned the approach, and Tromp appeared yet again in the Channel towards the end of July. This was to be his last battle. During the ferocious seafighting which eventually ensued, the gallant admiral lost his life in exactly the same way as did Nelson 150 years later; he was hit in the breast by a musket shot. As he fell, he called to his men: *Houdt goede, mijn kinderen! Met mij is het gedaan!* 'Keep good courage, my children! With me it is done!'

Grievously mourned throughout the Netherlands, Tromp was buried with great ceremony at Delft, where stands his monument.

AEMILIA

DUTCH

De Prins Willem

IN HER TIME, the *Prins Willem* was one of the world's finest merchantmen. Built at Middelburg in Zeeland and at something like 2,000 tons, she was easily the biggest vessel in the Dutch East India Company's (*de VOC*) fleet, their flagship and their great pride. With her keel laid down in 1649, she was launched on 1 January 1650, and fitted out in time to begin her maiden voyage to Batavia on 5 May 1651.

Although constructed by the shipwrights of Zeeland in the south of Holland, *Prins Willem* was built – as were every one of *de VOC*'s ships – using the Amsterdam measure; that is to say in multiples of the old Amsterdam foot of 28.31 centimetres, near-enough equal to the English foot of twelve inches. By this standard, she was 181 feet from stem to stern, had a full-bellied depth of 18 feet, and was 45 feet on the beam. She was designed with only two full decks, but her generous depth of hold permitted the addition later of a 'cow-deck' or orlop, laid down above the cargo hold to afford accommodation for the extra fighting men required in times of war. In accordance with what was then the custom, her three, square-rigged masts were placed in precise order. The main deck was measured off into 11 equal parts, and the foremast was stepped well for'ard at a distance of one part from the stem. The main mast was set near or at centre, and the mizzen just one part from the stern. It was a very successful mode.

As to her sail plan, the old Dutch sailmakers employed a method of calculation which also worked extremely well. To assess the optimum requirement they multiplied the piece width of their very fine and heavy canvas (usually 30 'thumbs', a measure which constituted one *el*, or roughly one English yard) by the number of feet on the beam, added a zero, then divided by six to arrive at the total number of *ellen* needed for a full suit of sail. So, a ship with a 30-foot-beam would use 30 × 30 = 900, plus a zero = 9,000, divided by 6 = 1,500 *ellen*. This ingenious formula was employed by the Dutch throughout the 17th and well into the 18th centuries.

Quite aside from her practical conception, *Prins Willem* was a work of great beauty. Her ornamentation by way of decorative carvings was a marvel of delight. The massive two-ton figure-head of a pouncing lion was only one of scores of hardwood sculptures which elaborated her stern, rails, and beak to enhance her from bowsprit to rudder, and this in spite of the fact that the thrifty Dutch burghers did not normally concern themselves with such frivolity. Indeed, so much was paid in wages to the *Prins Willem* wood-carvers, those who came later to paint the

ship were restricted to a total budget of only 160 florins. The artists and painters overcame this parsimony by means of a clever device; unable to afford final gilding, they first painted the figures an ochrous yellow, then added a covering of resin mixed with sulphur. In sunshine, or reflecting the light from her three enormous lanterns, the result was an appearance of costly gold and the high stern especially must have looked beautiful. Its embellishments included the shields of *de VOC* and of Middelburg, a painted carving of Prins Willem II flanked by lions and saluted by trumpeting angels, also warriors, water nymphs and dolphins. Much of the carving was fretted, or open, to allow the wind to blow through.

Prins Willem was manned in times of peace by a crew of about 150 and like almost all Indiamen, both English and Dutch, she was quite well armed. She had provision in her capacity as a merchant ship for the mounting of 32 guns; 24 black iron pieces each weighing two and a half tons and firing a shot of up to 24 pounds, a further six firing shots of between 18 and 29 pounds, and a pair of light bronze *mignon* or small anti-personnel cannon which were probably mounted topsides. Most surprising to us now is the fact that although *de VOC* was a commercial conglomerate run by seventeen 'directors' from seven largely-autonomous provinces, its rules of conduct were clear and un-equivocal and resulted in marvellous efficiency. Each ship had two 'masters', the captain, and the merchant. The latter was vested with complete authority in all matters concerning cargo and destinations, the former being responsible for navigation, discipline and safety of passage.

So far as *Prins Willem* was concerned, this arrangement was initially short-lived. After only one round voyage to the east – she sailed out of Batavia on 19 December and completed her home run to Holland on 28 June 1652 – she was loaned by *de VOC*, together with four other of their ships, for service with the Lands Vloot in the war with England. As a man-o'-war, she needed at least 40 heavy cannon, and this necessitated the cutting-out of more gun-ports. It is thought, too, that in order to facilitate this extra armament, her forecastle head and much of her forecastle was removed. The refit must have been carried out hastily because, by October of that year, she was actively engaged in the Battle of the Downs under the command of that most intriguing character, Witte Corneliszoon de With (1599–1658).

The names of Tromp and de Ruyter are of course legendary, but not quite so much is generally known about the controver-

sial figure of de With. He was, and from a very early age, a man with a great rage to live. Aggressive and belligerent by nature, and impetuously brave to the point of rash folly, he had a temper which even in times of repose simmered just below boiling point. This was his unfortunately-dominant dark side. On the other hand, he was clever and resourceful, and possessed of that sort of restless intellect which owes nothing to formal education. Son of a fisherman destined to an early watery grave, de With (pronounced 'Witt') was born in Den Briel in 1599 and raised by his widowed mother in the restrictive Baptist faith. Being as he was an inveterate brawler, and fighting being a sin, he soon abandoned his mother's religion and ran off to sea in a merchant-man when he was barely 17 years old. He wound up in Jacatra, where he rapidly became so troublesome that, in order to be rid of him, the governor there wrote him a glowing testimonial and packed him off back home.

This was in 1620, when de With was 21 years old. He used the Governor of Jacatra's testimonial to procure for himself a post in the Lands Vloot, and was commissioned as a lieutenant in 1621. He took part in many expeditions to the West Indies and South America, and eventually rose to the rank of flag captain under Admiral Piet Hein, a very gallant sailor whose wise and prudent nature could not have been in greater contrast. One was a perfect foil to the other, and it was while sailing together in South American waters that they attacked and captured the Spanish silver fleet in the Bay of Matanza before returning in triumph to Holland. They were lauded as heroes, but not for long. Soon afterwards, following the death of Piet Hein, the Lands Vloot fell into a state of decay, its ships neglected and their crews demoralised. Many officers resigned, not least among them Tromp and de With. Inevitably, though, there quickly came a time when the services of such seasoned mariners were again desperately needed, and in 1637 they were asked to return to duty. Both agreed, but the circumstances marked an end to what had hitherto been a firm friendship. Witte de With, one year younger than Tromp but with much wider experience at sea, fully expected to be appointed Lieutenant Admiral with Tromp as his second in command. Instead, and doubtless with regard to de With's headstrong nature, that order was reversed and de With became Tromp's bitter rival. Yet he served faithfully under Tromp in several major encounters including, in 1639, the first Battle of the Downs. Together they attacked a fleet of 75 Spanish warships carrying troops to fight in Holland, blockaded them in English territorial waters whilst waiting for reinforcements to

DE PRINS WILLEM

DE PRINS WILLEM

arrive, then utterly destroyed the Spaniards with fire-ships and cannon-shot.

Much later, in August 1652, Tromp resigned following a quarrel with the Admiralty, and de With succeeded at long last to the post he felt he had all along deserved. But his promotion to Lieutenant Admiral was by no means a popular one. Before he could take his place in the flagship *De Brederode*, the officers and men of Tromp's old command issued notice to the States General that the moment de With stepped on board would be the moment they all stepped ashore. With uncharacteristic restraint, de With backed off from this confrontation, opting instead to hoist his flag on the big East Indiaman. In fairness to de With, it must be recorded that he was by no means solely responsible for the mutinous atmosphere then prevalent throughout the Lands Vloot. Tromp's resignation had been in protest against a government neglect affecting every officer and man afloat and this, with a war against England plainly imminent, was a situation crying out for remedy. Tromp was almost immediately pressed back into service, and so the old rivalry was re-established. However, as before when close collaboration was imperative, all antagonism was directed against the common enemy.

After suffering defeat at the Battle of Newport in June 1653, de With's command of 30 ships was blockaded at Texel by an English force under George Monck, later Duke of Albermarle. Tromp sent a signal to de With that he would try to draw Monck off station so that he (de With) could get out of the shallow waters in which his ships were trapped. Tromp's ploy succeeded, but de With remained in trouble. A raging storm blew up, and because the beacons which marked the narrow channel had been removed in order to foil the English, any attempt to put to sea would be tantamount to inviting disaster. Regardless of his ragings, every one of de With's pilots refused to accept responsibility for the safety of their ships, and his squadron remained as securely trapped as when Monck was waiting out there.

It is easy for a seaman to imagine how closely the fury of Witte de With matched that of the dark, storm-lashed night. Less easy to conceive is the means by which he conquered his dilemma. He rounded up every fisherman on the island, commanded them to take out their boats, and lining each side of the narrow channel, anchor on the sandbanks burning torches to mark his way. Then, taking personal charge of the sounding-lead on board of his big East Indiaman, he led his squadron safely out and into the open sea, and what self-respecting sailor would not follow such a man.

His force joined that of Tromp late the following afternoon, and they engaged the English in a battle off Scheveningen on 31 July 1653. It was, and truly, a battle of giants. Tromp was killed in the conflict, but contrary to his expectations, de With was not appointed to succeed him as commander in chief. Nevertheless, he continued in his naval career and died in battle – ironically in Tromp's old flagship *De Brederode* – in October 1658 during Holland's war with Sweden.

In the meantime, *Prins Willem* was returned to her owners *de VOC*, and resumed her role as merchantman. In all, she made 17 round voyages, most of them between Zeeland and Batavia, the final one commencing on 13 December 1661. Having made vast fortunes for each of the shareholders of *de VOC*, she was wrecked on the Isle of Brandon, near Mauritius, on 10 or 11 February 1662.

Curiously, because the original never sailed to their country, the Japanese paid several millions of pounds for the building at Makkum during 1984–85 of an exact replica of *Prins Willem*. Guided by old paintings and a fine contemporary model in Amsterdam's Scheepvaart Museum, the Netherlands craftsmen did a wonderful job, and *Prins Willem* lies now in all of her old glory in an especially re-created 'Dutch' harbour at Nagasaki. Where, thanks almost entirely to the lifelong love and labour of Dutch maritime historian Herman Ketting, she looks and *feels* exactly as she did when she was a champion of the seas.

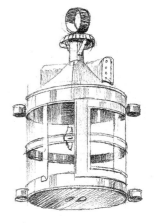

DUTCH

De Zeven Provinciën

FLAGSHIP OF THE FAMOUS Admiral Michiel Adriaanszoon de Ruyter, *De Zeven Provinciën* of around 800 tons ranked very high in her time amongst the world's most formidable men-o'-war. Her design and construction embodied the finest skills and materials then extant, and much that was innovative. She was also a great work of art, combining all the practical qualities of a superb fighting ship with the magnificent decorative features of a royal ceremonial barge.

Built by Pieter van Zwijnsdrecht at Delfshaven in 1664–65, *De Zeven Provinciën* was 163 feet long, 43 feet wide, and had a hull depth ex-superstructures of 16 feet 6 inches. She was capable of devastating firepower, mounting no fewer than 80 guns. On the lower (and main) gun deck, 28, big 36-pounders; on the upper deck 26, a mix of 18- and 12-pounders; in the forecastle and afterdeck, a total of 26, bronze 6-pounders. This hull design of only two through decks was common to all Dutch fighting ships of that era, as were the square-rigged sails on all three masts, with a steering spur on the mizzen. Marine historians hold differing opinions as to the size of her crew, but the figure of 500–530 quoted by the writer of an article in the February 1959 issue of Holland's premier nautical magazine *De Blauwe Wimpel* (The Blue Peter) seems to be excessive. We know that Tromp's 46 guns flagship *Aemilia* carried a maximum complement of 200, so although somewhat bigger and heavier the 163-foot *Zeven Provinciën* would have been hard pressed indeed to accommodate and provision for 500 seamen, even with bunks three-tiered in the foc'sle head and hammocks slung over the guns on both decks.

Having regard to her enormous wealth of embellishment, it is probably fair to assume that *De Zeven Provinciën* was commissioned by a grateful Dutch government as a splendid tribute to her greatest living admiral (Tromp was long dead, killed fighting the English in 1653), an assumption borne out by the elaborate carving on her stern, just above the rudder post, of the two crossed anchors which represented de Ruyter's family crest. Flanking and surmounting these, a great profusion of other deeply-carved armorial bearings including those of Holland, Friesland and Groningen, and Gelderland, Zeeland and Utrecht. The high wide stern, with its typical flat tuck, must have presented a riot of colour, the coats of arms all blue on a yellow (not gold, as on English ships) ground, and the ranks of heraldic beasts and figures painted every conceivable hue. Topsides, she

was bedecked when dressed overall with a multitude of flags and pennants, and must then have offered a spectacle to stir every Dutchman's heart.

But *De Zeven Provinciën*'s outward splendour was always firmly subjugate to her prime and efficient function. Every inboard nook and cranny, and not excluding the senior officers' quarters, was designed to provide for the mounting of cannon or for the handy stowage of powder and shot. The admiral's great cabin, located as usual astern on the quarter deck, was the only exception permitted. Master gunners and their mates had free access at all times, even when the ship lay at anchor and when officers might be entertaining friends from ashore. Unimaginable on an English ship, it was this brand of unilateral discipline which made de Ruyter an outstanding leader of men, and which enabled him to score brilliant victories often against daunting odds.

Returning to the question of crew, and before going on to her performance at sea in the imminent second war with England, it is interesting to quote from a report by de Ruyter regarding the state of his ship on 29 March 1666, barely one year after her launching. In it, he advised his government that due to higher pay and much better conditions then being offered to seamen by the merchant service, *De Zeven Provinciën* could muster only 190 hands, and some of them not seasoned. There was no such paucity of officers, because officers enjoyed vastly better conditions, and also the security of a proper term of employment. As with other navies, common seamen were taken on *ad hoc* and sometimes but not always paid off – should they survive – at the end of current hostilities. However, and regardless of his manning problems, de Ruyter sailed his great ship *De Zeven Provinciën* into world-wide maritime history.

As for the man, de Ruyter was born at Vlissingen in Holland on 24 March 1607 and he, like so many of his countrymen, went to sea as a young lad. He signed on as a boatswain's boy in 1618 and in 1638, at the age of 31, he became the captain of his own merchant ship. In 1641 he served with the Dutch navy, and acquitted himself well at a battle off Cape St Vincent in which the Netherlands assisted Portugal in a war against Spain. He returned to his merchantman in 1642 but was persuaded 10 years later, at the outbreak of the first Dutch-English war, again to accept a command in the navy. He served under Admiral Tromp

in the battles off Plymouth and Dungeness in 1652, and in the Three Days' Battle in the English Channel in 1653, and was highly commended for his skill and courage.

With the great Tromp dead, killed during the last of these fierce Channel battles, de Ruyter was offered a permanent commission in the navy, and in November of 1653 the Amsterdam admiralty board appointed him Vice Admiral of Holland. He spent all but two of the next 10 years in the Mediterranean (in 1659 he was recalled and sent into the Baltic, where he helped the Danes in their war with Sweden), protecting Dutch merchantmen against the depredations of Barbary pirates and French privateers. In 1664 he sailed for the Guinea Coast and there, acting on secret orders, took reprisals against English ships for their raids on Dutch settlements. He succeeded in chastising the English, but sailing on from there to a similar campaign in the West Indies he suffered a series of defeats. On his return to the Netherlands, however, he was promoted to the grand position of Lieutenant Admiral of Holland, and he worked with Johan de Witt on the important task of strengthening the Dutch navy in preparation for yet another war with England. Soon came the launching of de Ruyter's *De Zeven Provinciën,* a most important event in Dutch naval history because together the man and the ship forged its everlasting glory.

There have been a number of fascinating books about famous battles at sea, and de Ruyter's triumphs are adequately recorded, but one vital factor missing from most of these accounts is this: de Ruyter taught the English a lesson which they were not slow to learn, and adopt. The second of the Anglo-Dutch wars was fought in the narrow waters between the Dutch and English coasts and the English ships, bigger and much more heavily armed, lacked the sea-room in which they might best have employed their advantage. Admiral de Ruyter's resounding victory in the Four Days Battle of June 1666 was thanks in part to the superior manoeuvrability of his ships, but most of all to the rapid re-load and fire of his easily-handled, 18- and 12-pounders and the constant raking fire of his light, bronze cannon. In such close quarters, the big, 100-guns ships of the English fleet were ponderous to tack and bring about, and the rate of fire from their heavy 38- and 43-pound guns was woefully slow for such fast and furious short-range gunnery. The mighty *Royal Prince* was forced aground on the Galloper Shoals off East Anglia, set on

DE ZEVEN PROVINCIËN

fire and her entire crew made captive. The opposing fleets re-grouped each night, when the fighting ceased, and the four day action was broken off only when a persistent, dense fog hid the ships from one another. The mist was probably fortuitous, because such was the stubborn courage of both opposing forces, they might otherwise have battled on until hardly a ship was left afloat.

In the event, the fight was resumed two months later, when the same forces met again off the North Foreland of Kent. This time the English commander, the Duke of Albermarle, employed new tactics and de Ruyter was forced into retreat. Albermarle routed de Ruyter's ships, chasing them back into their native harbours, and then set out upon a campaign of pillage and destruction. He burned Dutch villages, wrecked their harbours and destroyed a great many merchant ships. However, the fact was that the Dutch and the English were much too evenly matched at the time for either side ever decisively to win, and de Ruyter extracted a crushing revenge. Exactly one year later, when England was reeling under the after-effects of the Great

Plague and the Fire of London, de Ruyter in *De Zeven Provinciën* led his famous raid on the Medway. He breached the heavy chain which formed its defensive boom and wrought terrible havoc upon the English men-o'-war laid up there in harbour for lack of men and resources. He burned the skeleton-crewed English fleet and chose the flagship *Royal Charles* as a prize to be taken in tow for transport back to Holland. It was the most crushing and humiliating attack on England since the conquest of 1066.

There was more to come. During the third and last of the Anglo-Dutch wars (1672–74) de Ruyter, in *De Zeven Provinciën,* inflicted even more heavy damage upon England's royal ships. In the long and furious Battle of Southwold Bay, he and his ship were singled out for a concerted attack by two much bigger ships, the 100-guns (new) *Royal Charles,* and the 96-guns *St Andrew*. Both were forced to break off the engagement and *De Zeven Provinciën,* with only minor damage, went on to lead the Dutch fleet into a resounding victory. The following year, 1674, de Ruyter commanded his flagship in further great triumphs at the battles of Schoneveld and Kijkduin, when he repulsed

the invasion of Holland by a combined Anglo-French fleet.

With peace in Europe established, de Ruyter was sent by his government to deal once again with Holland's enemies in the Mediterranean. He accepted the order under protest, and in hind-sight his reluctance was sadly prophetic. He was mortally stricken at the Battle of Syracuse, off Sicily, on 22 April 1676, and died of his wounds one week later. His body was carried back to Holland in *De Eendracht* and laid to rest in the Nieuwe Kerk in Amsterdam.

But his famous ship lived on and, ironically, fought her last great battle – the Battle of Le Hogue in 1692 – as an ally of England in her war against France. The grand old flagship was badly damaged and hauled into Portsmouth for repairs. Although she returned to Holland under her own sail, she was then sold for demolition and broken up at a wharf near Delfs-haven, the place where she was built.

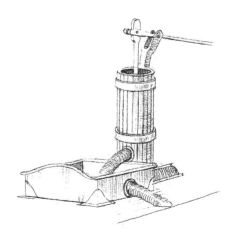

DE ZEVEN PROVINCIËN

De Noach

THIS BEAUTIFUL medium clipper, launched at Kinderdijk in 1857, was built and owned by the remarkable Fop Smit, grand old man of a shipbuilding and shipowning family famous throughout the world. *Noach* was the first of no fewer than six grand clippers destined to bear the same name, all of them built and owned by one or another of the Smits, but none of these successors ever gained more fame and she has always been regarded as easily the best of the lot.

A ship of 892 old tons, *Noach* had a wooden hull with little or no deadrise, not much keel, and a rounded stern. She was 47.5 metres in length and, with a width at maximum of 11.2 metres, rather broad in the beam. Nevertheless, and even though she lacked the fine sharp entrance and elegant narrow grace of the extreme clippers then being built in British yards, she was without doubt an extremely handsome vessel. With her distinctive figurehead of an outwards-gazing Noah, she was richly decorated at bows and stern with very fine carved-and-gilded scrollwork, and the fitting-out of her well ventilated passenger accommodation was done without regard to expense.

Noach was an unusual ship. With her very tall masts, enormous bowsprit and jib-boom she had to be heavily rigged, and was in fact the first Dutch ship ever to carry the iron-wire standing rigging (made for her by the English firm of Newall & Co) introduced in British yards about 1850. Later, her rigging was lowered in for reasons of economy, but even from the first she could ship more cargo than her foreign counterparts and be sailed quite efficiently by a crew of only 27 as opposed to the British clipper requirement of 32–34. This lively interest in money saving appears to have been characteristic of Fop Smit. He liked to be asked why he chose this particular name for his ships and to chuckle, it is said, over his answer. Noah, he would explain, must have been a very shrewd old individual; he timed the launching of his ark to coincide with the flood, and he sailed with only his own family on board leaving behind – to drown unpaid! – all those who had helped him to build it. *De Noach* remained his proudest possession until he died in 1866, when ownership passed to his son Fop Smit Junior.

Noach's first master, Captain P Wierikx, startled the shipping world in 1858 with a claim that his ship had made a 24-hour run on her maiden voyage which beat any then recorded by the champion British tea clippers. Whatever the truth or otherwise, Captain Wierikx was certainly a great sail-carrier and the *Noach* under his command made some very fast passages indeed. His best time homeward from Batavia to Brouwershaven, deep-laden with sugar, ore, and a transport of soldiers, was set up in 1863 and never bettered by any of his successors. His astonishing time was 71 days port to port, 65½ days land to land, a passage of which the master of *any* ship could feel justifiably proud.

Examination of *Noach*'s passages reveals the curious fact that she was almost invariably a good deal faster on the homeward leg of her voyage, but her fastest time outward, made in 1866 under the command of Captain Lüpcke, was a noteworthy exception. Lüpcke sailed from Broewershaven to Batavia, land to land, in 65 days and port to port in 71 days. The fact remains however that over 13 consecutive voyages made under five different captains, *Noach* averaged 87½ days for her outward passages against 85½ days homeward bound. Much the most intriguing aspect of all this is the fact that *Noach* was not purpose-built for speed, but rather with an eye for cargo and passenger-carrying capacities. Old Fop Smit was not much interested in the ocean races then being run by ships in the China trade; his prime concern lay in the area of revenues, and in this he was brilliantly successful. Passengers revelled in the ease and comfort of *Noach*'s luxurious accommodation (each cabin had its own well-stocked liquor cabinet) and were attracted also by her unrivalled reputation for consistent regularity. Anyone booking a passage in the *Noach* could feel reasonably confident of arriving at the port of his destination in close to record time. Another novel feature: on 5 May 1864, on a passage from Brouwershaven to Batavia, Captain J R Ulrich surprised his passengers by producing what might well have been the first-ever ship's newspaper.

The *Noach* set out on her longest voyage in 1859, one which proved to be her most eventful. On a passage to Australia she ran into a tremendous gale which ripped away her foremast and jib-boom, and much of her copper sheathing. Forced into Port Jackson for repairs, she sailed on later to Sydney, and on then to Newcastle, New South Wales to pick up a cargo of coal for Batavia. After discharging her coal, she took on rice and a supercargo of 80 coolies bound for Macao. Back then to Batavia, before heading home via Semarang. When at last she docked back in Brouwershaven in 1861, she had been away 532 days.

The last of her very fast passages was made in 1871, when Captain van Schelven sailed her from Zierikzee to Batavia, port to port, in 72 days; a disappointment for the young skipper, as he failed by just one day to equal Captain Lüpcke's record run of 1866.

In 1877 an ageing *Noach* was re-rigged as a barque, and went on to offer sterling service to her owner until she was finally demolished in 1884. But even then she continued useful, as much of her was salvaged for use in the construction of the *Thorbecke*, last of all the clipper ships built in Holland's yards.

The other five Smit ships of this same name ranged in size from 945 old tons to 1,503 old tons and were built at Slikkerveer in 1867, 1869, 1874, 1877 and 1878. Of these five, *Noach III* came closest to approaching the fame of her original namesake, not least because her maiden voyage was a narrowly-averted disaster. Her outward passage to Batavia was smooth and uneventful, but she was saved from a tragic end on her passage home only by Captain Kruyt's superb seamanship and iron control.

She left Batavia during the night of 11–12 March 1870, laden deep with cargo and a full complement of passengers. Dawn brought a furious storm and she was driven hard on to Pasop Reef. Her mainmast was broken off, tearing down the mizen as it fell, and the yards caught up in the rigging and lashed by pounding waves threatened to smash holes in her hull. Kruyt had masts and rigging cut away, and managed to keep his ship from being torn asunder on the reef until help arrived in the form of the steamship *Tjiliwong*. It speaks volumes for the qualities of both ship and captain that, with only her foremast left intact and without stopping over for repairs in port, Kruyt nursed his ship back home to Brouwershaven in a passage of only 97 days.

Another distinguishing feature of the career of *Noach III* is that she was the only one out of all six *Noachs* to keep her high masts and rigging right to the end of her days. At 1,117 old tons, she was the first *Noach* to exceed 1,000 and yet her lines, according to a Melbourne newspaper of the day, were '. . . as beautiful as those of any yacht.' Fop Smit Junior sold her in 1890 to a Norwegian owner who changed her name to *Gudvang* and used her as a timber ship.

DE NOACH

Tjerimai

ALTHOUGH THE *Tjerimai* created no sailing records and was never noted for any particular, exciting performance, she holds a very special place in the hearts of all those many Dutchmen who love the old, tall ships. She was, and remains, the most celebrated of the splendid bark-rigged clippers built in Holland (the famous *Noach*s were square rigged), combining great, weatherly strength with elegance, beauty and a respectable turn of speed. She never once lay idle during a lifespan of more than 40 years, and must have repaid each of her three owners many times her purchase price.

She was built in 1883 by J F Meursing (son of W H) at the family's Nachtegaal shipyard in Amsterdam. The Meursings specialised in the design of composite ships; sturdy clippers with iron frames and knees, the wooden hulls sheathed in copper plates against the ravages of tropical marine parasites. Other fine vessels out of the Nachtegaal yard include the *Merapi* of 850 old tons built in 1870, the *Sindoro* of 993 old tons built in 1874, the *Slamat* of 916 new tons built in 1876, and the *Smeroe* of 1,000 new tons built in 1878. The Meursing family also built all seven ships of the famous series which bore the same name of *Thorbecke*.

These mighty *Thorbecke* sisters apart, *Tjerimai* was the biggest clipper ever constructed in the Nachtegaal yard. Built for the Amsterdam shipping firm of A Hendrichs & Co, she was a three-masted bark of 1,013 new tons with a length of 188.3 feet, a beam of 36.7 feet, and a depth of 21.1 feet. This relative measurement of length at roughly five times that of beam, together with a rather full entrance and a somewhat dated and unattractive flat stern, was typical of Meursing design. Speed of passage was not the prime concern; the Meursings built for cargo capacity, economy of handling and sailing, and durability. It was by concentrating on these qualities to the exclusion of all others that Meursing and Hendrichs are now generally accepted as being the first people in Holland, if not in Europe, to recognise the fact that the era of speed-above-all was very rapidly drawing to a close.

Nevertheless, the *Tjerimai* had the overall appearance of a splendid, medium clipper and in 1893, when her then-captain, F Diepenbroek, brought her home from Batavia to Ijmuiden in a praiseworthy 93 days, she was already 10 years old. In all of the 11 round voyages she made under the Dutch flag, this was her best-ever passage, and she never improved on it before Hendrichs sold her to a Russian shipowner in 1898. It is interesting now to speculate that Hendrichs might have had cause to regret

that sale, because this wonderful ship went on to give sterling service to her subsequent owners for a further 27 years.

Aside from the fact that she was never laid up, or modified, little is known about the *Tjerimai* until, some 15 years later, she became the property of the Swedish/Finnish shipowner Gustaf Erikson. This final change of ownership, in 1913, marks one of the most significant events in the entire history of tall ships. It heralded the founding of a one-man renaissance, and the realisation of a dream.

The name of Captain Gustaf Erikson will live forever as that of the man who, far more than any other, maintained a stubborn faith in the power and majesty of sail many long years after all others had dismissed the notion as archaic. The son of a farmer on Aland, biggest of all the numerous islands in the Baltic, Erikson went to sea as a small boy, became a sea-cook when he was 13 years old, and went on to sail before the mast throughout the rest of his active life. At the age of 18 he was first mate of a timber ship trading in the Baltic, and at 19 he gained his first full command as the master of another Baltic timber ship. Later, he sailed the world's oceans, first as mate on a full-rigged ship, and then with his own commands.

In 1913, and after 25 years at sea, Erikson had saved enough money to fulfill his life's ambition. He became the owner of his first tall ship and that one, the fore-runner of many which would later wear his house flag, was the Dutch-built clipper *Tjerimai*.* Erikson was a remarkable individual, a man with a deep feeling for tradition; his very first action when he acquired the *Tjerimai* was to remove the Russian lettering on her bows and sternboard, and give her back her original name. He did the same with every ship he ever bought, always restoring to them the name under which they were launched.

All of Erikson's subsequent fame and fortune derived from the little *Tjerimai*. He employed her as a timber ship and she rapidly earned him enough money to buy a second tall ship, and soon after that, a third. At that time, many fine sailing ships were being sold cheap and Erikson took full advantage of a buyers' market. By the year 1917 the 'mother ship' had spawned another eight of her kind, and in 1924 the Erikson fleet of sailing ships had grown to an impressive 16. He ran them out to Australia, often in ballast but sometimes with coal for South Africa, to return with cargoes of grain along the old, long routes around Cape Horn.

In the 22 years between 1913 and 1935 Erikson bought a total

of more than 40 tall ships, some of which he re-sold after only a few years. But he knew his business better than any man alive, and he always kept the best. As late as 1932 the town of Mariehamn on Finland's island of Aland was home port to no fewer than 20 majestic ships, by 1934 that number had risen to 27. It was during the following year, 1935, that Erikson bought the last of his darlings and the *Moshulu*, at 4,900 tons, was the biggest ship he had ever possessed.

Lovers of sail can only marvel at Erikson's devotion to the craft. Starting with one ship, the *Tjerimai*, he built up a great fleet of 'antique' vessels which combined beauty with utility over a period of more than 40 years. When he added *Moshulu* to his fleet she joined a company of sister ships with immaculate pedigrees and famous names, from the finest shipyards in Europe. They included the *Viking* of 4,000 tons, the *Pamir* (4,500), *L'Avenir* (3,650), the *Passat* (4,700), the *Pommern* (4,050), the *Herzogin Cecilie* (4,350), the *Olivebank* (4,400) and the *Archibald Russell* of 3,950.

Until his death after the Second World War, Gustaf Erikson gave pride of place in his offices at Mariehamn to a model of his first and favourite ship, the *Tjerimai;* and although the company turned long ago to modern steamers, that model might still be there today. After a long and hard-working career, *Tjerimai* went down fighting for her life following a collision in the North Sea, on 14 August 1925, with the steam trawler *Christina Catherina*.

Ironically, the *Christina Catherina* was a trawler out of Ijmuiden, in Holland.

* Accounts of Erikson's life differ. Some have it that his first acquisition (also in 1913) was from Germany, a four-masted ship, the Renne Rickmers, *built in 1887 by Russell & Co of Port Glasgow. Erikson is said by some to have re-named her the* Aland, *but whether or not he was the actual sole owner appears to be in doubt. In any event, the* Aland *was wrecked on her very first voyage under that name, whilst* Tjerimai *went on to sail under the Erikson house flag for a further 12 busy years.*

TJERIMAI

Geertruida Gerarda

THERE WERE TWO Dutch vessels of this name, both of them built by J & K Smit in their yard at Krimpen aan de Lek, and both to the order of shipowner P van der Hoog. Both (perhaps unfortunately) had hulls of steel and both might reasonably lay claim to having been clippers, although neither one was ever a mighty sailer. The first had a short and fairly unremarkable life, but the second remains fixed in seafaring memory as a grand and unusual ship.

The original *Geertruida Gerarda* was a three-masted bark of 1,360 new tons, laid down in 1891 and launched the following year. Her short career was marked with only one memorable passage and that was in 1899, when she was eight years old. She was lying in New York together with another Dutch ship, the *Nicolaas Witsen,* and as both vessels were bound for Australia their captains decided to make a race of it. The *Nicolaas Witsen* set sail on 3 June bound for Melbourne, and the *Geertruida G* left on the following day bound for Adelaide. Both ships made a passage of 104 days, arriving respectively on the 15 and 16 September. Although *Geertruida* had the somewhat shorter run to Adelaide her performance remains very creditable, because the *Nicolaas Witsen* was a much sharper-built ship and was capable also of carrying a good deal more canvas.

The first *Geertruida* was wrecked on 1 May 1901 on a passage from Surabaya in Java to Newcastle in New South Wales. She was badly damaged by shifting ballast and broken spars in a heavy storm, and her captain was forced to cut away masts and rigging. Most of the crew took to the lifeboats and reached South Africa after a gruelling three weeks of short rations and little water. The rest of the crew were taken off by a steamer and the hulk was left to drift across the Indian Ocean before sinking, finally, near Mauritius.

At 2,505 new tons and with four masts instead of three, the second *Geertruida* was almost twice the size of her predecessor. Launched on 19 November 1904, she measured 85 metres in length, had a beam of 13.60 metres and a depth of 8.25 metres. Her rigging was made at Vlaardingen by the firm of Hoogerwerf. She was the very last, blue-water sailing ship to be built in Holland, and she was also the biggest. Another notable feature was that she was the only Dutch-built clipper ship ever to be rigged as a four-masted bark, with the single exception of her J & K Smit/van der Hoog sister ship the *Jeanette Francoise.* However, in spite of carrying double topgallants, the rigging of these big, steel barks was far from heavy, and although they were fine, handsome ships, neither of them was ever noted for speed of passage. All else equal, they followed the sound old Dutch traditions of seaworthiness, high cargo capacity, and economy of handling.

This new *Geertruida Gerarda* was given to Captain J Kuipers, who remained in command throughout the rest of her years under the Netherlands national flag. She began her maiden voyage on 20 April 1905 out of Rotterdam with a mixed cargo for the East Indies, rounding the Cape of Good Hope on 27 June and arriving at Batavia on 7 August. She returned with sugar for the Port of London, but P van der Hoog had died during her absence, and his two big barks had been sold to the Rotterdam shipowner C J Lels.

It was a difficult time for sailing ships, but *Geertruida* did not lay idle for long. Her second voyage, in 1906, was out to Melbourne with a cargo of Norwegian timber, and she was able to secure a return cargo of wheat from Geelong destined for the French port of Dunkirk. After discharging her wheat, she sailed directly to Port Talbot in Wales to take on coal for the Chilean port of Mexilonnes. She left Port Talbot on 24 September 1907 and ran reasonably fair down to the southern latitudes; she was sighted on 20 November at 44° south and 60° west, about 400 miles due north of the Falkland Islands. This, though, was the last report of her until she was so many weeks overdue at her destination that anxiety over her had become acute. Captain Kuipers later described what happened in a letter to his son.

As he attempted to pass the Falklands, his ship was battered by furious head-on gales which roared up out of the south west and engulfed her for days and nights on end with crashing mountains of white water. He described the conditions as the worst he had ever encountered, with *Geertruida* labouring to hold her own in seas which smashed so fiercely over her that it was well nigh impossible, even with lifelines, for a man to venture out on deck. Hatch covers were splintered, and *Geertruida* shipped so much water that the crew was soaked as completely between decks as they were up top. Even during those short intervals when the storm did ease, Captain Kuipers was hardly able to muster a sufficient number of fit or uninjured men to get some sail on her before the tempest blew up yet again and he was forced to revert to bare poles. Some of his crew were genuinely ill, others feigned illness in order to avoid the risk of being swept overboard into seas from which there could be no hope of rescue.

That Captain Kuipers was a brave and stubborn man there can be no doubt, but due to the fact that he had an inadequate complement – fewer than 30 men, probably only 28 – and that most of the men had no previous experience of those terrible waters, he did not succeed in making that particular traverse around Cape Horn. He tried three times, was three times driven back, and was forced after an abortive fourth attempt to put up the helm and set an easterly course for a passage all the way around the bottom of the world. He sighted the Cape of Good Hope on 19 December, and having gone on then to circumnavigate the globe, he finally reached Mexillones on 14 March 1908, almost six months out of Port Talbot and long after many – including Lloyds of London – had begun to fear the worst.

Her coal at last discharged, the *Geertruida* was laden with salt-petre and made an uneventful passage back to Ostend. But what sad ignominy attended the twilight years of these proud, tall ships. She was sent at once to Rotterdam to blacken her holds with coke and be outward bound again for Chile, and again around Cape Horn. This time, however, Captain Kuipers met with better weather and he negotiated the Straits of Magellan with little trouble. His ship was much easier to handle because coke, although every bit as bulky as coal, is a great deal lighter and much less likely to cause problems of shifting during storms or in heavy seas.

Upon his return to home port in 1910, Captain Kuipers retired from the sea and the *Geertruida Gerarda* was sold to a German firm of shipowners in Hamburg, who re-named her the *Olympia.* The new owners kept her on the Cape Horn run, very probably with coal or coke, and as she dropped out of sight after the outbreak in 1914 of conflict in Europe, it is generally accepted that she spent the war years in Chile.

Olympia passed at some time after the war into the hands of Italian owners, and research suggests that the first post-war sighting of her was by Captain D Molenaar who, by coincidence, happened to have been second mate on the old *Geertruida* when she sailed on her maiden voyage. Captain Molenaar spotted her in 1920 as she lay alongside at Livorno in Italy, still being used as a coal vessel. Just a few years later, in 1924, she was damaged by fire, and rather than try to save her, the Italians broke her up.

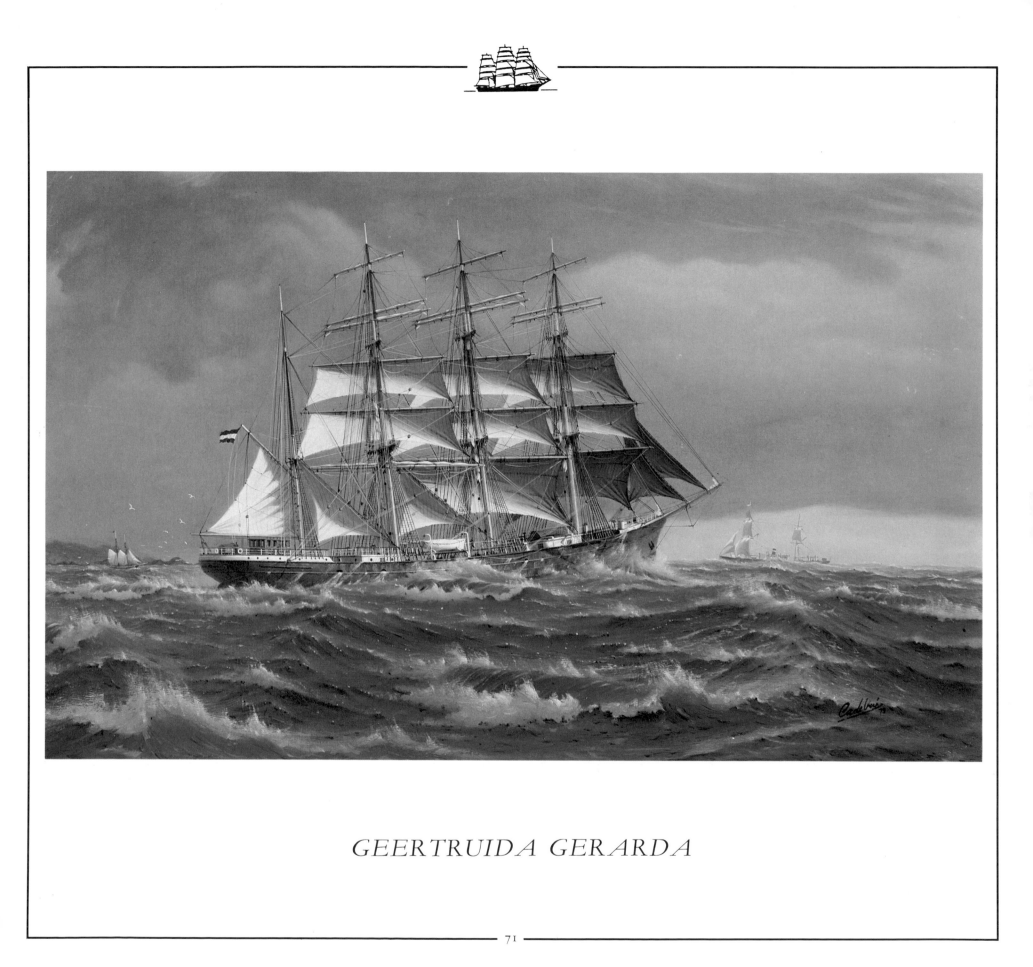

GEERTRUIDA GERARDA

DUTCH

Europa

THERE WILL, of course, always be argument, but many marine historians – and not only those of the Netherlands – hold firmly to the opinion that *Europa* was the best and most famous clipper ship ever to come out of Holland. She certainly was an extremely graceful vessel, and so very fast of passage that she set up a number of sailing records never bettered, or even closely approached, by any other sailing ship of any other nation. In several important respects she was unique.

Constructed by Huygens & Van Gelder at their Concordia shipyard, the steel-hulled *Europa,* laid down in 1897 and launched in 1898, was the last of only five ships ever built in Amsterdam by that company, all of them completed between 1886 and 1898 and all of them to the order of shipowner W A Huygens of Bussum. Her less-illustrious predecessors were the iron barks *Concordia* and *Oostenburg,* the steel bark *Amsterdam,* and the steel frigate *Nederland.* The *Europa,* last of this short series, was also the last of the big, tall ships ever to originate in Amsterdam. Even as she was being fitted out, plans for the creation of a new railway terminal were already well advanced, and when this huge Central Station began to rise over what had once been Amsterdam's great shipyards, the way out to the open sea was forever blocked and cut off. This might well be the one and only time in the history of sail when tall ships were forced to succumb, not to the power of steam at sea but to the advance of steam on land. *Sic transit gloria mundi.*

Square-rigged on three high masts, with a fine sharp entrance, rounded stern and a magnificent bowsprit almost 100 feet long, *Europa* was every inch a beautiful clipper of 1,911 new tons. Her dimensions as registered in English measure by Lloyds of London show her hull as having had lines a good deal sharper than was common in Netherlands design, lending her more the configuration of a ship out of Scotland's yards. With an overall hull length of 258.7 feet, she had a beam of only 42 feet, a ratio of just over six to one as opposed to the usual five. She had a depth of 23.6 feet, and a height from keel to topgallant mast-head of 188 feet. With all canvas spread, she carried 2,037 square metres of sail and all of which, in spite of their having no assistance from any donkey-engine, could competently be handled by a crew of only 25 men. Credit for this super efficiency, and indeed for all other detail of build and rigging, was due to her prospective captain, Gunther Bona, who personally supervised *Europa's* construction from the laying-down of her keel to her final fitting-out.

Europa's prime function was that of a fast cargo vessel, but with a poop of 44 feet and a 24-foot forecastle head she was able to accommodate a small number of first-class passengers and to carry four apprentice seamen. These apprentices were required to pay for the privilege, but after their first year at sea, and if they were then considered to be worthy of further training, they were paid thereafter at the rate of ten florins (about two English pounds, or eight US dollars) a month.

It seemed to take Captain Bona a long time to get the feel of his new ship, because his performance on her maiden voyage was inordinately poor. The passage out to Batavia took 99 days, whereas the *Noach* made the same passage 35 years earlier in 71 days and promptly made the much more difficult return passage also in 71 days. But those who wrote *Europa* off as a disappointment wrote her off too soon, because she proceeded the following year – still under Captain Bona – to set up sailing records so astonishing they have never been beaten to this day. On 9 March 1899 she left New York bound for Adelaide full laden with casks of paraffin, and arrived at the Australian port on 19 May. This stunning passage of only 71 days created great excitement in the shipping community and earned for *Europa* the nickname by which she quickly became known the world over. She was invariably referred to as 'The Flying Dutchman'; and as though to reinforce her right to this appellation she came close to repeating her tremendous performance on the first leg of her very next voyage. In 1900 she sailed again from New York to Adelaide, and made the passage in 77 days. However, although this was six days outside of her previous time, it was then and still remains two days faster than any other tall ship.

Having found her stride, as it were, Europa was quick to show her paces again. On two consecutive passages between New Zealand and Batavia via the turbulent Straits of Torres, The Flying Dutchman ran from port to port, the first time in 42 days, the second time in 44. Other noteworthy voyages under Captain Bona included Gravesend to New York in 36 days, New York to Melbourne in 90 days, then Newcastle, New South Wales to Falmouth *via* San Francisco in 135 days. Next came Liverpool to Wellington, New Zealand in 95 days, Dunedin, New Zealand to Tocopilla in Chile in 42 days, and Tocopilla to the Isle of Wight in 99 days.

Captain Bona left *Europa* in 1904, relinquishing his command to Captain Wiebes. It was the end of a legend; Wiebes was not a man to 'carry on', and The Flying Dutchman flew no more. In 1906 she set out upon what was to be her last voyage under the Dutch flag, and it was a voyage which ended in financial disaster.

At first all went well. Captain Wiebes took his ship up to Frederikshald in Norway, dumped her ballast and took on timber for Australia. Oddly enough, considering all which was to follow, he went on from there to make his best-ever passage in *Europa,* sailing from Dungeness out to Melbourne in a very creditable 90 days. But this proved to be the only profitable leg of a voyage planned to take 15 months: Norway to Melbourne with timber, Melbourne to Newcastle, New South Wales, in ballast and from there to Chile with coal, and from Chile back home with saltpetre. In the event, *Europa* did not see Holland again for 26 months.

The passage from Newcastle to Chile showed no profit, because Huygens had chartered for 12 shillings a ton just in order to pay expenses. He was relying for his rewards on the 20 shillings a ton for saltpetre out of Chile. But his contract stipulated loading at Caleta Colosa by 15 September 1907, and two factors conjoined to militate against any such eventuality. First; no great sail carrier, Captain Wiebes was hampered by rough weather and was very late to reach Caleta, and second; the price of saltpetre was steadily falling. *Europa's* coal was not off-loaded until after the 15 September deadline and Huygens refused a new offer of 18 shillings a ton for saltpetre, preferring to send *Europa* back to Australia in ballast and load there with grain for England at the current rate of 31 shillings a ton. But it was as though the *Europa* was carrying a Jonah. By the time she had returned to Australia, grain prices too had fallen and the cargo Huygens had confidently expected just did not materialise. There was nothing for it but to sail around to Port Pirie and pick up a cargo of nickel ore for transport to Dunkirk at only 17 shillings a ton.

Again *Europa* made a rough, slow passage, and when towards the end of 1908 she finally returned to her home port, a disgusted and disgruntled W A Huygens promptly put her up for sale. She was bought for £4,800 by J A Henschien of Lillesand in Norway, who re-named her the *Lotos.* Henschien sold her in 1916 to Heiskein & Son of Kristiaansand who changed her name again, this time to the *Asra.*

It was under this name that the old Flying Dutchman, last of Holland's tall ships ever to sail in blue water, met a cruel and unjustified end. On the afternoon of 5 May 1917 she was torpedoed and sunk in the Atlantic whilst on a passage from Belfast to New York. Fortunately, her crew was picked up and landed safely at Balderic in north-west Ireland.

A beautiful model of the *Europa* stands now in Amsterdam's Nederlandsch Historisch Scheepvaartmuseum, donated by the heirs of W A Huygen. Also to be seen in the museum are the original shipwrights' drawings.

EUROPA

Ranger

THE *Ranger* is a prime example of a ship made famous not so much for any intrinsic quality of design or innovation but rather by the exploits and character of her most remarkable captain, John Paul Jones. Constructed in 1777 to an order of Congress, she was built at Portsmouth, New Hampshire by the Hackett family of shipwrights, and just preceded her sister ship the *Hampden*, launched from the same yard. The two were almost identical in hull, having a length between perpendiculars of 97 feet, a beam of 29 feet, and both were of 308 tons. But whereas the *Ranger* was a square-rigged Continental corvette, the *Hampden* was rigged as a brigantine. This made for extra room on the latter's quarterdeck, and allowed her to mount 22 guns as opposed to *Ranger*'s 18.

The events leading up to John Paul Jones' appointment as commander of the new American warship were colourful to say the least, but any historian attempting an objective assessment of the man is faced with a difficult task. The many accounts of his life are almost equally divided between *pro* and *con*, according to the affinities of their authors. So far as some American chroniclers are concerned, he was a patriot and a hero; to all of the British, he was a traitor and a scoundrel. Having regard to the basic known facts, the reader must judge for himself.

Jones' real name was John Paul (the 'Jones' was assumed later in an attempt to conceal his true identity) and he was born in Scotland in 1747, the son of a landscape gardener. In 1766 he was granted a warrant as a midshipman in the British Navy. Why the warrant was almost immediately rescinded is not to be found in navy records, but he shipped out to the West Indies in a merchantman that same year and was soon engaged in the nefarious slave trade as third mate in a brigantine. In 1770, during a passage home from Jamaica to Scotland, he flogged the ship's carpenter literally to death, and was charged on landing with murder. He jumped his bail by shipping out to the West Indies yet again and three years later, in 1773, he killed another seaman, allegedly a mutineer. Having managed to avoid retribution a second time, and unable to return to his native Scotland, he threw in his lot with the American revolutionaries and was given a commission as first lieutenant in the emerging Continental navy. He was given command of the newly-launched *Ranger* on 14 June 1777, with orders to sail for France. There, on 14 February 1778, the *Ranger*'s flag bearing the new Stars and Stripes became the very first ever to be officially recognised and saluted by another warship of a foreign (France was then at war with the British) nation.

Jones sailed from Brest on 10 April, outward bound on a passage through St George's Channel and into the Irish Sea. Some accounts of this voyage assert that *Ranger* 'captured a few prizes and sank several ships', but there is a curious absence of any definite record. We do, however, have a record of Jones' shore attack on the little town of Whitehaven up on England's north-west coast. *Ranger* was brought to anchor at dawn on 23 April, and Jones led a hit-and-run assault on Whitehaven's two small forts. But it must have been the briefest of encounters, because by noon on that same day he had sailed north to the tiny island of St Mary's up in the Solway Firth, home of his native countryman Lord Selkirk, intending to seize the nobleman as hostage. Selkirk, however, was not in residence at the time and so, having only a few servants to contend with, Jones and his crew looted the house of everything they could carry away, including a great quantity of silver plate bearing Selkirk's coat of arms. Some years later, and perhaps with the thought of redeeming himself in the eyes of his natural compatriots, John Paul returned the plate to its rightful owners.

The following day, 24 April 1778, *Ranger* came upon HMS *Drake* off Carrickfergus in Ireland, and a short but furious battle ensued. In spite of the fact that *Drake* was not a warship – she was a small, converted merchantman armed only with light 4-pound guns – she held off *Ranger* for more than an hour before, having taken a tremendous battering from her opponent's heavier guns, she was forced to strike her colours with the loss of 42 killed or wounded men. Jones lost only eight of his crew, and sailed triumphantly back into Brest to be hailed by the French as a hero. This was on 8 May, and following a request by the French minister of marine, Jones was seconded to the French navy in order that he might lead a full scale expedition against the British. Command of the *Ranger* passed to Jones' disaffected first officer, Lieutenant Thomas Simpson, on 27 July, and on 26 September Simpson sailed her out of Brest on a passage home to New England.

In the meantime, Jones was left for a whole year to cool his heels ashore, and it was not until 14 August 1779 that the overdue expedition finally put to sea. The force consisted of Jones' flagship the *Bon Homme Richard* of 42 guns; the *Alliance*, a new US frigate just arrived in France mounting 36 guns; the *Pallas*, a French ship of 32 guns, and a much smaller Frenchman, the *Vengeance* of 12 guns. This small fleet, which was accompanied by three motley-crewed privateers, attempted an attack on Edinburgh's port of Leith, but failed to negotiate the tricky currents of the approaches in the Firth of Forth. Further south, off the Yorkshire fishing town of Scarborough, Jones' command was more successful. He intercepted a merchant fleet escorted by HMS *Serapis* of 54 guns, and the little HMS *Countess of Scarborough* of 20 guns. The *Bon Homme Richard* and the *Alliance* attacked *Serapis* by moonlight, whilst *Pallas* and *Vengeance* took on the *Countess of Scarborough*. HMS *Serapis* struck her colours when, after more than three hours of constant engagement, she

was set on fire, and when the *Bon Homme Richard* was rapidly sinking with the loss of over 300 men. Jones transferred what was left of his crew to *Serapis* and sailed her, together with the *Countess of Scarborough* – taken by *Pallas* and *Vengeance* – back to France, where he was again applauded as a great victor.

But opinion was not unanimous. There seems no doubt that Jones was a fractious and ill-tempered character. Thomas Simpson in *Ranger* was driven almost to the point of mutiny and Peter Landais, French captain of *Alliance* and Jones' second-in-command, had quarrelled incessantly with Jones throughout the expedition. On reaching port, Jones preferred charges against the Frenchman and arbitrarily took over the US 36-guns ship. However, and with what can only have been tacit acquiescence of the French minister of marine, Landais seized *Alliance* at L'Orient in June 1770 and sailed her out of harbour whilst Jones was occupied on shore. A furious Jones then returned to his adopted country, where he was promised command of the US *America*, a big ship of 72 guns then under construction at Portsmouth in New Hampshire. For reasons known only to Congress the promise was never fulfilled and Jones returned to France, there to offer his wayward allegiance. The offer was not taken up, and he offered his services next to Denmark. Nothing there either, and in 1788 he accepted the post of Rear Admiral in the navy of Catherine the Great of Russia. Almost at once his orders were questioned by the senior officers of his command, and he was accused at St Petersburg in March 1789 of a vicious criminal assault upon a young girl. Catherine (herself a notorious libertine) dismissed him, and he went back again to France. He died there at the age of 45 on 17 July 1792, never having put to sea again. His remains were shipped to America over 100 years later, and his crypt in the naval chapel at Annapolis is regarded by some as a national shrine.

Returning to *Ranger*, Thomas Simpson was given permanent command of the ship and sailed her out of New England in July 1779 in the company of two other US warships, the *Providence* and the *Queen of France*, with orders to patrol up the coast of Newfoundland. This was *Ranger*'s most successful voyage ever. The three-ship fleet took British merchantmen prizes amounting in value to over one million dollars, by far the richest single haul in the entire revolutionary war. Unfortunately for *Ranger*, her victories were short-lived. Before the end of that year she was taken by the British during an action off Charleston in South Carolina (the *Queen of France* had been sunk) and re-named HMS *Halifax*. But the British sold her out of Royal service only two years later, in October 1781, and what became of her afterwards might never now be known.

RANGER

AMERICAN

USS Constitution

Now preserved and cared for by the American nation in much the same way as the British revere their HMS *Victory*, the USS *Constitution* had a very long and active career. She was one of a group of six warships whose construction was authorised by Congress in March 1794. Congress however had an almost immediate change of heart, and building was halted for four years, at the end of which time work was resumed on only half of the original order. *Constitution* was one of the three reprieved, and after two abortive attempts at launching she finally slid off the ways at Edmund Hart's shipyard in Boston on 31 December, 1797.

Her remarkable catalogue of rebuild and refit started before she was even off the stocks. Originally laid down as a ship of 74 guns, and built with scantling massive enough to support such heavy ordnance, it was decided at some stage to finish her off as some breed of super frigate capable of out-gunning all other frigates and of out-sailing any heavier opposition. She had an overall length of 204 feet, a gun deck between perpendiculars of 174 feet and a breadth, moulded, of 43 feet 6 inches. The depth of her hold was 14 feet 3 inches, and she had a draught of 21 feet forward and 23 feet aft. She measured 1,444 American tons (1,533 British) and displaced 2,200 tons. Instead of the first-intended 74 guns she was armed at launching with 56: 30, 24-pounders on the main deck, 18, 42-pounder carronades on the quarter-deck, plus six 42-pounder carronades and two 24-pounders on the forecastle. So, with her scantling equal to that of a British 74, and armed almost as heavily as a British third rate, she was more than a match for any Royal Navy frigate and later, in the war of 1812, she was able to demonstrate this to good effect.

Constitution first saw action as the US Navy flagship in the American attack on Tripoli on 3 August 1804. Weary of harrassment by Arab privateers, and of the levies imposed by local sultans on its merchant ships trading in the Mediterranean, America sent a fleet of warships to put an end to these humiliations once and for all. The only damage suffered by *Constitution* was wrought when she ran foul of her sister ship the *President* and lost her splendid figurehead of Hercules in the collision. She was later presented with a replacement by President Jackson himself.

Soon after the declaration of war with Great Britain, on 16 July 1812, *Constitution* was chased near the New Jersey shore by a squadron of five British ships; HMS *Africa*, a 74, and the frigates *Shannon*, *Belvidera*, *Aeolus* and *Guerriére*. Suddenly the wind failed, and Captain Isaac Hull found himself in the middle of a dead flat calm. He put out all boats, and had his ship towed towards a

point at which he knew there were shallows. When he had a sounding of 26 fathoms, Hull sent relays of boats on ahead to put down kedge anchors, and *Constitution* was hauled on by her own capstan. This enormous effort was sustained throughout three days and two nights of intermittant calms and light airs, and when at last a wind sprang up, *Constitution* was off and away. Captain Hull was said to have had a lucky escape, but luck played no part in it. He saved his ship by tactical excellence, and 60 hours of unremitting toil. Of his pursuers, only *Belvidera* came close enough to fire on him, and most of the shots fell short.

Hull's next encounter with the British came very soon afterwards, on 19 August, and this time he really was lucky. HMS *Guerriére* had left her squadron and was sailing back into port for a refit. *Constitution* overhauled the 48 gun frigate, and after a furious two-hours engagement *Guerriére* was dismasted and defeated, and *Constitution* took her first prize. Two months later, with her armament slightly altered and now under the command of Commodore William Bainbridge, she scored her second victory. This was not so easily achieved. A one-to-one action in the South Atlantic against the frigate HMS *Java*, 46, lasted almost four hours and ended with *Java* so severely damaged that she had to be sunk.

Constitution saw no further notable action for over a year until, on 14 February 1814, she easily took the schooner *Picton* of 14 guns. In the meantime she had been 'improved' yet again, this time with a furnace for the provision of red-hot shot, and was under the command of Captain Charles Stewart. She was sighted and chased on 3 April by HMS *Junor* and HMS *Tenedos*, both frigates of 38 guns, but was comfortably able to outrun the two smaller ships. In fact, and considering her bulk, *Constitution* was a remarkably fast sailer. Fifty years later, and then on a passage from Newport to Annapolis under Commander George Dewey, she touched on 14 knots.

But the action for which 'Old Ironsides', as she then became known, is perhaps most famous occurred off Madeira on 20 February 1815, when she fought two British sloops, the *Cyane* of 32 guns and the *Levant* of 20 guns. She far out-matched both sloops combined and could out-manoeuvre them at will; and thanks to her greater range of fire, and no less to Stewart's fast backing and filling, she was able to avoid a broadside from either one whilst she herself was raking the other. Stewart won the day, and captured both of his adversaries, but his triumph was short lived. *Constitution* and her prizes were chased to the Cape Verde Islands by three British warships, HMS *Leander* and HMS *New-*

castle both of 50 guns, and the fifth rate HMS *Acasta* of 40. The pursuit was hectic, and *Cyane* escaped her captor early. When *Levant* attempted a similar run for freedom, into the neutral haven of the Portuguese harbour at Porto Praya, the Royal Navy chose to abandon its chase of *Constitution* and escort *Levant* into safety. So, and once again, 'Old Ironsides' had a narrow escape.

Significantly, this historically-recent event serves to emphasise the fallibility of old ships' portraits. On his return to home port, Captain Stewart employed an American artist to depict his victory over *Cyane* and *Levant*, instructing the painter to portray the two sloops as full-blown British frigates. Engravings made afterwards reached a vast newspaper audience, and were widely accepted as being accurate.

Long after the war of 1812, during the American Civil War of 1861–65, *Constitution* was spared from confiscation by the Confederate forces when she was towed by the Unionists into a safe berth at Newport, and there left to rest. More than 10 years after the Civil War had ended, she was given a refit and used for the transport to Le Havre of American items for the great Paris Exhibition of 1878. Having delivered her cargo she ran aground on the passage home and was saved, ironically, only with the help of the Royal Navy. She was brought to dock at Portsmouth in England and made fit for the voyage home.

After her return passage she was employed for some years as a training ship, and this was to be her final period of service at sea. She was paid off at New York in 1884 and relegated to the role of receiving ship at Portsmouth, New Hampshire. She fulfilled that purpose until 1897, when she was towed up to Boston, the scene of her launching 100 years before. Appropriately, the US Navy assembled the whole of its North Atlantic fleet to welcome 'Old Ironsides' back to the place of her birth.

At the time of this writing, visitors do not see the old warrior as she was decked out in her heyday. She is painted now in a trim of sombre black and white, a dress far removed from that she wore at her launching. Then, according to some records, her colours were much more striking. Her hull was all of bright ochre with a black wale strake, the two uppermost panels of her planking and topsides pale blue. Her figurehead of Hercules was magnificently adorned, much of her head and taffrail heavily gilded, her rails all black and her deck furniture red.

Many great sailing ships were built in American yards, but of all those designed as men-o'-war, *Constitution* is justly the most renowned.

USS CONSTITUTION

Chesapeake and Shannon

THESE TWO SHIPS gained lasting fame for their respective parts in a single and very short engagement. Neither one distinguished herself in any other way, and the lives of both were comparatively brief. Indeed, had it not been for one man's rash and impulsive conduct, their names might now be long forgotten.

The US frigate *Chesapeake* was built at Fox's Yard in Norfolk, Virginia, and launched in 1799. Her designer, Mr Humphreys, had specified an armament of 44 guns, but at some time between the laying down of her keel and her subsequent fitting out she was reduced to a 38. (Some historians have her as a 36.) She was 163 feet 6 inches long, was 40 feet in the beam, and had a depth of 13 feet 6 inches.

Construction of the Royal Navy fifth-rate HMS *Shannon* followed a similar pattern. Built in Brindley's Yard at Frinsbury in 1806, she was designed to mount 46 guns, but this number was also later reduced to 38. Her measurements, too, were similar to *Chesapeake*: length 150 feet, breadth 40 feet, depth 13 feet. So, although *Shannon* was slightly smaller, the frigates were fairly evenly matched. Both were ships of around 1,100 English tons.

Chesapeake first entered the records in 1807, when she was engaged in an irregular fracas with the British frigate HMS *Leopard*. With outright war between the two nations still five years away, the incident was nevertheless only one of many such clashes – all involving searches by British commanders for Royal Navy deserters. Captain Humphreys of *Leopard* had information that several of these were among the *Chesapeake*'s crew, and having waylaid the US frigate in the Atlantic, he signalled her to heave to. When she ignored the signal, shots were fired from *Leopard* and *Chesapeake*'s captain chose discretion as the better part of valour. Humphreys led a strong boarding party, mustered all hands on deck, and identified three of them as the men he was looking for. He took them back aboard *Leopard*, and they later received due punishment. Two were flogged around the fleet, and the third was hung.

HMS *Shannon* saw her first and only really notable action some six years later, when she was in service on the North Atlantic station based at Halifax under the command of Captain Sir Philip Bowes Vere Broke. At sea, the war between Great Britain and America had been a somewhat desultory affair, with no great battles between fleets and no resounding victories on either side. In *Shannon*, the impatient Captain Broke was suffering the frustration of never being able to find an opponent, and when he learned that *Chesapeake* was lying in harbour at Boston he sent a message to her commander, Captain James Lawrence, daring him to come out and fight. Whether Lawrence sailed out in response to the challenge, or whether he had already left port in order to engage *Shannon*, is the subject of controversy. But Lawrence did sail out to meet Broke, and his decision to do so is regarded by many as an act of foolish bravado. The decisive factor in any battle between two equal frigates had long been well accepted: victory was determined by the swift and expert handling of sail, and a masterly use of the guns. Lawrence had a raw crew of both officers and men, most of them only days in the ship and with no experience of her behaviour at sea. Broke had a crew of seasoned hands, seamen and gunners virtually without equal anywhere.

The two ships met in Boston Bay on 1 June 1813. It was a short and inglorious fight, although the bravery of Lawrence and his men was quite without question and must forever be admired. But the speed and dispatch with which Broke first raked and then boarded *Chesapeake* was in classic affirmation of the foregoing rule concerning encounters by single frigates, and of the ancient adage that a ship is only as good as the men who sail in her. *Chesapeake* was crippled by just two broadsides from *Shannon*, both of them fired within the space of five minutes.

Captain Lawrence paid the ultimate price for his hasty oversight. He was mortally wounded at the outset of the action, and his last order as he was carried below – 'Do not surrender the ship' – has echoed down the years of American naval tradition. His final words are less known, and less noble; he died protesting the correctitude of his decision to attack *Shannon*, and blaming the ineptitude of his officers for having lost the fight.

Captain Broke is not on record as having spoken to the dying Lawrence, but Broke certainly led his own boarding party, which met with little or no resistance. He put a prize crew on board *Chesapeake* and escorted her into harbour at Halifax on 6 June to the cheering of a huge crowd waiting there to witness the event. This painting by Cornelis de Vries (after an original by the contemporary artist John Christian Schetky, Marine Painter to King George III) faithfully depicts the triumphal entry.

Boston Bay was the scene of *Shannon*'s first and last victory. Some time afterwards, she was re-named *St Lawrence* and put into service as a receiving ship at Sheerness. She was broken up at Chatham in November 1859.

CHESAPEAKE AND SHANNON

Charles W Morgan

IF ANY ONE SHIP might be said to typify the American whaler, that ship is the *Charles W Morgan*. Her name is known the world over, and features large in a voluminous literature.

Early texts show that men have hunted whales for over a thousand years, and it is known that the Basques and Gascoynes were so successful during the 12th, 13th, and 14th centuries that the Bay of Biscay was veritably 'fished out'. Dutch and English whalers were active around Iceland and Spitsbergen in the 16th and 17th centuries, as to a lesser degree were those of Germany, France and Denmark. However, so far as sailing ships are concerned, the industry was raised to its greatest height by the men who colonised New England.

When Captain John Smith sailed to America in 1614 he carried with him a royal charter to 'fish' for whales, and this prerogative was actively exercised from the colony's earliest days. At first, they probably employed the native Indians' method of putting out in small boats to take blackfish, a small catacea about 25 feet in length, sighted from watchtowers and towed ashore after killing for flensing and 'trying-out' on the beach. However, the hardy and adventurous colonist rapidly evolved his own way of hunting, and had created by the middle of the 17th century the foundations of a great national industry. Other nations competed sporadically over the next 200 years, but in spite of several often-serious setbacks, America's dominance of the trade continued throughout the days of sail. In 1842, New England had 652 whalers, whilst all the rest of the world put together could muster a mere 230.

According to C W Ashley in his masterly *The Yankee Whaler* (first published 1926, later edition Halcyon House, New York, 1942) it all began – as an *organised* business – around 1645, when the inhabitants of eastern Long Island formed proper whaling companies. They were first in the field, but were rapidly overtaken by the denizens of Nantucket. The entire island was originally populated by Quakers who, on a very broad basis of all-for-one-and-one-for-all, made whaling a complete way of life. The island remained supreme as the centre of American whaling until well into the 19th century, but as severe depletion of the Atlantic migration schools necessitated the use of larger ships for hunting in distant waters, a sandbar across the harbour entrance forced its whalers into the deeper harbours of Martha's Vineyard and New Bedford, and the latter, by 1850, had become home port to some 400 vessels, more than half of all the whalers in the world. In 1857, New Bedford's whaling fleet earned for this town of only 2,000 inhabitants an enormous six million dollars. Other thriving whaling ports included Cold Spring Harbour and Mystic Seaport.

The *Charles W Morgan*, launched at Fairhaven, near New Bedford in 1841, was one of numerous such blunt and ponderous vessels said by one contemporary wit to have been '... built by the mile and so much chopped off as needed.' She was a full-rigged ship of 351 tons, 106 feet long, and 27 feet on the beam. With her three masts sticking up like broomsticks and a bowsprit set at an angle approaching 45 degrees her hull and rigging offered an antique appearance resembling ships which pre-dated her by 200 years than those – the wonderful Yankee clippers – which followed within a decade. Seen in their present form her bows look bereft of any entrance, but they were further encumbered originally by reinforcements of solid oak all of 4 feet thick. This extra protection against pressures of ice was subsequently removed, but although the *Morgan* could never have been a beautiful ship, her qualities as a practical work-horse were veritably unsurpassed. She was, and remains, a living legend.

To describe the *Morgan* is to describe almost every other New England whaler; the vast majority were rigged as barks in order to facilitate ease of handling when most of the crew had taken to the boats. However, most, though not all, contemporary portrayals of the *Morgan* – including the painting made at Round Hills in 1925 four years after her last voyage – depict her as a full ship with one small gaff under three square sails on the mizzen. Other portrayals, including one by the American artist John Leavitt, show her as a bark. It would seem, therefore, that periodic changes were made.

For the rest the *Morgan* was flush-decked with a small after-house at her stern, a midship shelter on top of which were stowed the one or perhaps two spare boats, and a try-works shelter just abaft the foremast. The try-works were two large cauldrons set in a solid brick range, their fires started with wood but kept blazing afterwards by rendered-out scraps of blubber. Beneath the try-works, a shallow brick water-filled pan, called the duck pen, insulated the deck from the heat of the fires. Hard alongside of the try-works, a large rectangular metal tank was used to cool the whale oil before it was transferred into casks for stowage in the hold. The most recognisable feature of a whaler when cruising was the (usually) five long whaleboats slung on her thick wooden davits, three on the port side and two on the starboard, or when trying-out after a kill, it was the glow and smoke from her try-works. Close to, the smell was enough, although it has often been protested that a whaler between try-outs was kept as sweet and clean as any other ship.

The only truly elegant aspect of the *Morgan* was her boats. Typically, they were about 28 feet long, and double-ended to provide for immediate change of direction. Planked with cedar only half an inch thick, they were extraordinarily light and swift. Weighing a bare 1,000 pounds, they were capable nevertheless of stowing the same weight of gear, plus the weight of six men. Five of these, each pulling on an oar from 14 to 18 feet long could propel the craft at a steady five knots; but for the covering of any considerable distance they stepped a mast and hoist a sail. Gear carried in the boat included three or four harpoons and the same number of lances and marking flags. Also, a water keg, a baling bucket, broad–bladed paddles and up to half a mile of whale line coiled in two open wooden tubs placed near the centreboard. One end of the line was passed aft around a loggerhead at the stern and then strung for'ard to pass through a chock at the bow. Incredible as it might seem to us now, it was from these frail cockleshells that men attacked and killed the largest animals – including dinosaurs – ever to have lived on this planet.

Over the course of a long and active life the *Morgan* took inummerable whales, the most highly-prized of which were those of the species, sperm. The sperm's massive head, almost a third of its bulk, was largely composed of a white fatty substance which yielded a special oil called spermaceti. Spermaceti rendered out so marvellously fine as to burn – and especially when used for the making of candles – with a pure, clear, smokeless flame. When on 27 May 1853 the *Morgan* returned to New Bedford after one of her early voyages, her hold was stacked with 1,150 barrels of oil, much of it spermaceti, and each barrel holding a minimum of 30 gallons. (The *average* male sperm whale was 60 feet long and weighed some 65 tons.) These, together with a cash cargo of New Zealand kauri gum, grossed for her owners a total of $44,138. As was the custom, this sum was divided into three equal parts: one for the owners, one for refitting the ship, and one to be shared among the crew. These crew shares were vastly disproportionate. Captain Samson received about $4,000, harpooner Haley got $400 – less the $200 he had already drawn in advances and spent on goods from the ship's slop chest. It was, he remarked, 'A slow way to get rich.' Haley went on however to become himself a captain, and doubtless retired with a considerable fortune.

Huge as it was, this profit for the *Morgan*'s owners represented but a drop in the ocean. She made six round voyages between 1841 and 1865, 14 years during which the value of whale oil

CHARLES W MORGAN

CHARLES W MORGAN

increased by a factor of three, baleen by a factor of four, and the price of spermaceti rose to $1.61 per gallon. In the 80 years of her working life the *Morgan* made no fewer than 37 voyages and earned profits for her owners of almost two million dollars. She was built, rigging not included, for $23,000; and she, of course, was only one such ship among hundreds. In 1818, New England whalers garnered 16,000 tons of oil; in 1841 the figure topped 233,000, and all of this aside from the thousands of tons of baleen which, at its peak, was worth $6 per *pound*. The baleen from a single whale might easily fetch $15,000, and great numbers of bowheads were slaughtered just for their bone and carcasses, blubber and all cast adrift to feed the sharks. Demand for baleen, which continued well into the 20th century, prompted Dr Frederick A Lucas to write in his book *The Passing of the Sperm Whale* (New York, 1908) 'Nothing can possibly prevent the extermination of the bowhead but the discovery of some perfect substitute for whalebone ...'. There was, too, always the chance that a sperm whale might yield ambergris, a substance sometimes formed in the animal's intestines. Prized in the East as a spice and in the West as a fixative for perfumes and ointments, ambergris was so highly valued that in 1858 one single lump was sold for what in those days was the enormous sum of $10,000.

So what brought about the decline of this tremendously profitable industry? Some historians blame ship losses during the Civil War of 1861–65, but these were no greater than depredations during the Revolutionary War and the War of 1812, after both of which conflicts the whaling fleet rose Pheonix-like to even dizzier heights. Similarly, icing-in and wreckages during the Arctic winters of 1871 and 1876 accounted in total for only 48 ships, and this at a time when the yards of New England were turning out ships by the dozen. The 1859 discovery of petroleum in Pennsylvania did indeed pose a threat to whaling, but gas had already been used for illumination for roughly 50 years, so that particular problem was surely not insurmountable. Besides, whale products were valuable for uses other than lamp oil and lubricants, and rival nations – notably Norway, following Svend Foyn's invention of the harpoon cannon – promptly took up where New England left off and continued to reap rich rewards beyond the turn of the century and up to the present day.

The writer leans towards a view that the main root cause was a persistent over-fishing of *those five species* (sperm, right, humpback, bowhead, and gray) *which men were capable of killing from boats* in waters economically accessible to small ships under sail. As depletion of stocks in the Arctic migration patterns forced

whalers to hunt ever further afield, voyages began to take as many years as once they had taken months. One such voyage, that of the *Nile* out of New Haven, lasted almost 11 years. She sailed in May 1858 and did not return until April 1869. Also boat-whaling was a cruelly hard and hazardous business, and the time had come for a major transition to new and better methods. But owners, captains, and not least seamen were presented during the third quarter of the 19th century with a fortuitous and very attractive alternative to whaling: the fabulous Yankee clippers were born.

The *Charles W Morgan* completed her last voyage in 1921 and after being used in a film, 'Down to the Sea in Ships', was beached in 1925 at Round Hills. There, she was saved from destruction by Harry Neyland, who raised the money for her purchase and offered her to the aldermen of New Bedford. His offer was declined, and the cost of her maintenance was taken up by Colonel E H R Green. In 1941 she was hauled to South Dartmouth, where she lay neglected for 32 years. Then, in 1973, the old lady was towed to Mystic Seaport and given a face-lift which restored her completely. Now, she lies there in the harbour museum, a monument to the industry which created New England's wealth.

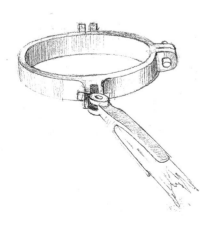

AMERICAN

Flying Cloud

ONSTRUCTED TO THE ORDER of Mr Enoch Train for his White Diamond Packets line, *Flying Cloud* was yet another in that long list of Yankee clippers whose names are logged in maritime history. Designed and built in his Boston yards by Donald Mackay, she was launched on 15 April 1851, a vessel of 1,793 tons. From knighthead to taffrail she measured 225 feet, and she was 208 feet on the keel. Her depth of hold was 21 feet 6 inches, and she was 40 feet 8 inches on her beam. She had a 20-inch dead-rise at half floor (compared with the 40 inches of Mackay's first clipper, the *Staghound*, built the previous year) suggesting that the great designer was already making efforts to produce a fast vessel with a full midship section. Topside, a long campaign or poop provided luxury accommodation for passengers, and she had a 40-foot-thwartships deckhouse just abaft her foremast. Adorning her stem was a beautiful figurehead of an angel blowing a trumpet. Her rigging was fairly orthodox. Like most American clippers, she crossed skysail yards on all three masts, but her main yard was slightly less wide than that of her predecessor, 82 feet against *Staghound*'s 86. She carried royal stunsails, had a reef band in her topgallants, a swinging boom and a passaree to spread her fore lower stunsails and haul out her foresail clews.

That there appeared to be nothing really remarkable about her is evident from the fact that Enoch Train sold *Flying Cloud* whilst she was still on the ways to shipowners Grinnell, Minturn & Co, proprietors of the Swallow Tail line. But the *Cloud* lived up to her name from the moment she rode blue water, and Train is said to have regretted the sale all the rest of his life.

Flying Cloud's maiden voyage began on 3 June 1851 when she sailed out of New York and cleared the Hook, running before light, westerly airs. She was bound for San Francisco with a full complement of passengers and cargo, under the command of her appointed captain, Josiah Perkins Creesy. The voyage was to prove, in several ways, a very memorable one. Captain Creesy was acknowledged by all as being amongst the finest sailors of his era, but his character as a human being left much to be desired. His reputation as a tyrannical skipper was never quite so awful as that of his countryman, Bully Forbes, but like many another God-fearing New Englander he was a harsh disciplinarian who ran his ships with a rod of iron – or, in sailor's parlance, on a diet of knuckle-duster biscuit and belaying-pin soup. He was as hard on the vessels he commanded as he was on himself and their crews, but the damage he inflicted on spars and rigging was usually compensated for by a skilfull saving in perilous situations of vessel, crew and all.

Barely two days out, the westerly airs began to freshen fast, becoming a blow which soon developed into a dangerous gale. Typically, and with utter disregard for the alarm of his first officer, Creesy clung grimly to all three of his skysails, and even to royal stunsails. Inevitably, spars strained far beyond breaking point began to snap like breadsticks, and on 6 June away went her main topsail yard and main topgallant masts. Undaunted, and heedless of the risk to life and limb in those conditions of howling wind and water, Creesy bullied his crew into sending up replacements. Next day brought a slight abatement of the gale and on the following day, the 8th, Creesy gave the order to set all possible sail. There were no further spar losses, but *Flying Cloud* was still most brutally hard-pressed, and it was discovered on 14 June that her main mast was badly sprung. Captain Creesy had it fished, and continued to 'carry on'.

On the 15th the wind went suddenly away and there followed a period of near-flat calms which reduced the *Cloud*'s 24-hour runs over four consecutive days to 101, 82, 52, and 53 miles respectively. But she still went on to cross the line only 21 days out of New York, although this remarkable performance was not achieved without constant work aloft, and Creesy's hard-driven crew was goaded into rebellion. He clapped the ringleaders in irons, and forcing those who were left to take up the slack, went on to pursue his relentless determination. The consequences are recorded by this relevant section from archives of his original abstract log:

July 11 Very severe thunder and lightning. Double reefed topsails – latter part blowing a hard gale, close reefed topsails, split fore and main topmast staysails. At 1 pm discovered that mainmast had sprung again. Sent down royal and topgallant yards and studding sail boom off lower and topsail yards to relieve the mast. Heavy sea running and shipping large quantities of water over lee rail.

July 12 Heavy south-west gales. Distance 40 miles.

July 13 Let men out of irons in consequence of wanting their services, with the understanding that they would be *taken care of** on arriving at San Francisco. At 6 pm carried away main topsail tye and truss band around main-mast. Single reefed topsails.

July 19 Crossed latitude 50° south.

July 20 At 4 am close-reefed topsails and furled courses. Hard gale with thick weather and snow.

July 23 Passed through the Straits of Le Maire. At 8 am Cape Horn north at 5 miles distant, whole coast covered with snow.

July 26 Crossed latitude 50° south in the Pacific, 7 days from same latitude in Atlantic.

July 31 Fresh breezes and fine weather. All sail set. At 2 pm wind south east. At 6 pm equally, in lower and topgallant studding sails. 7 pm in royals, 2 am in foretopmast studding sails. Latter part strong gales and high seas running ship very wet fore and aft. Distance run day by observation 374 miles. During squalls 18 knots of line were not sufficient to measure rate of speed. Topgallant sails set.

August 1 Strong gales and squally. At 6 pm in topgallant sails, double reefed fore and mizzen topsails. Heavy sea running. At 4 am made sail again. Distance run 334 miles.

August 3 Suspended first officer from duty, in consequence of his arrogating to himself the privilege of cutting up rigging contrary to my orders, and long continued neglect of duty.

August 25 Spoke barque *Amelia Pacquet* 180 days out of London bound to San Francisco.

August 29 Lost fore-topgallant mast.

August 30 Sent up fore-topgallant mast. Night strong and squally. 6 am made South Farallones bearing north east ½ east. 7 am took a pilot. Anchored in San Francisco Harbour at 11 30 am after a passage of 89 days and 21 hours

Sandy Hook to equator	21 days.
Equator to 50° south	25 ,,
50° South Atlantic to 50°	
South Pacific	7 ,,
50° South Pacific to equator	17 ,,
Equator to San Francisco	19 ,,
Total	89 days

* *Author's italics*

Three years later, *Flying Cloud* was to clip 13 hours off this stunning record time, a feat never accomplished by any sailing ship, and she was generally regarded for more than 10 years as undisputed champion of the seas. At the end of that maiden voyage however, and although she was greeted in San Francisco with wild acclaim, older hands pointed to the evidence of harsh punishment – splintered spars, chain lashings around the tops of her poles, emergency stays and a broken flying jib-boom. Her average speed for the entire voyage (including those days in the doldrums) of 222 statute miles per 24 hours had not been achieved with impunity. There were other dire consequences, too. The sacked first mate and other members of the crew

AMERICAN

FLYING CLOUD

thrown ashore in San Francisco hired themselves a lawyer and sued Creesy for cruel treatment and wrongful dismissal. In order to foil prosecution, the owners announced the death of their famous captain at sea and later, when he picked up a parcel of American newspapers half way across the Indian Ocean, Creesy had the unusual experience of reading his own obituary notices.

After this first outstanding passage around the Horn, *Flying Cloud* sailed from San Francisco on to Canton. On her first full day out she ran 374 knots, or 428 statute miles, and crossed to Honolulu in 12 days. She left Canton on 6 January 1852, and arrived in New York on 10 April. Respectable though it was, this 94-day passage underlined the fact that *Flying Cloud* was a typical Mackay ship: virtually unbeatable in whole sail and hard breezes, she could not compete with the smaller clippers in light winds. The little *N B Palmer*, under her wealthy skipper Charles P Low, left Canton three full days after *Flying Cloud*, and arrived in New York 10 days ahead. Captain Low's triumph was short lived. On her second voyage around the Horn, *Flying Cloud* overhauled her rival off the coast of Brazil, and the vessels lay side by side in a flat calm. When, at four o'clock in the afternoon, a light ripple of wind rose suddenly to a whole sail breeze, *Flying Cloud* went away with it and by daybreak next morning had run the *NB Palmer* hull down. Eight hours later she had the ocean to herself, and reached San Francisco three weeks ahead of Low's ship.

Her third voyage was not remarkable, but when on her fourth she beat her own record time to San Francisco, Captain Creesy was presented on his return to New York with a service of silver plate. On her fifth voyage, during which she made her astonishing best-ever 24-hour run of 402 sea miles, she came very close to total loss. Homeward bound out of Canton with a load of tea worth almost one million dollars, she ran aground on a coral reef in the China Seas. She lost the shoe off her keel, and the keel itself was thrust up through the bottom planking. Creesy managed somehow to float her off, and although she was leaking badly, he would not put into port for repairs. By having the pumps manned 24 hours a day he struggled home unaided, saving not only his valuable cargo, but an estimated $30,000 in port repairs. This time, the owners presented him with a silver tea set.

The end of this voyage coincided with the start of America's 1856–57 depression, and the *Cloud* was laid up in New York for two and a half years. Captain Creesy retired, and her first voyage after the depression, under the command of Captain Reynard, was a disaster. She was badly damaged whilst rounding the Horn, and forced to put back into Montevideo for costly repairs. Captain Creesy was coaxed out of retirement and continued as master of his wonderful clipper until she was sold, at the outbreak of the Civil War, to the English Black Ball line. In 1870, with her ageing timbers now water-sodden, she astounded the shipping world by carrying 385 emigrants out to New Zealand in only 87 days. In the meantime, her famous captain died at his home in Salem at the age of 57.

Reduced in the end to carrying timber, *Flying Cloud* ran aground on Beacon Island off the coast of New Brunswick in September 1873, and was broken up in the harbour at St John when found to be beyond repair. For 23 years, since her very first voyage, she had been a living legend.

- 84 -

FLYING CLOUD

AMERICAN

Witch of the Wave

OF ALL THE MANY fine Yankee clippers *not* built by either Webb or Mackay, *Witch of the Wave* was perhaps the most famous. The masterpiece of George Raynes, she was commissioned by the Salem shipowners Gliddon & Williams and launched at Raynes' yard in Portsmouth, New Hampshire in the spring of 1851. Known throughout New England as the 'Pride of Salem', this remarkably graceful vessel fully deserved the name. Her elegant lines embodied all the best attributes of a very sharp, extreme clipper, and she was rigged and fitted out using the most expensive materials available. 202 feet long between perpendiculars (about 220 feet on the rail) with a beam of 40 feet and a depth of 21, her lavish decoration excited admiration wherever she sailed. Her beautiful figurehead, mounted under a sea-shell canopy, was of a young woman dressed in flowing garments of white and gold holding aloft a wind-blown scarf. The golden foliage on which she stood trailed away in swags to curl around the hawse-holes. The black varnished hull was encircled by a bright red stripe and the stern was embellished by a carving of Venus, also gold and white, riding on a shell towed by dolphins. Two more dolphins, port and starboard, had cherubs riding on their backs. Surmounting the Venus, the *Witch*'s hail and name were carved and gilded above a bed of roses, the whole enclosed in a gilded frame. Her decks below were equally magnificent, with the furnishings of her passenger accommodation said to be as good if not better than those of any other ship afloat.

That the *Witch* was much more than just a model of perfection was amply demonstrated by her maiden voyage. So heavily overladen with a cargo of 1,900 tons that her rails seemed almost awash, she nevertheless made a traverse of the Horn in foul midwinter weather and in spite of having been becalmed in the North Pacific for eight consecutive days, entered harbour at San Francisco 121 days out of Boston. Her master, Captain J Hardy Millet, was congratulated as being one of the very few skippers whose ship escaped that season without heavy loss of spars. From San Francisco, Millet took the *Witch* across to China and after loading some 20,000 chests of tea, she sailed from Whampoa on the Canton River on 5 January 1852 bound for the Port of London. By 13 January she had cleared Sunda Strait, and after making the run (which included one day's work of 338 miles) from Java Head to the Cape of Good Hope in 29 days, took up her pilot at Dungeness on 6 April. This record passage of 1852, only 90 days land to land, generated tremendous British interest in Rayne's splendid clipper, and American clippers in general.

On reaching Boston at the completion of his round voyage, Millet relinquished command of the *Witch* to Captain Benjamin

Tay. This reputable seaman made no great showing on the outward leg of his first voyage in the *Witch*, but his performance homeward-bound left the competition hull-down. The *Witch* left Saugor on 13 April 1853, flew before the wind from Sand Heads to the Cape in only 37 days, and docked at Boston on 3 July after a wonderful passage of 81 days. In doing so, she established a double-record never bettered by any other ship under sail.

Two years later, in the spring of 1855, Gliddon & Williams astonished the shipping world by announcing that *Witch of the Wave* was up for sale. The staggering news aroused a storm of wild speculation: had the owners discovered some hidden flaw in her? Had she suffered from too much hard chasing, so that the wave turbulence created by her long hollow entrance had affected the alignment of her timbers? Credence was even given to the fanciful story that her old sailmaker had heard her canvas groaning, begging for rest at the bottom of the sea. As these and other wierd rumours gained currency, it began to be generally accepted that there must be something wrong with the *Witch*, else why were Gliddon & Williams so patently anxious to sell her?

The owners found no takers in America or England, but the *Witch* was sold in June 1855 to the Dutch firm of van Eeghen & Co, who examined her thoroughly on arrival at Nieuwediep. It was found that, although she seemed basically very sound, with her beautiful furbishings still largely intact, the large sum of 20,000 florins would need to be spent on renewing her so-called 'household'. She needed new instruments such as chronometers and compasses, new hawsers, and the replacement of some of her running rigging.

The *Witch* was re-named *Electra*, and there quickly arose the serious question as to whether or not those rumours about her were indeed based on fact. It certainly looked at first as though her new Dutch owners had laid out $43,000 to buy a 'pig in a poke'. On her first voyage out to the East Indies, *Electra* made so much water that her pumps were more or less constantly manned, and although her second voyage was much less troubled, and despite the fact that she must over ensuing years have earned a fair return on van Eeghen's investment, she was never again regarded as anything like a crack ship. She made some respectable passages but was often plagued by mishap, as shown by her logs still in archive.

Following restoration work at Nieuwediep, *Electra* sailed on 9 August 1855 bound at first for Liverpool to pick up a cargo and a body of British soldiers destined for Melbourne in Australia. She was leaking so badly after her short 11 days passage that work at Liverpool on her hull occupied all of two months and her mas-

ter, Captain H Wegman, had trouble with his idle crew. However, when *Electra* did finally leave the Pool, on 15 November, she regained some part of her earlier glory by making a passage out to Australia in a creditable 76 days. After dicharging her cargo at Melbourne, she lay there at anchor for six weeks, then sailed for Holland via Batavia. Once through Sunda Strait she showed her old form with runs over five consecutive days of 234, 214, 230, 225 and 210 miles. Soon afterwards, she did one splendid day's work of 280. Unfortunately, these excellent performances were followed by 16 days of hellish weather during which she made little or no headway; then, the best part of another day wasted whilst spent hove-to for the ceremony of a burial at sea. So, altogether, that voyage home took a disappointing 111 days.

Electra's second voyage, just like her first, was beset at the outcome by difficulties. Towed out into the roads at Brouwershaven, she had to wait two whole weeks for the freshening up of a breeze and once again, as at Liverpool, Captain Wegman was burdened with crew, troops, all of their necessary supplies, and the task of maintaining some semblance of discipline. The mood and conduct of so many 'imprisoned' men might only too well be imagined. On her eventual arrival at Semerang in Indonesia, *Electra*'s deck was fitted out with horse boxes and after embarking the animals she was towed to Boni by the Dutch Royal Navy steamer *Groningen*. Heavy seas caused difficulties, and in the storm-swept darkness of a midnight watch *Electra* began to overhaul the *Groningen* with her tow-ropes a tangled rat's nest. Despite the frantic use of loud-hailers, Captain Wegman was unable to hear *Groningen*'s skipper for the snorts and squealing of terrified horses, and because, without any sail on her, *Electra* was denied manoeuvre, she rammed the *Groningen* port side. Marvellous seamanship resolved the ensuing chaos, and the horses were later disembarked at Bouhain, taken off by rafts.

On her very next voyage, once more under Captain Wegman, *Electra* exhibited her old spirit by making a run on one particular day of 289 miles. She continued to sail under the flag of van Eeghen & Co, until 1875, when the firm decided to sell her. Offers for the lovely ship from French and German owners were miserable in the extreme, and she was finally sold to another Dutch firm, Reiger & Co, of Amsterdam. Reigers butchered the old *Witch*, hacking down her lofty rigging to that of a lowly bark, and sold her in 1882 to a Norwegian shipping company who gave her the name of *Ruth*. That which happened to her afterwards is lost in the mist of time, but *Witch of the Wave* will always be remembered as one of the most beautiful sailing ships ever to plough the seas.

WITCH OF THE WAVE

AMERICAN

Challenge

IT HAS OFTEN BEEN SAID that the performance of any sailing ship, no matter how excellent in design and construction, can only be as good as the men who take her to sea, and never was the truism made more manifest than in William Webb's notorious *Challenge*. Built by America's foremost shipwright and regarded by many as his most beautiful creation, this magnificent clipper was vilified by having as her first captain the most infamous monster in maritime history. R H Waterman was beastiality personified. He took the marvellous *Challenge* and made her name a poisonous stench in the nostrils of seamen throughout the ports of the world. Compared with Waterman, his hated contemporary 'Bully' Forbes was gentle as a lamb.

But first the ship, and looking at her dimensions it is easy to understand the excitement she generated among the crowds of people who flocked to witness her construction in Webb's yard on the East River. At 2,006 tons, she was the biggest vessel yet built in New York, and it is recorded that her bowsprit jutted high above the roofs of Pine Street's dockside warehouses. Webb had set out to design and build the sharpest clipper afloat, and with 42 inches of dead-rise, he might well have succeeded. She was 230.6 feet long, 43.6 on the beam, and had a depth of 27.6. She had been ordered by N L & G Griswald, and the fact that these shipowners were commonly known as 'No Loss and all Gain Griswald' is perhaps reflected in their hiring of Captain Waterman. One of the most costly wooden vessels ever built in New York, her hull was originally painted all black with a broad gold stripe, and in striking contrast to the gleaming white masts and yards of other Yankee clippers, hers were the doom-laden colour of her hull. Her rigging, too, was different. The truck of her mainmast towered 197 feet above the deck, and her main yard of 90 feet was extended by lower studding sails to a tremendous 160 feet boom-end to boom-end. Her mainsail measured 80 feet on the head, 100 feet on the foot, and had a drop of 47 feet 3 inches with 49 feet 6 inches on the leach. Her lovely, snow-white cotton canvas, all 12,780 running yards of it, was especially woven for her by the Colt Manufacturing Company.

Launched in 1851, *Challenge* began her maiden voyage from Pier 19, at the foot of what is now Wall St, in July of that same year, under the command of 'Bully' Waterman. Waterman came fresh off *Sea Witch* and his awful reputation had preceded him, so it might at first seem inconceivable that the owners, having paid an unprecedented sum for their splendid new ship, should have entrusted her to so terrible a man. However, owners in those days were very much less concerned with people than they were

with profits and Waterman, in spite of his fearsome personality, was entitled to make an astonishing claim: throughout his career as ships' master, he had never cost owners one single penny due to loss of mast or spar.

So, when he sailed out of New York on a passage to San Francisco the Griswald clan, together with a party of friends, sailed in *Challenge* as far as Sandy Hook. Before disembarking there, they officiated at a customary mustering of all hands, and were dismayed at the abysmal quality of such a motley crew. Of the 64 men and boys willing to serve under Waterman, all but 10 were ignorant landsmen. Only six were capable of taking the wheel, and only four could speak English! The senior Griswald wanted to put back into port and recruit more men of experience but Waterman, now formally appointed as master, would not hear of it. This was exactly the sort of situation in which he revelled. He looked at his sad collection of the sweepings-up of nations and said, in effect: 'I'll make 'em sailors, or I'll make 'em mincemeat.' Concerning the latter option, no man ever spoke truer word. No sooner had *Challenge* hoist anchor than he asserted his despotic authority by hacking at the skull of a careless negro steward with a heavy carving knife. The man was severely injured with cuts about the head and face, but all in all, he got off lightly. Many others suffered much worse before the passage was over and some, indeed, were killed.

This is not a work of fiction. It is a record of sober fact, with all essentials solemnly sworn to in a USA court of law. Bully Waterman was a Jekyll and Hyde. Ashore, he was a big, swaggering dandy dressed always at the height of fashion in fancy frills and raw-silk suits, a frequenter of the very best hotels. At sea he became a fiend incarnate, subject to uncontrollable fits of rage. His first act after stepping on board was to change into rough clothes which he never took off – he slept only in cat-naps on a sofa in the chart room – until the passage was made. Second, he called for a bucket of salt water with which to 'wash away my shore-face'. He was universally hated, and the story goes that when Griswalds asked him to take command of *Challenge,* the offer was fortuitous. On the final leg of his last voyage in *Sea Witch* his first mate, Fraser or Frazer, confronted the master in his cabin and placed two loaded pistols on the table between them with the words: 'One of us is going to have to leave this ship.' Waterman backed down, but they were patently two of a kind. Four years later in 1885 when *Sea Witch* put into Rio, she did so with the dead body of Captain Frazer, murdered by his own first mate.

The record of *Challenge*'s first passage, which proved to be Waterman's last, reads like a catalogue of unrestricted mayhem. Her first mate, Jim Douglas, and her second mate, Cole, were each as big and tough a 'bucko' as the 'old man' himself, and scarcely a day passed without the spilling of someone's blood.

During the 55 days it took *Challenge* to fetch Cape Horn her crew became so weakened by sickness and ill-treatment she was lucky to have had moderate winds and fine weather. A change for the worse as she embarked upon the traverse caused a series of incidents almost beyond belief. One afternoon, with the captain snatching one of his cat-naps, Douglas was on deck as officer in charge and Cole aloft with the watch, struggling to furl the mizzen topsail in freezing gale and blinding hailstones. The sail was being whipped up over the yard like a living thing gone mad and the exhausted men, hands, feet and limbs numb with cold, were unable to control it. Down below, the furious Jim Douglas yelled louder than the storm: 'Get 'em out, mister! Get them — out on the yard!' Clinging on to the tye, Cole hauled himself up onto the yard and lashed out with his feet in a frenzied effort to drive the men out onto the foot-ropes, and three of them were booted clean off. Two hit the brace bumpkin and rebounded into the sea where mercifully, in those sub-zero temperatures, they must have perished instantly. The third man crashed down onto the poop and lay there groaning, barely conscious, a bag of broken bones. Douglas rushed at him like a man demented, screaming as he kicked the shattered man, 'Why ain't you dead, you ——? You *are* dead, you ——!' Then, turning to the men on deck he yelled down at them. 'Has this —— got a blanket? Bring up his —— blanket!'

With sailmaker's palm and needle, Douglas personally sewed up the living man in his blanket and heaved him, still groaning, over the rail and into the sea.

Some small justice was visited upon the second mate when *Challenge* was barely around the Horn. Cole was in charge of hands bracing the yards and in the eyes of Waterman, up on the poop, making a slack show of the job. Having turned the air around him blue with foul language, the skipper suddenly lost control of himself and made a rush for his second officer with heaver at the ready. Unfortunately he stumbled on the ladder and Cole, who was dashing to meet the assault, got in first with a hammer-like fist which laid Bully Waterman out cold. Jim Douglas, also up on the poop, hurled an iron marlin spike at Cole, but missed him. Douglas then tried to scramble below, presumably to grab a pistol, but was overtaken by the enraged

CHALLENGE

CHALLENGE

Cole and knocked flying into the fore-topsail halliards. With both master and mate sprawled out unconscious, Cole then turned to the gaping crew and shouted 'Here's the ship then, you ———s! If you want her, take her!'

His offer was met with averted eyes. For the crime of mutiny there was only one punishment, and every man knew what it was. They also knew that both Waterman and Douglas would need to be killed, and none had the stomach for such a deed. So, seeing himself without support, Cole had the stunned officers carried below and calmly resumed his watch. Half an hour later Waterman, on the pretence of affecting a reconciliation, asked Cole to join him in his cabin for a drink. The rum was drugged, and Cole woke up to find himself lying on the thwarts of the port quarter life-boat, his wrists and ankles shackled in irons. He was kept there with no shelter for 52 days, fed only on bread and water, until *Challenge* docked at San Francisco.

But perhaps the most heinous of crimes committed in *Challenge* was the brutal murder of an aged Italian. One day when the old man failed to muster for his afternoon watch, Waterman charged into the fo'c'sle to drag him out on deck. Mumbling weakly in the only language he knew, the recalcitrant pointed to his feet. They were black with gangrene. Someone had stolen his boots, and he had worked barefoot in the freezing weather all around Cape Horn, until now he was unable to stand. With a yell of 'Speak English, you dago ———!' Waterman swung his heaver and crushed the skull of the sick, old greybeard with one tremendous blow. Yet another wretched soul was dumped in Davy Jones's locker.

Knowing what he might expect when word of his atrocities spread, Bully Waterman slipped ashore by boat before his ship dropped anchor. As well that he did. Soon after *Challenge* docked at Pacific Wharf she was boarded by a swarming mob armed with guns and crowbars, fully intent on lynching all three of her officers. Too late. The only man then on board was gentle, old John Land, ex-captain of the famous *Rainbow,* hurriedly placed in charge by Alsop & Co, Griswalds' agents. Fired by blood lust, the mob prepared to lynch Captain Land, but the innocent old man was saved by a team of lawmen led by the city marshall, who managed to calm them with a fervent promise that Waterman would be brought to justice.

The marshall kept his word, but the 'justice' to which Waterman was eventually brought afforded no consolation to the ghosts of his many victims. Today, when serving officers of our armed forces are held accountable for any over-zealous performance of their duties, it seems inconceivable that Bully Waterman could walk out of court a free man. Yet, walk out free he did, just like every other Yankee clipper master. He never again set foot on a deck, but being already a rich man he had no need to. Furthermore, he prospered mightily. Once 'on the beach' he put on his 'shore face', exchanged his heaver for a Bible, and went about converting sinners to the ways of righteousness. Incredibly, he was appointed to the important office of Port Warden & Inspector of Halls in San Francisco and went on, after retiring to his extensive land holdings in Solano County to found the city of Fairfield. He died on his ranch in 1884, at the age of 76. Douglas and Cole were also cleared of all charges, and both of them went scot-free.

All very well for her diabolical officers, but after only one passage, the beautiful *Challenge* was cursed forever with the stigma of hell-ship. She had proved her worth with one particular day's run of 346 miles, and went on from San Francisco to make a very fine run to Shanghai, and from there with tea for England. She was so admired as she lay in the Blackwall dock that her lines were taken off for the British Admiralty, and it is believed by some that she was bought then by Green & Co, who changed her name to *Result*. In fact, the subsequent career of Webb's poor beauty is shrouded in uncertainty, so many other vessels were launched or re-launched as *Challenge*, and the original trying to live down her name. It would seem beyond question, however, that Webb's tragic beauty was finally owned by Captain Joseph Wilson of Sunderland, who described her end in a letter to Basil Lubbock dated 17 May 1892. Known at the time as *Golden City,* and her rig very much cut down from that with which she was launched, she was wrecked off Aberbrache on the coast of France in 1876, at a loss to Captain Wilson of £10,000.

Seldom, if ever, has any ship been the subject of greater controversy. Over the years, many respected writers have offered widely divergent accounts of that 1851 maiden voyage, some even going so far as to assert that Bully Waterman was an innocent victim of malicious falsehood, and that contemporary accounts were based upon a tissue of false testimonies by a vindictive crew. Whatever the truth, the fact remains that at least nine men died or were killed on the passage from New York, and as many again lay sick or badly injured when *Challenge* docked at San Francisco.

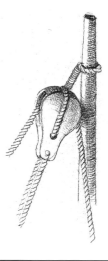

Lightning

CONTROVERSY AS TO whether this or that sailing vessel was or was not a true clipper has simmered for over a hundred years and will probably simmer hundreds more, but *Lightning* is very well to the fore of all those many splendid ships about which there can be no doubt.

When James Baines, Liverpudlian founder of the (English) Black Ball Line, decided in the early 1850s to expand his fleet he looked across the Atlantic to the legendary Donald Mackay for the design and building of four new ships – the *James Baines,* the *Donald Mackay, Champion of the Seas* and *Lightning.* Baines was a remarkable character. From one small room at the back of his mother's cake shop he built up a mighty line of 80 ships and 3,500 officers and men, only to die in a miserable lodging house without a penny to his name.

Donald Mackay of Boston, Massachusetts, assuredly one of the greatest shipbuilders the world has ever known, built numerous very fine clippers and never once had a failure. This was not due to any rigid mode of design, because every one of his masterly creations had its individual character. All four ships ordered by Baines, when Mackay visited Liverpool in the summer of 1853, differed in some way from each other. *Lightning* was a real extreme clipper, with a sharp, hollow entrance and a long, concave run. The *James Baines,* whilst also regarded as an extreme clipper, had hull contours somewhat less fine, and *Champion of the Seas* was slightly fuller in the ends than either. The *Donald Mackay* was a medium clipper with a deep, flat-floored hull.

Construction of the first of Baines' quartet began in 1853 and after her launching and fitting-out at Boston, she was delivered to Baines in March of the following year. According to David MacGregor in his book *Fast Sailing Ships* she was a vessel of 2,084 tons with a length on deck of 237.5 feet, 44 feet on the beam, and a depth in hold of 23 feet. (Other writers have her as being of lesser tonnage, but MacGregor is most probably correct.) She was built almost entirely of wood, with knees of white oak and decks of pine, her hull beneath the water-line fully sheathed with copper. By usual British standards her mid-section was rather full, with near-flat floors rounding down to low bilges and above, a marked tumble-home. She had rather more beam in proportion to length than most British clippers and having been designed to carry passengers in preference to heavy cargo, her draught line was deliberately set low in order to keep her dry in big seas. She had headroom between decks of eight feet and her total of 10 large staterooms plus other cabins provided accommodation, according to a newspaper advertisement published to

announce her first voyage to Australia, '... unequalled, and supplied with beds, bedding, and every other requisite, including stewards' attendance and stewardesses for the ladies.' The advertisement went on to claim that *Lightning* was '... the fastest ship in the world ... carried a full band of music, and bullion safes, and will be well-armed.'

Topsides, her provision for cabin accommodation was made manifest by the deck of her topgallant forecastle joining the top of the big deckhouse abaft the foremast, with gangways port and starboard leading on to the forward end of a long poop. A refit carried out later linked poop and forecastle together, so making a further continuous deck guarded by bulwark railings. *Lightning* was never graced with a figurehead, but enhancement by decoration was one thing she never did need.

As to her rigging, Mackay equipped his *Lightning* to carry a lot of sail. His original plans show a main yard all of 95 feet long, but – and curiously – with a sky sail only on the main. Curiously because almost all contemporary illustrations depict her with sky sails on all three masts, and some of them with a moon sail above the sky sail on the main. It therefore seems most likely that new and taller topgallant masts were fidded in England either before or soon after her maiden voyage to the Antipodes. Much less likely is the school of opinion which suggests a fidding of separate royal masts, or sliding gunter masts. But little matter; *Lightning* with all sail set must indeed have resembled a flying cloud, the actual name of her older Mackay sister launched in 1851.

Lightning showed her paces from the moment her bows sheered blue water. On her delivery across the Atlantic from Boston to Liverpool she made, from noon on 28 February to noon on 1 March, with 'her lee rail under and rigging slack' a run of 436 sea miles, giving her an average over the 24 hours of slightly over 18 knots. More was to follow. Her very first passage under the Black Ball flag, from Liverpool to Melbourne via the Cape of Good Hope, was made in just 77 days and this when a passage of 90 days was regarded as rather good. On her first homeward-bound passage, sailing ever eastwards around Cape Horn, she went on to set up a record never since approached by any ship under sail: a passage from Melbourne to Liverpool, 13,800 nautical miles, in 64 days 3 hours and 10 minutes. However, although her record time for this sailing passage remains intact up to the present day and probably now for ever, *Lightning* was not quite so fast in optimum conditions as a few of her sister ships. The speed of some Mackay vessels was

phenomenal. On her maiden passage from London to Melbourne in 1854 the *James Baines,* carrying 700 passengers, 1,400 tons of cargo, and 350 sacks of mail, made the 14,000 sea miles port to port in 63½ days. Heavily laden, she made her return passage in 69½ days, so completing the circumnavigation of almost 28,000 sea miles in a total of 130 days. It was by no means unusual for *James Baines* to log 21 knots, but even she was beaten at times by her sister ship *Champion of the Seas.* The *Champion* lived up to her name whilst running her easting down on her maiden voyage out to Australia, when she logged 465 nautical miles in 24 hours, an *average* speed of 20 knots. Another great Mackay clipper, the *Sovereign of the Seas,* topped 22 knots on her record run from New York to Liverpool in a passage of 13½ days. It was common at the time for sceptical rivals to question these tremendous runs, but the evidence provided by ships' logs and not least, times of departure and arrival were irrefutable. Certainly in the early 1850s and possibly throughout that whole decade, Donald Mackay and his fellow American, W H Webb, built clipper ships the like of which had never before been seen.

As always, however, individual performances depended to a very large extent upon the vagaries of two major factors; sailing conditions, and the determination of captains to 'carry on' at whatever the risk to spars and rigging, or indeed to the vessel itself. Equally matched in these respects, and fast as *Lightning* was, she could never outrun the crack British ships built especially for the China trade. In the light weather and doldrums between the tropics of Cancer and Capricorn, the swift little tea clippers always beat the big Black Ballers hands down. On 20 September 1855 *Lightning* crossed the tropic of Cancer and took 25 days to Capricorn. Robert Steele's *Ariel,* built at Greenock, crossed Cancer two days later, on the 22nd, and made the run to Capricorn in only 18 days.

In the matter of her skippers, *Lightning* had two (among others) whose names are legendary; the famous Captain Anthony Enwright, who left his crack ship *Chrysolite* to take command of Mackay's great Black Baller, and the notorious 'Bully' Forbes. Both were the best of sailors, but were very different in character. The former was bold and daring, the latter hard and stubborn to the point of having reckless disregard for passengers, crew and ship. Once, in *Lightning,* the passengers so feared for their lives that they appointed a spokesman to beg Captain Forbes to shorten sail. His reply was 'No, by God! It is hell or Melbourne!' So saying, he continued to 'carry on' until the crew was driven to the point of mutiny, whereupon Forbes

LIGHTNING

had padlocks clamped on the sheets and stood on the poop with a loaded pistol in each fist, swearing to shoot dead any man jack who dared to lay hand on a rope.

But for all of his absolute tyranny, Forbes commanded respect by proving himself, time and again, to be the toughest man on board. Once, for a bet, he hauled himself hand over hand all the way up and across the standing rigging whilst *Lightning* was at sea, from spanker boom to shark's fin on the jib-boom, a prodigious feat of brute strength and courage. And, almost as though to test and challenge the loyalty of his crew, he used often to climb out onto the end of the swinging boom when the stunsails were set, for the sheer delight of watching his ship roaring along before the westerlies. By adopting such a perilous perch, he placed his life in the hands of the helmsman. One slight turn

of the wheel to bring the ship only one or two points closer to the wind, and Bully Forbes would have gone to his Maker.

Lightning went on and on, together with others of her kind, to make passage after passage along the fabled Clipper Way – out from England to Australia via the Cape of Good Hope and back again around stormy Cape Horn – positively the most romantic sailing route ever known. Ironically, though, it was one which brought about the ruin of its principal protagonist. Overfull of confidence, James Baines committed his marvellous Black Ballers to regular feats of sailing impossible ever to maintain. In order to crush competition from the White Star Line out of Aberdeen, he signed a contract with His Majesty's Government to deliver the *monthly* mail to Australia within a maximum of 65 days, and rashly put his name to a penalty clause which cost him

£100 per day for every day over and above. It was a guarantee which lost him his fortune, and brought about his downfall.

In 1857, Mackay's beautiful *Lightning* was contracted out to carry British troops to India to suppress the historic mutiny. She afterwards returned to the emigrant trade, and continued to give sterling service until she was burned and sunk at Victoria, in Australia, in 1869.

What must it have been like to have sailed in ships such as *Lightning*? No wonder Bully Forbes climbed out onto the end of her swinging boom. Aside from viewing her from another ship, it was the one and only way he could watch her cleaving the ocean and see her at her glorious best.

LIGHTNING

AMERICAN

Young America

Of all the 150 ships built in New York by William H Webb the *Young America*, launched in 1853 at a cost of $140,000, was always his personal favourite. He was not alone in his choice. Many others regarded her as the finest clipper built during that zenith year of US shipbuilding, and possibly the finest of all time. A big ship in her day – Donald McKay's *Great Republic,* launched that same year, was of course a monstrous oddity – the *Young America* was a vessel of 1,961 old tons, 1,439 new tons, with a length on deck of 243 feet, a beam of 43.2 feet, and a depth in hold of almost 27 feet. She had a mean draft of 22 feet, and a 20-inch deadrise at half floor. Her bow lines were lean and graceful, her run was long and clean and this very elegant sheer, together with an eliptical stern of deep counter and overhang, gave her a lovely yacht-like profile much admired and remarked upon. She was never graced by a figurehead, but her trail boards were heavily carved and handsomely topped by a fine, gilded, billet head. She was a thing of beauty and a joy, although not forever, certainly for a very long time.

Young America owed her striking design to the genius of W H Webb, but construction throughout was supervised by the man who was destined to command her and who later became boss of the Pacific Steam Ship Company, Captain David S Babcock. Of the many tall ships which were battered whilst sailing Down East, she was probably the one best fitted to survive; her iron frames were diagonally braced, and set only four feet apart. She had three decks, and her 42-foot-long poop was smartly fitted out with cabins for several passengers. Her sail plan was both lofty and square. She crossed three skysail yards and her mainyard, before eventually and inevitably she was cut down, spanned an enormous 104 feet. So vast a spread of canvas demanded a lot of handling, and when *Young America* set out on her maiden voyage on 10 June 1853 she was manned by a crew of 75, including four mates and 60 able seamen. There were a lot of wages to be paid, but owner Mr George Daniels doubtless consoled himself with the knowledge that his grand new ship was laden for the voyage with an unprecedented $86,400 worth of freight. She continued to make similar huge sums of money for her various owners throughout an unusually-long life, and considering the terrible poundings she took on her many traverses of the Cape, she cost them relatively little in broken masts and lost spars.

That first outwards passage to San Francisco was made in 111 days. The following year, 1854, Captain Babcock 'clipped' one full day off this time and on his third attempt, in 1856, he sailed this always-more-difficult, east-west passage in 107 days. These were very fast passages indeed and yet in 1873, when *Young America* was 20 years old, the famous sail-carrying Captain George Cummings dropped anchor at San Francisco exactly 100 days out of New York. In 1879, and after a quarter of a century of Cape Horn battering, the marvellous old lady made the east-west passage under Captain E C Baker in only 102 days. The best-ever time put up by her greatest rival, the *David Crockett,* was the latter's passage of 103 days made in 1872.

As was inevitable during her long years of work in the world's most dangerous waters, *Young America* was subjected to some grinding punishment. She began the third of her Down East voyages on 29 March 1856, and the night of 18 May saw her hove-to off Cape Horn in a storm so furious it threatened to crush her timbers. It smashed in bulwarks, tore away her boats, broke through her deck-house hatches and snapped off her massive jib-boom as if it were a breadstick. But Captain Babcock rode it out, and went on afterwards to make his own record passage of 107 days.

Young America averted another near-disaster on 30 October 1862 when, at 9° south and 32° west, she ran into a tornado whilst bound out of Calloa for Antwerp. The towering squall ripped away her fore topmast, her main topgallant mast, and her main topsail yard. Captain Carlisle got her jury-rigged at sea and put into Plymouth for yard repairs on 30 October before sailing on to Antwerp and later home to New York. Once again she had survived, but her worst encounter with the elements was yet to come. On 3 December 1868, when she was 41 days out of New York and bound once again for San Francisco, a raging pampero swept down off the Andes and caught her full aback. The icy wind hurled her over onto her beam ends and broke off her mizzen topmast which, in falling, carried away two others, her main topgallant and fore royal. With his ship back on an even keel, Captain Cummings faced a hard decision; whether to put in for costly repairs at nearby Monte Video, or to risk a makeshift refit at sea with the 'Cape Stiff' traverse yet ahead of him.

He opted for the latter choice, but for 24 hours after the pampero struck *Young America* she was swamped by a heavy cross-sea, and all hands were required to take shifts at the pumps in order to keep her from foundering. Cummings knew that with his ship awash below decks, she was in terrible danger of her cargo of railway iron shifting to leeward, in which case she was doomed. Once the water below was more or less under control, Cummings set half of his tired men to claw the wreckage of masts and spars hard alongside and hoist it inboard. Then, after a gruelling week's work during which *Young America* was jury-rigged on the mizzen, a full gale blew up out of the south west and threatened to undo that tortuous effort. The men were exhausted almost to the point of mutiny, but Captain Cummings drove them on by sheer force of will, and the newly-crossed mizzen topsail was cut down from a four-reef sail to a three. A brief period of calm followed the sou'wester, and the main topgallant mast was fidded and the sail was bent on 15 December. Only five days later, however, there blew up a Cape Horn snorter the like of which even Cummings had never before experienced, and he was forced yet again to bully the crew into carrying on with their duties.

This last storm finally blew itself out on the evening of the 24th, and Christmas Day brought fine clear weather. *Young America* went spanking around the Horn, and fetched San Francisco on 17 February 1869. This was a passage of 117 days and one which, but for all that lost time, must surely have been an all-time record. As it was, the underwriters rewarded Captain Cummings' superb feat of seamanship with a purse of $1,000. It was money well deserved. Cummings had saved a ship so badly damaged that she cost $18,000 to repair.

Young America set up two record passages during her long life, both under Captain Cummings, and several record runs. Deep laden, she left San Francisco bound for New York on 15 March 1870. She crossed the Equator in the Pacific 16 days out, traversed the Cape 42 days out, and crossed the Equator in the Atlantic 64 days out. At 8 am on 4 June, only 81 days out, she was off Sandy Hook but unable to see the lightship because of dense fog. The fog prevented her from finding a pilot until late the following day, and so it was not until 6 June that she dropped anchor in New York harbour. Even so, her time of 83 days was then and still is a record for the west-east passage by a loaded ship.

She made her second record passage when she sailed out of Liverpool bound for San Francisco on 12 October 1872, ran to the Equator in 15 days, and was off Pernambuco only two and a half days later. Her average 24-hour run over the first 10 days of this passage was 249 miles. She was within 100 miles of the Golden Gate on 18 January 1873, only 94 days out.

Later, when homeward bound from San Francisco in 1876, she ran 1,423 miles in four days with consecutive 24-hour runs of 365, 358, 360 and 340 miles. But perhaps the most remarkable of her performances was when, on the first leg of that same voyage, she traversed the Horn from Atlantic to Pacific between 17 and 23 July, 1876. A traverse of just six days.

The wonderful *Young America* changed hands several times before February 1886 when, sailing under the Austrian flag and re-named the *Miroslar,* she was posted as 'missing' on a passage between Delaware in the USA and Finme (now Rijeka) in Yugoslavia.

YOUNG AMERICA

Great Republic

MANY OF THE world's sailing ships won glory, but the *Great Republic* remains forever unique; she was vastly famous right from the start of the laying down of her keel. When Donald McKay announced his intention to build, entirely at his own expense, a vessel almost three times the size of any then afloat, the nabobs of the shipping trade shook their heads and pronounced him mad. There was heavy betting on both sides of the Atlantic as to whether or not McKay would ever complete his ambitious project and that, even if he did, such an uneconomical monster would ruin the Boston man. The prophets of doom were right, but they were right for all the wong reasons.

McKay did build his ship, and she was launched on 4 October 1853 amidst scenes of great excitement. The Boston city fathers announced a public holiday, and some 60,000 people massed to cheer her down the ways. Longfellow wrote a poem to commemorate the occasion, and the *Great Republic* looked set to fulfill her destiny as the largest, finest, fastest sailing ship ever known.

Certainly, her dimensions were staggering. Designed as a four-masted shipentine, or barque, she was 335 feet long with a beam of 53 feet and a depth of 38 feet. Each of her four laid decks had an unprecedented eight feet of headroom, and her masts and yards were immense. The truck of her mainmast towered a full 228 feet, and at lower-mast level was 44 inches in diameter. She crossed a tremendous main yard, 120 feet long and 28 inches in diameter, and with all other masts and yards in proportion her total sail area amounted to almost 16,000 yards. She was enhanced by two huge, carved and gilded eagles, one at her stem and the other with wings outstretched across her stern-board.

Alas, this marvel of human craftsmanship was never to grace the seas. After being thrown open to the public – at a dime a head, all proceeds to the Seamen's Aid Society – she was taken down to New York and loaded ready for her maiden voyage. There, on 26 December 1853, Donald McKay suffered the greatest disaster of his life. Fire broke out in a dockside bakery, and sparks from the conflagration ignited the great ship's rigging. Her crew made heroic efforts to stop the flames from spreading, hauling water up to the tops in attempts to drench the bent sails, and hacking desperately to cut away from the spars that canvas already ablaze. They were driven down by heat and danger, and could only watch helplessly as burning masts and yards crashed down and smashed through the upper deck, setting fire to the cargo below. Two other ships were totally destroyed in the holocaust, and the *Great Republic* sustained terrible damage. A decision to scuttle her in order to save the cargo resulted in only part submersion, and the consequences were dire. She was

laden with grain which, swollen by the water trapped between decks, severely strained her hull.

The effect on McKay of the loss of his leviathan might well be imagined, and he never attempted her like again. He left the work of salvage and reconstruction in the hands of Captain Nathaniel Palmer, and sold the resurrected giant to the firm of A A Low & Brother. Inevitably, the ship which sailed out of New York in 1855 under the command of Captain Joseph Limeburner was very different from the one envisaged by her creator. She had lost her top deck, her masts had been cut down, and her lower yards were shorter by 20 feet. Her stem was bereft of its beautiful golden eagle, and without it the plain billet-head looked unattractively utilitarian. Nevertheless, she went on bravely to vindicate her inspired conception with performances of which any ship might justly boast.

She left New York on 24 February, and arrived at Liverpool 13 days out. Those who had predicted her failure must have felt smug when she was unable to dock due to her excessive draught. There was more satisfaction for her detractors when, after sailing round to London, she encountered the very same problem and her cargo had to be taken off by lighters. But Captain Limeburner was not dismayed. He took his ship back to Liverpool, embarked 1,600 British soldiers for a passage to Marseilles, and then went on charter to the French government for the transport of troops to the Crimea.

Great Republic returned to New York at the end of 1856, and soon began her years of fame in the hazardous Cape Horn trade. She was converted to a three skysail-yarder by the removal of her jigger mast and then, carrying a massive 5,000 tons of general cargo, she proceeded to show her paces. On her first voyage as a Cape Horner, out of New York in December 1856 bound for San Francisco, Captain Limeburner sailed her from the Sandy Hook lightship down to the Equator in a record time of 15 days. On the fifth of these days she ran 413 miles, most of them at the astounding rate of over 19 knots. She rounded the Cape with skysails set, and only one week later was at 50° south in the Pacific. Sailing north, she re-crossed the line on 17 February 1857, and but for a delay of five whole days in calms and fogs, must surely have beaten the east-west record set up by the fast clipper, *Flying Cloud*. Even so, and heavily laden as she was, she made the world's most difficult passage in a remarkable 92 days.

The writer is bemused by a nagging fancy that the *Great Republic* was plagued from her conception by a jealousy even exceeding that of human kind. Because of his ship's vast size, Limeburner was unable to contract for a viable cargo back to home port, and so was compelled to look further afield and

besmirch her with 4,500 tons of Chincha Islands guano out of Callao for London. Heavy seas south of the Horn broached *Great Republic* amidships, stoving in her planking and fouling her provisions with the inrush of tainted water. Limeburner was forced into Port Stanley in the Falklands, where he carried out repairs and hired the schooner *Nancy* to fetch fresh stores from Monte Video in Argentina. After this delay, he brought his stinking ship up into London's river on 11 January 1858.

Great Republic continued to be beset by problems throughout the rest of her life, but was fortunate in having for her master one of the greatest tall ships captains of all time. Joseph Limeburner tackled and overcame each of her misfortunes as they arose with skills and fortitude well beyond the demands of normal duty, always steadfast in his conviction that, come what may, his ship was the finest ever built. After unloading in London he took her back home, made three more round voyages in the Cape Horn trade, and set out from San Francisco in 1861 with a cargo of grain for Liverpool. He made a splendid passage, but this was the year which saw the start of the American Civil War and because a majority of her shares were held by Southerners, *Great Republic* was seized on her return to New York by the US Government. A A Low & Brother resolved this predicament by buying out their Southern partners, and in February 1862 their vessel was put to work as a transport for Union forces. She was twice run aground during this service, once in the Mississippi River, but survived both mishaps with only superficial damage. This was thanks entirely to the superlative handling by Captain Limeburner, whose ability to bring his enormous ship safely to anchorage under all plain sail had long been legendary. He could clew up and haul down, round until his topsails were all aback, strip her of canvas as she was losing way, and begin to make a harbour stow before the order was given to let go. A feat of seamanship which had actually to be seen to be believed.

Limeburner's last voyage in *Great Republic* ill befitted his marvellous record. After discharging a cargo of guano at London he returned to New York in May 1864, and his ship was paid off. He then retired from the sea, and *Great Republic* was laid up for two years. She was bought in 1866 by J S Hatfield of Nova Scotia, who sold her in Liverpool in 1868 to the Merchant's Trading Company for a measly £3,500. She was put back into service as the *Denmark,* but seemed to accept her demise with the loss of her illustrious name. On 5 March 1872, on a passage to Rio de Janeiro, she succumbed to a storm off Bermuda. Those surviving, old, deep-sea sailors inclined by sentiment to endow great ships with souls of their own will doubtless agree, without hesitation, that she went down with no regrets.

GREAT REPUBLIC

GERMAN

Preussen

THE 30 years between 1890 and 1921 saw the launching on the continent of Europe of seven huge vessels which, because all were five-masted sailing ships, formed a tiny elite never seen before, or since. They were the *France I* of 1890, (owners A D Bordes of France), *Maria Rickmers* 1890 (Rickmers, Germany), *Potosi* 1895 (Laeisz, Germany), *Preussen* 1902 (Laeisz, Germany), *R C Rickmers* 1906 (Rickmers, Germany), *France II* 1911 (Societé des Navires Mixtes, France), and *Kobenhavn* 1921 (Det Ostasiatiske Komp., Denmark). Even within this tiny group, unique in the history of sail, *Preussen* was herself unique. She was the only one full-rigged overall; all of the others were barks.

Preussen was built for the most famous of all German ship owners, F C Laeisz of Hamburg. She was designed by W Claussen, a director in the shipbuilding firm of Johann C Tecklenborg, and when launched from their yard at Geestemünde was undoubtedly the finest vessel ever to slip down the ways. She was a triumph and a colossus and probably, with a displacement of well over 11,000 tons, the biggest sailing ship ever built. Steel on steel, hull and spars alike, her proportions were awesome. Of a registered 5,081 tons, she could (although seldom did) ship cargoes in excess of 8,000 tons. A magnificent giant from bowsprit to taffrail of 490 feet, she was 54 feet on the beam and had a depth in hold of 27 feet – the height of a modern three-storey building – the whole being heavily reinforced to take the strain imposed by gigantic spars. Her main masts, almost 10 feet in circumference at deck level, towered 227 feet to the truck, more than one and a half times the height of Nelson's Column. With lower yards over 100 feet long and two feet in diameter at centre and each weighing six and a half tons, the aggregate of her standing and running rigging was enormous: 15 miles of wire and 10 miles of hemp and manilla rove through no fewer than 1,260 blocks. In addition, some 800 yards of heavy cable chain.

To haul her laden weight of 11,160 tons at speeds of up to 18 knots, *Preussen* needed to hoist more canvas than any other ship afloat. With the largest of her 46 sails having a spread of 3,500 square feet and each one weighing half a ton, she carried a total sail area of 60,000 square feet. Prior to the introduction of mechanical aids, the handling of such a monster would of course have been virtually impossible. In fact, the mighty *Preussen* was sailed by a crew of only 48 men, whereas many an earlier 2000-ton clipper was hard pressed to manage with 50. Even so, her two deck-mounted steam engines were used in the main for cargo winches, pumps, and anchor hoisting, and were linked only occasionally to the steering gear. It frequently took at least six men to handle the wheel, and yards were braced with iron-cogged winches powered by what sailors used wryly to term 'the good old Armstrong method'. Hardly surprising therefore that whilst she performed magnificently in rolling blue water, *Preussen* was far from nimble in narrow confines and was usually towed out of harbour all the way to Start Point, where the English Channel begins to open out. Her second captain Heinrich Nissen (late of *Potosi*) was wont to remark: 'It was always I who chose the course for *Potosi,* but sometimes *Preussen* chose the course for me.'

There can be no story about the *Preussen* without a brief account of the company whose flag she wore. In 1825 Ferdinand B Laeisz set himself up in a one-man business selling silk hats to the gentry of Hamburg. Very soon, this extraordinary young entrepreneur was exporting his hats, and other divers wares, to the large German colony in South America. In 1852, when he took his 24-year-old son into partnership, Ferdinand had already bought his first ship, and had ordered the building of a brand new vessel to be called the *Sophie* in honour of Carl's recent bride. But Sophie Laeisz was rarely addressed by her given name. Due to her great mass of curly hair she was affectionately known as 'Pudel', a nick-name which rapidly became attached to the ship. Ever thereafter, and as was then the custom, the name of every ship owned by Laeisz began with the letter 'P', and so was born the famous emblem of the P-Line. Later, as Laeisz ships built up a reputation for speed and reliability, this was commonly changed in maritime circles to the Flying P-Line with ships called *Potosi, Pamir, Pitlochry, Padua, Peking, Priwall,* etc, etc.

Old Ferdinand was a man of great enterprise and vision, and Carl was a real 'chip off the old block'. Main architect of the fast-growing line, he issued a set of written orders to captains and crews alike. He knew that sail could compete with steam only by the exercise of rigid disciplines, not least of which was economy. Wages and conditions were good and fair, but his ships fell short of being undermanned by the merest possible fraction, with every man on board expected to pull every ounce of his weight. When at sea, 14-hour days were commonplace, seven days a week. Captains were not permitted to authorise any but the most vital repair or replacement except when in the home port of Hamburg, where Carl could personally negotiate costs. Any employee reported drunk aboard ship was instantly dismissed, whether skipper, mate or deck hand. Further, Carl kept a 'black book' in which was listed the personal and professional records of every ships' officer, and they were up- or down-graded according to conduct and performance.

Most of the Flying P ships were engaged in the South American nitrates trade and *Preussen,* like her predecessor *Potosi,* was designed specifically for this purpose. Trade was largely one-way and many ships made the outward passage only half- or even less than half-laden with mixed cargoes, usually including coal out of Wales to be discharged at Rio for Brazilian railway engines. It was an arduous regime, punishing to ships and men alike, every round voyage necessitating as it did a double traverse around Cape Horn. For the owners, too, the business was frought with risk; the ever-present scarcity of freight out of Europe, and loss of or damage to vessels in waters generally accepted as the most dangerous in the world. Not surprising, then, that Laeisz had only one serious competitor, the French firm of Bordes et Fils. Even less surprising, this was also a family business, founded and run by a man after Laeisz's own heart, Antoine Dominique Bordes. With ships, among many others, such as *France I* and *France II* this great French shipping line might never easily be dismissed, but *Preussen* was the pride and joy not only of Carl Laeisz, but of the entire German nation. She was celebrated, too, in England as the only five-masted sailing ship ever to be registered A1 at Lloyds.

No-one really knows why Carl Laeisz chose to launch his new flagship as the *Preussen.* She was his sixty-second purchase, and he already owned a vessel of that name, a small but very fine steel four-master of 1,761 tons built in Hamburg by Blohm & Voss. This one, which he re-named *Posen,* became a total loss in 1909 when she caught fire in mid-Atlantic on a passage across to New York. Because her cargo included 500 crates of dynamite, *Posen's* crew took to the boats without even attempting to fight the fire, and every man jack survived uninjured. The new *Preussen's* ultimate fate was hardly less dramatic, but before it came about she made 13 round voyages, all but one of them to and from Chile for cargoes of nitrates. Ostensibly, these were imported into Germany for use as fertilizers, but hindsight suggests that much of the tonnage was destined for the manufacture of explosives.

Although *Preussen* never competed with other windjammers in contests such as the grain races out of southern Australia, she was universally recognised as being an exceptionally fast ship, with an average speed over the whole of her albeit-brief career of something like seven knots. In ideal conditions, she often came within a whisker of 18 knots, beating her closest rival and sister-

PREUSSEN

PREUSSEN

ship *Potosi* by not very much, but enough. The fact, now seen clearly, is that she was just too big. A marvellous sailer when properly laden, she was hampered on many an outward-bound occasion and especially when beating against strong westerlies, by the dangerous slopping-around of her water-ballast.

When in 1902 she sailed out of Hamburg on her maiden voyage, *Preussen* was commanded by Carl Laeisz's favoured master, Captain Boye Petersen. She made fast but otherwise uneventful passages to and from Chile, the first of 10 consecutive round trips. Her eleventh voyage was different. Out on charter to the Standard Oil Company, she left Cuxhaven on 11 March 1908 and docked in New York on 13 April after a passage of 33 days. There, she took on a cargo of oil before leaving on 27 May, bound for Yokohama. Fully laden for once, she showed her excellent paces by fetching the Japanese port on 16 September, 112 days out. For Laeisz, it was her most profitable venture. She completed the round voyage by sailing on from Japan to pick up a cargo of nitrates in Chile before returning home to Europe.

There appears to be no extant account of Carl Laeisz's reason for then relieving Captain Petersen of his Flying P Line flagship command. It might be that Petersen retired. In any event, when *Preussen* made her next two voyages to the western coast of South America she did so under the command of Heinrich Nissen, who joined her from *Potosi*. As previously, she sailed out with a mixed cargo, laden far below capacity, and returned with nitrates. The second of these voyages, her thirteenth, proved to be her last.

On 31 October 1910 this huge and beautiful five-master left the port of Hamburg bound for Valparaiso with her holds part-filled with general cargo, including a load of coal. The weather was bad: rain, fog and a heavy swell, but very little wind. Carl Laeisz gave permission for a hiring of the steam tug *President Lion* to pull his ship down the Elbe, across the North Sea, and through the English Channel. Dover was sighted in the late afternoon of 5 November. There was still a good deal of patchy mist, but the breeze appeared to be freshening and Captain Nissen – probably frustrated by five days and nights under tow, and conscious also of what it was costing his penny-pinching owner – determined to cast off from the *President Lion* and set all appropriate sail. Reached as it was by a seasoned windjammer skipper, it was a curiously bad decision. *Preussen* lay squarely in the neck of a very narrow channel which formed the busiest sea lane in the world, and with only one more day of towing she could have been off and away to a safe run from Start Point.

It was not to be. Even as *Preussen*'s crewmen were spreading sail, and shooting off fog-rockets to warn other vessels of her position, the for'ard lookout yelled a report of smoke from a steamer approaching fast off the starboard bow. It was the cross-channel ferry *Brighton* on her regular run from Newhaven to Dieppe. Each ship saw the other, and there has never been any question but that *Brighton*'s captain blatantly disregarded that most-sacred rule of the sea which decrees that steam must *always* give way to sail. The excuse he gave later, that he underestimated

Preussen's speed, was no excuse at all. His plain and bounden duty was to slow down, and even hove-to, in order to pass well astern. He called instead for more steam, intending to cut across the windjammer's bows, and the two ships met in heavy collision.

After the initial chaos, the badly-holed *Brighton* struggled back into Newhaven, leaving Captain Nissen to survey the damage inflicted upon *Preussen*. Sea pouring in through a great rent in her starboard bow had filled her for'ard holds with water, but he reckoned that his steam pumps could render her seaworthy enough to limp as far as Portsmouth for repairs. Again, it was not to be. The weather made another fickle turn, this time for the worse, and Nissen was forced to seek anchorage. He found a temporary haven, but then a gale blew up, and he made a desperate call for three tugs to haul his stricken ship into Dover.

That which followed reads like a catalogue of terrible misfortune. Broken tow-ropes made fast again by dint of super-human effort snapped again and again, and the helpless wallowing *Preussen* was hurled by the storming gale onto rocks under the cliffs of Dover. There, she stuck fast with a broken back. Ironically, the next day dawned calm, and Nissen was able to discharge his cargo into lighters. All in vain. His wonderful ship *Preussen* was battered beyond repair.

Captain Nissen was completely exonerated from any blame at the inquiry which followed, but it is safe to assume that his name was marked down in Carl Laeisz's 'little black book'.

Passat

CLOSELY FOLLOWING its 1910 disaster with the oversized *Preussen,* and apparently having learned from that experience, F M Laeisz & Co ordered the construction of two new vessels, each much smaller, to replace the ill-fated giant. Built at their old wharf on the North Elbe by Blohm & Voss, the ships were listed in that firm's order books as Nos 205 and 206. The former was launched as *Peking,* the latter as *Passat.* Both were splendid steel ships, and both went on greatly to enhance the proud reputation of Laeisz's Flying P Line.

Passat was and is a four-masted bark of 3,180 tons with an overall length of 115 metres, a beam of 14.40, and a draught when laden of 6.70. With a headmast from deck to truck of 52 metres, her 34 sails had a total area of 4,100 square metres, but she could safely be handled by a crew of about 35 experienced men aided by varying numbers of boys under training. Her keel was laid down on 2 March 1911, and after launching on 20 September she was fitted out and made ready for sea by 25 November. Her final cost was exactly the same as that of her twin sister, 680,000 marks. Command was given to Captain Wendler, and *Passat* sailed down the Elbe on Christmas Eve of 1911, bound on her maiden voyage for the port of Valparaiso. She fulfilled Laeisz's hopes and expectations by making a passage out of only 73 days before rounding the Horn to pick up a cargo of nitrates in Chile, and made a further five round voyages before being detained in South America, together with other German ships, at the outbreak of the First World War in 1914. When at last her then-master Captain Pieper was able, on 27 May 1921, to set sail for Europe with 4,700 tons of saltpetre, her homecoming was a sad one. *Passat* had been awarded to France in the 1918 peace negotiations. However, the French did not want yet another four-masted bark, and Laeisz was permitted to buy back his own ship for the sum of £13,000. She was boarded at Marseilles by a German crew on 3 January 1922, and returned to Hamburg for extensive renovations.

Laeisz put her back into the nitrates trade, and the next 10 years of *Passat*'s life brought a mixture of triumph and trouble. She made some outstanding passages, the best-ever in 1927 when she ran from Start Point to Corral in 67 days. She sailed on then to Caleta Buena, loaded close on 5,000 tons of nitrates, and was back in the Channel out of Caleta in 75 days. On her next round voyage, in 1928, she excelled herself by clipping two days off this time. But she suffered on her next time out from the first of two major setbacks. Outward bound on 25 August she collided off Dungeness with the French steamer *Daphne.* The

steamer sank, but although *Passat* sustained considerable damage, she was able to put about and sail back into Rotterdam for repairs. Her next misfortune came exactly 10 months later, late in the evening of 25 June, 1929, when bound with a general cargo for Talcuahana in Chile.

This time, at least, her skipper was entirely without fault. The night was fair and clear and *Passat,* in full sail, was passing once again through the Channel in sight of the lightship *Royal Sovereign.* Well ahead, the freighter *British Governor* was on course to pass across her bows. The steamer had plenty of sea room, but her captain panicked and altered course in an attempt to pass astern. It was a serious error of judgment. Doing all of 10 knots, the *British Governor* rammed the sailer's port bow. Once again, *Passat* was forced to limp back to Rotterdam. She later resumed her voyage but Laeisz, sensing perhaps that her luck had run out, sold *Passat* in 1932 to Gustaf Erikson of Aland for the knockdown sum of £6,500. (Erikson had, in fact, considered buying *Passat* when the French government put her up for sale in 1921, but had chosen instead to buy *Herzogin Cecilie.*)

Erikson put his new ship into the Australian grain trade and she served him well until 1939, when trade was suspended by the Second World War. She was first laid up in her home port of Mariehamn on the island of Aland, then used for two years as a floating warehouse in the harbour at Stockholm. After the war, she was given a face-lift and dispatched in 1946 with cargo for South Africa en route to Australia, there to pick up grain for delivery at Cardiff in Wales. It was her last voyage under the Erikson flag. Old Gustaf, saviour of so many tall ships, died in 1947 and *Passat,* together with her old sister-ship *Pamir,* were chartered for two years by the British government. The British wanted then to convert both ships to steam, but a clause in Erikson's will specifically forebade any such measure, and the ships were sent to Antwerp in Belgium, there to be broken up.

News of the threatened vandalism aroused a great outcry in Germany, and the old windjammer skipper Captain Helmut Grubbe was instrumental in the purchase by Lubeck shipowner Heinz Schleiwen of both ships. Reprieved and rejuvenated by Howalt-Werk of Kiel at a cost of 2,700,000 marks, *Passat* was returned to useful life on 12 February 1952, outward bound for Brasil and Argentina with her holds packed with bags of cement. She returned at the end of June with Australian grain. Away again the following month, she was back home at Travemünde near Lübeck in February 1953. By this time of course the commercial viability of sailing ships was really a thing of the past and

Heinz Schleiwen, faced with the necessity to apply once again for a Letter of Licence, reluctantly decided to call a halt. Captain Heuer and his crew were paid off, and *Passat* was laid up at Travemünde along with her sister ship *Pamir.*

In 1954, a group of 40 German shipowners formed a consortium to save the ships, and put them to use as cargo-carrying training vessels for the *Segelschulschiff der Deutschen Handelsmarine,* the German merchant navy. In this sail-training programme, *Passat* made five round voyages to South America under the command of Captain Helmut Grubbe, and it was during the last of these that she almost came to grief.

Passat left Buenos Aires bound for Hamburg with a cargo of loose barley in September 1957, and ran into difficulties right from the start. Soon after clearing the River Plate, the notorious Brazil currents forced her to sail first south, then east, before resuming a true course for home. In the meantime, Captain Grubbe put his crew of 96 seamen and cadets to the never-ending task of chipping-off and re-painting, and to the preparation of his ship for the North Atlantic autumn gales. This entailed the stripping-off of all sails and the bending-on of *Passat*'s best canvas – a full suit of which cost 170,000 deutschmarks. This major exercise was completed just in time. On 3 November, after passing the Azores, there were ominous indications of an approaching north-west gale, and the rapidly-burgeoning storm brought grave concern. Only a few weeks earlier, Captain Grubbe had received the terrible news that *Pamir,* carrying the very same cargo, had gone down in that very same area with a loss of all but six of her 86-man crew.

By the afternoon of 4 November the wind had risen to a raging force 10, and *Passat* was battered by 50-foot waves which engulfed her decks from stem to stern in continuous torrents of green water. The crew worked like demons at their dangerous work of taking off sail until only top and under-topgallants remained together with the staysails. Then, with the storm at its height, the mizzen staysail was ripped out of its leeches, and there happened that which Captain Grubbe feared most. Pounding seas smashed through a hatch and began to flood the holds. This caused a shifting of *Passat*'s cargo, and the saturated barley began to swell. A sleepless Captain Grubbe was only too well aware that these were precisely the conditions which had finished *Pamir,* and he must have thought that his ship was doomed to the same fate. He was nothing, however, if not a fighter. With his foundering ship listing heavily to port, he ordered the flooding of her starboard cargo compartments in an attempt to restore

PASSAT

a balance. His ploy succeeded, but *Passat* now lay perilously low in the water with her deck almost constantly awash.

Throughout his endless battle with the elements, Captain Grubbe had been sending out SOS signals, and the passenger liner *Rangitiki* had responded with a signal that she would reach him within six hours. Such was the storm's ferocity, though, the *Rangitiki* herself became endangered, and she was forced to rescind the offer. So *Passat* struggled on unaided but providently, and just when it seemed that her fate was sealed, the gale began to lose its fury. After four days and nights during which he had never left the bridge, the exhausted Captain Grubbe was able to

order the setting of restricted sail before succumbing at last to sleep. Afterwards, with his brave ship wallowing like a dying whale, he managed to coax her into the nearest port. There, in Lisbon, that part of her cargo ruined by sea-water was taken off and the undamaged portion re-stowed. Then, with the worst of her structural wreckage repaired, *Passat* set sail for home.

But her trials were not yet over. As she neared the Elbe estuary, and with sanctuary almost in sight, she was buffeted again by an ugly storm and was able to enter the river only after surviving once more those elemental forces which had threatened her in the North Atlantic. Captain Grubbe's masterly handling

brought her safely into dock at Hamburg, but the tragic loss of *Pamir* and the fearsome tribulations of *Passat* stamped that year of 1957 with a permanent place in history. *Passat* came to dock on 8 December, the last great cargo-carrying sailing ship ever to plough blue water. Her deep-sea days ended, she lay in Hamburg for just over two years before being bought by the city of Lübeck to serve as a floating monument. On 5 January 1960 she was hauled to Travemünde, where now she lies against the wall, visited annually by many thousands of enthusiasts come to marvel at the manner of ship which, under sail, made many a passage through waters still feared by the modern vessels of this day.

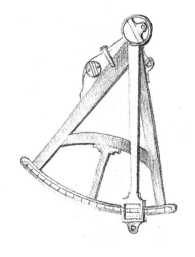

PASSAT

Herzogin Cecilie

ENTHUSIASTS HAVE ALWAYS differed as to which ships were or were not true clippers, and which were Down Easters or Cape Horners; but when it comes to windjammers there is little room for doubt. These huge and magnificent works of man, last of the great sailing ships, were crewed by real sailors, not a few of whom are still very much alive. Mainly employed in the South American nitrates and Australian grain trades, some were launched in Britain, but the vast majority of European 'jammers were built and first owned in Germany and France. And just as there can be no question regarding the special qualities which went into the making of a windjammer, there is overwhelming support for the proposition that *Herzogin Cecilie* was the best and most beautiful of all. Named after the Duchess Cecilie of Mecklenburg, she was built for the North German Lloyd Co by R C Rickmers of Bremerhaven and launched there on 22 April 1922 at a cost of £43,000.

By no means the biggest of windjammers, *Herzogin* was designed to be the finest. She had to be. On placing the order, Norddeutscher Lloyd had specified their needs in great detail: the ship, a four-masted bark, was required to be of superb construction, and to combine great elegance of line with practical utility, a high cargo-capacity with first-class accommodation for officers and crew and also for 60 fee-paying apprentices or cadets. The result was a splendid steel vessel of 3,242 registered tons with a length between perpendiculars of 313 feet, a beam of 43.6, and a depth in hold of 24.2. She was capable on a draught of 23 feet of carrying a cargo, often exceeded, of 4,200 tons. Her hull was double-bottomed for the taking on of water ballast, and the steel of her two full decks was overlaid with hardwood planking. Officers and cadets were quartered topside under a poop extending almost two thirds of her length, with bunks for the crew in a for'ard deck-house. The fo'c'sle was divided into paint locker, stores space and a pigsty. The lines of her brilliant-white hull were robust without being clumsy, although she did appear to be a trifle full in the stern. She had bulwarks only at her mainmast section, so that when she did ship green water, it poured off easily through the rails. However, such was the height of her freeboard that her decks became awash only in the very worst of weather.

Herzogin was a tall ship, with the truck of her mainmast 200 feet above keel level. Her spars were of steel and wood, the main and royal yards being 95 and 49 feet respectively. She was rigged with double topsails and double topgallants and her spanker, like those of most German ships, was divided. Not surprising,

therefore, that none of her 32 sails had reefs. When all were spread, she carried 56,000 square feet of canvas, and must at such times have presented a truly glorious spectacle. Her figurehead, a fine bust of the Duchess Cecilie, was mounted on an elaborate scroll the sides of which bore stands of flags and shields of the Norddeutscher Line. But *Herzogin* was more than just a beauty. She was equipped with steam winches for the working of cargo and subsequently, in 1912, with wireless telegraphy. Her steering gear was duplicated, with one set of huge double-wheels placed amidships and another, connected directly to the rudder head, astern. The latter was not housed, because steering was normally done from the protected midships position.

This lovely 'Bride of the Wind' began her maiden voyage on 27 June 1902 under the command of Captain Dietrich, bound for Astoria near Portland, one of the most northerly ports on the western seaboard of North America. It was a very long voyage for any ship and one which, for *Herzogin Cecilie*, came close to being cut short by disaster. Somewhere off the mouth of the River Plate she was hit by a pampero, a sudden enormous gust of wind peculiar to those regions, which in only a matter of minutes ripped away canvas, rigging, and spars. She was forced to put into Montevideo with damage so extensive that repairs took a full six weeks. After this initial misfortune, she sailed around the Horn and all the way north to Astoria in a passage of 69 days, an excellent performance which proved to be the forerunner of many. During her 12 years of valuable service with Norddeutscher Lloyd, mainly in the nitrates trade, 24-hour runs of 300 miles were not exceptional, and she could generally be relied upon to average seven knots.

The first major turnaround in *Herzogin*'s eventful career was occasioned by the outbreak of the First World War. Commanded at that time by Captain Ballehr she arrived at Herradura Bay on the coast of Chile on 25 July 1914, laden with coal or coke and carrying an extra large number of cadets. Knowing that his ship was to be detained there for the duration, Captain Ballehr did his best to make it impossible for the enemy powers to seize her. Anchoring in the deepest water of the bay, he removed her three-ton rudder and the most vital components of steering gear, and placed them on deck ready for easy and immediate ditching. When, with the passing of months into years, it became evident that the war would be a protracted one, most of the crew and all but 11 of the young apprentices left the ship for good and sought to make new lives ashore. Some returned at the cessation of hostilities, only to leave again during the two further years

which passed before *Herzogin*'s fate was finally decided. Then, in 1920, Captain Ballehr received a signal ordering him to make her ready for sailing.

It was an order easy to issue, but difficult to execute. After six years of idleness and neglect, *Herzogin*'s bottom was totally encrusted with marine growth, many of the shells as big as large cauliflowers. Not quite so bad had there been a handy dry drock, but with no such facility available, Captain Ballehr was forced to improvise. First, he pumped the port side ballast tanks so full of water that the ship heeled over almost onto her beam ends. In this way, and by afterwards reversing the process, he was able with the help of local labour to careen the greater part of *Herzogin*'s hull, and make her ready for sea. Then, with his depleted complement reinforced by a scruffy international crew recruited in Famagusta, he took on a cargo of nitrates and set sail for Ostend. Once back in Europe, *Herzogin Cecilie* was alloted by the peace negotiations to France but the French, with many of their own windjammers lying idle, had no use for yet another one and so the 'wind bride' was offered for sail. With no-one wishing to buy her, she lay once again in limbo.

Until, that is, 10 December 1921, when she was rescued from an ignominious end by a tall-ships skipper, Captain Ruben de Cloux. Apalled at the thought that so beautiful a work of art was destined for the breakers yard, the Belgian sailor made urgent contact with that great saviour of threatened sailing ships, Gustav Erikson of Aland. Without hesitation, Erikson authorised de Cloux to put in a bid and *Herzogin Cecilie* was bought for £4,250, less than one tenth of her building cost. Erikson knew as well as anyone else in the shipping business that the days of sail were fast running out, but his love of these ships was so all-consuming that he strove to the end of his life to keep his fleet at sea, only managing to do so by rigorous economies and iron control. Significantly, though, he made concessions when it came to his pride and joy. The hulls of all of his 22 ships were painted black, because black paint was cheaper than any other colour. But, just as he always restored to his ships the names under which they were launched, he kept his lovely *Herzogin Cecilie* in a coat of shining white.

'Old Gusta' spent a considerable sum on re-fitting his great 'new' flagship, but she went on to justify his unusual extravagence by making numerous profitable voyages. Old as she was, and in spite of her vicissitudes, her speed when fully laden continued to be phenomenal. Her best day's work under the Erikson flag was a stunning 336 miles and she was often logged, during

HERZOGIN CECILIE

HERZOGIN CECILIE

ideal conditions, as making over 18 knots. Alan Villiers, sailor-author of many authoratative books on tall ships, sailed before the mast in *Herzogin Cecilie* when she was once again first ship home in 1928. She left Port Lincoln laden to capacity with 4,500 tons of grain and arrived at Falmouth well ahead of the competition in a passage of 96 days. Ironically, her very best time in the grain races, Port Victoria to Falmouth in 86 days, was also her last.

Captain de Cloux was master of *Herzogin* until his retirement in 1929. She was then taken over by his 25-year-old first mate Mathias Sven Eriksson (no relation to Gustav Erikson), who remained in command to the end. Like most of Erikson employees, this young man was strong, tough and dedicated, the product of generations of Aland Island seafarers. His father, both grandfathers and both of his brothers were ships' captains who, like himself, had started their lives at sea as little cabin boys. Sven Eriksson loved his 'Bride of the Wind', but he drove her to the limits of her capabilities. October of 1934 saw her in the South Atlantic outward bound for Australia, when she encountered a passenger steamer running on a converging course. In

order to give his passengers a better view of the windjammer, the liner's captain called for full steam with the intention of passing alongside. Eriksson responded by hoisting all sail, and as the steamer fell astern her captain dipped his flag and hooted his foghorn in tribute and salute. In a wind approaching gale force, *Herzogin* was making close on 19 knots.

Even so, Eriksson might have felt disappointed, because three years earlier on a passage in 1931 between Wales and Finland up and around the north coast of Scotland, his *Herzogin* logged an all-time record windjammer speed of 20.45 knots. Flying in darkness before a strong, southerly wind she sped down through the Sont, overhauling steamers and firing rockets into the night sky to warn of her approach. Nobody on board slept that night, every off-watch seaman was up on deck anxiously watching the sails, waiting for the booming crack of an over-extended spar. Dawn brought an easing of the blow, and the white bark ran past Copenhagen at a less hazardous pace, not nearly so heeled over but still a wonderful sight. Incidentally, *Herzogin* was on her way home to Aland for scouring and careening, so what might her speed have been had her hull been smooth and clean?

The 24th of April 1936 might well be remembered as one of the blackest days in the history of sailing ships. At half past eight on the evening of that day, *Herzogin Cecilie* set sail out of Falmouth, bound for Ipswich on England's east coast. She sailed in heavy fog. At about 4 am, in the dark of night, she struck Ham Stone Rock off the coast of Devon and was thrown stern-seawards into the aptly named Sewer Mill Cove, where she ran aground at the foot of steep cliffs. In seafaring England the tragedy roused a huge wave of concern and incredibility. In those cruel days of widespread poverty, a sympathetic public donated the then-large sum, in pennies, sixpences and shillings, of over £1,000. Sadly, and although old Gustav Erikson was prepared to add several times this amount (he never insured any of his ships) it was not enough to rescue the old 'Bride'. She was hauled into Starehole Bay, but the shallows there which might have spared her proved, in fact, to be her undoing. A heavy swell on 17 July lifted and dumped the stricken *Herzogin* until she was smashed beyond repair. Her passing marked the end of a glorious era.

Santa Maria

THE MOST SIGNIFICANT fact about the *Santa Maria* is that nobody knows beyond doubt exactly what she looked like. Columbus himself described his flagship as a *nao*, but this was and remains a somewhat loose term used to denote a ship which differed in some way – in size or build or rigging – from the ubiquitous caravel. She most probably differed by varying degrees in all three of these respects, most widely in her sail plan, and her appearance as depicted by Cornelis de Vries is as close to the reality as any modern artist can aspire.

An historical consensus suggests that she was a vessel of between 80 and 100 tons, with an overall length of some 80 feet, about 26 feet on the beam, and drawing around six and half feet of water. She must have been rigged for ocean sailing with square sails on the fore and main masts, one sail on the fore and possibly two on the main, another under the bowsprit, and a lateen sail on the mizzen. She would probably have a crew, give or take two or three, of 40. This, having regard to contemporary knowledge of blue-water sailing, would make good sense.

Curiously, and despite a lack of knowledge of Columbus's flagship, we have fairly accurate descriptions of his two ancillaries, the *Pinta* and the *Santa Clara* – the latter being nicknamed, and much more widely known as, the *Niña*. Both were in the form known as *caravela redonda*. An improvement on the caravel, which was lateen-rigged overall, the redonda's foremast was stepped vertically on its heel and fitted with two square sails. The *Pinta* was of about 60 tons, the *Niña* of 50 or so, and they shared the admirable qualities of being large enough for ocean voyaging yet small enough and with sufficiently shallow draught to venture into unexplored bays and rivers. They also carried sweeps, and might easily be rowed in the absence of a favourable wind. *Pinta* and *Niña* shipped crews of around 35 and 30 respectively. Of the two, the smaller ship proved herself best.

We know that the *Niña* was slightly over-loaded with 51 tons of stores, but that she nevertheless remained stable and nimble. She was a splendidly built vessel, her two and a half inch thick oak hull planking fastened with oaken pegs and reinforced at stress points with iron bolts. She was close on 70 feet long, with a 22-foot-beam and a 9-foot-depth of hold. The stern part of her short quarter-deck was given over to a small cabin for the captain. Underneath the qaurter-deck was the helmsman's post, also two very tiny sleeping spaces for the master and the pilot. The rest of the crew slept, ate and lived on the open deck. She carried a small swivel-gun mounted on the quarter-deck rail, and an iron cannon in the waist fired three and a half inch round-shot. *Niña*

was chosen by Columbus as his flagship when *Santa Maria* was lost off Hispanolia.

This, then, was the brave little fleet fitted out at the small port of Palos, in the south-western province of Spain, for a voyage of exploration which was vastly to change the course of world history.

Christopher Columbus was born in Genoa in Italy, the son of a weaver, in or about 1446. There is no reliable account of his early life, and it is probably unwise to take much heed of the sympathetic biography written by his illegitimate son, Ferdinand. Some chroniclers have Columbus attending the university of Pavia to study astronomy, geometry and cosmography; other and more creditable writers have him sent to sea at 10 years of age and virtually illiterate until he was 23. All ignore the fact that Columbus himself once said that he began his life at sea when he was 14. In any event, he certainly spent the three years between 1470 and 1473 ashore and at home in Genoa, working in the family weaving business, and it is during this period that his formal education most probably began.

Five years later he was living in Portugal and married to Felipa Moniz de Perestrello whose father, Bartholomew Perestrello, was a captain in the service of Henry the Navigator and first colonial governor of Porto Santo. For a man of Columbus's abiding interests it was an excellent match, and when he and his wife paid a lengthy visit to Porto Santo there can be no doubt that the future discoverer of America was fascinated by his father-in-law's library of logs, charts and maps. He was certainly able by this time to read and write not only in his native Italian, but also in Latin and Portuguese, and further intensive studies led him firmly to believe that the world was round. But he also believed it to be very much smaller than in fact it actually is, and that the continent of Asia almost encircled the globe to form the main land mass which lay to the west of Spain.

Columbus endured 15 years of intense frustration during which the bishops and monarchs of Spain, France and Portugal listened carefully to his proposals for a great voyage of exploration and then, fearful of offending each other and not least of offending the Church, went on endlessly to procrastinate. At long last, Queen Isabella of Spain reached a firm decision to support the enterprise, and the three little ships sailed out of Palos on 3 August 1492. By this time, Columbus was 46 years old.

The ships fetched the Spanish-held Canary Islands in a passage of 10 days, during which time the *Pinta* sprang her rudder.

Whilst this was being repaired, *Niña* was refitted, her masts stepped upright and her sails cut and re-sewn to make her square-rigged on the main and fore masts. Laden with fresh provisions, the small fleet set sail again on 6 September. In spite of having had nearly six weeks respite, the crews were not in good spirits, and Columbus began early to falsify his log, fearing mutiny among the men should they learn their true distance from home. Ironically, he miscalculated so badly that of the two logs he kept, the 'false' one was much the most accurate.

Two factors militated against a happy crew: they were sailing ever westward across a vast uncharted ocean; also, many if not most of then, believed that the world was flat and that they might at any time plunge over the edge into a bottomless abyss. So, and in spite of favourable weather, their fears grew day by day, and when in mid-September they entered the Sargasso Sea a huge proliferation of weed convinced the men that they were caught in a God-sent tangle which would drag them down to their doom. Fortunately, the weed parted easily, and fears were allayed.

On 10 October, however, after an unprecedented 34 days at sea, Columbus began to have grave trouble even with his captains. Martin Alonso Pinzón of the *Pinta* was all for turning back, and so too was his younger brother Vicente Yanez Pinzón, who had command of the *Niña*. Both were troubled that the burgeoning easterly winds which were driving them on to their goal might prevent them from ever returning.

Just as well, then, that two days later, shortly after dawn on 12 October, the exhausted fleet sighted land. Columbus was sure he had reached the Indies, gateway to Cathay and fabulous cities of gold described by Marco Polo. His calculations were out by something like 10,000 miles but this, at the time, was of no consequence. He had brought his fearful crews to the promised landfall, and the fact that it was one of the islands (now known as Watlings) in the Bahamas made absolutely no difference at all. The awestruck natives were very friendly, showering the strangers with gifts – though not of gold, jewels and spices. These things, the islanders explained, belonged to the king of a mighty land which lay over the sea to the south-west.

After taking possession of the island in the names of Ferdinand and Isabella, the admiral sailed on a southerly course through a sea profusely dotted with islands, all of whose friendly inhabitants repeated the story that a great land to the south was ruled by a king who was lord over mountains of gold. Columbus's discoveries included islands which he named Santa

SANTA MARIA

Maria de la Concepcion (Rum Cay), Ferdinanda (Lord Island), Isabella (Crooked Island), Juana (Cuba), and Hispaniola (Haiti), or San Domingo. It was whilst off the coast of this last one that the helmsman of *Santa Maria*, grown careless after weeks of easy sailing, ran the flagship aground on a reef. There was no loss of life, but the ship was damaged beyond repair. Columbus abandoned her, leaving her crew on the island with orders that they use her timbers to build a small fort. He gave to this first-ever European settlement in the New World the name La Navidad.

Eager now to return home with the news of his discoveries, Columbus transferred to the *Niña*, loaded her with fresh supplies, and set sail on 4 January 1493 with her bows headed east. *Pinta* and *Niña* came together on the 6th but then a fierce storm drove the ships far apart and 45 days later, on 18 February, *Niña* limped alone into the port of Santa Maria in the Portuguese-held Azores. Columbus rested his crew for only six days before setting sail again, and he entered the Tagus to drop anchor off Lisbon on 4 March. All past ill-feeling forgotten, King John of Portugal entertained Columbus with the highest honours, detaining him for nine days. Then, on the 13th, *Niña* put out of the Tagus river bound for her home port of Palos, and entered harbour there on Friday the 15th to scenes of wild rejoicing. Incredibly, Martin Alonso Pinzón brought *Pinta* into harbour on the very same tide, and the two ships came together again after being separated for 62 days.

Columbus left ship to set out on the long land journey to Barcelona, seat of the royal court. He entered the city with the spoils of his voyage – gold, cotton, parrots, strange plants and animals, and the Indians he had brought back for baptism – in what amounted to a triumphal procession. Ferdinand and Isabella received him with great pomp, confirmed him in all of his titles and privileges, and conferred upon him a magnificent scutcheon blazoned with the royal castle and lion of Castile and Leon, combined with the five anchors of his own, previous coat of arms. Two months later Pope Alexander VI issued the controversial bull which granted to the Spanish rulers sovereign rights over all the lands discovered, *or yet to be discovered*, west of a line drawn 100 leagues beyond the Azores, and Columbus was given a virtual free hand to set about organising a new and very much larger expedition to secure and extend the discoveries already made.

Columbus went on to make a further three voyages to the New World, planting the flag of Spain on the Leeward and Virgin Islands, Puerto Rico, Trinidad, Venezuela, the Honduras, and on Panama; but all of these great triumphs were to be met by Isabella and Ferdinand with staggering ingratitude, and the latter part of his life was soured by an obsession that he was beset on all sides by those who wished him ill. He sailed again on 24 September 1493, and found on his first return to La Navidad that the men he left behind had been slaughtered by the natives. He spent a frustrating 18 months there in a futile attempt to found another colony, before returning to Spain for more men and materials.

His third expedition, with eight ships out of San Lucar on 30 May 1498, attracted 'colonizers' hungry only for gold, and with no interest at all in the agricultural and animal husbandry so vital to the establishment of a permanent settlement. With no precious metals easily to be found at La Navidad, they turned on their admiral governor and tried to kill him. Columbus rallied those still loyal to him, hung the rebels, and returned home to the wrath of his monarchs who accused him of mismanagement of 'their' colony. He was stripped of the titles they had previously conferred upon him 'in perpetuity', and condemned to live in disgrace.

Nevertheless, he somehow managed later to persuade his royal patrons that he be given one last chance to redeem himself, and set sail from Cadiz on 9 May 1502 with four caravels and 150 men. This fourth and last voyage was a triumph of navigation, but it culminated in disaster. By this time, the rapacious cruelty of the Europeans had become a byword among the natives, and Columbus found himself almost constantly under attack. Grieving and disillusioned, he left Jamaica on 28 June 1504 and sailed again into San Lucar on 7 November.

The man who, far more than any other, founded the vast wealth of Spain, and whose enormous feats of seamanship opened up the way to a circumnavigation of the globe, died bitter and broken in Valladolid on 20 May 1506, at the age of 60 years. The final accolade bestowed upon him, on 23 February 1505, was the right to ride on a mule.

SANTA MARIA

SPANISH

Réale

ALTHOUGH SHE WAS a galleas, and one which relied for power as much on oarsmen as on sail, *Réale* deserves mention here by virtue of her major role in the biggest (in terms of vessels engaged) sea battle of all time. Historically, the Battle of Lepanto in 1571 was easily the most significant since the Emperor Octavian defeated Anthony and Cleopatra at the Battle of Actium in 31 BC.

Réale was perhaps the most magnificent galleas ever launched. Designed and constructed by Reales Atarnazanas in 1568, she stepped two masts and so far as can be deduced from a sifting of contemporary accounts – and certainly according to the superb modern replica built in her native Spain for the Maritime Museum at Barcelona – her length on deck was 52.5 metres and her beam measured 6.20 metres. Her 60 oars, 30 on each side, were 11.5 metres long, and the fact that she carried 236 oarsmen suggests that allowing for casualties etc, she was rowed by 3 men to each oar. Resembling much more a splendid royal barge than a fighting ship, the whole of her high stern, panels and rails of her quarter galleries was one solid mass of beautiful carving, all of it covered with shining gold leaf. This so-called 'tabernacle' was protected from hot sun and wind by a huge tent-like structure composed of heavy, damask material richly embroidered with colourful silks and threads of silver and gold. Such was the flagship of Don Juan d'Austria, 22-year-old illegitimate son of Charles V of Spain, and therefore half-brother to the reigning Spanish king, Charles's elder son Philip II.

The tremendous battle in which *Réale* played so vital a role was the final outcome of an age-old struggle between Cross and Crescent – Christendom and Islam – for control of the Mediterranean. On the one side a Holy Alliance between Malta, Spain and the several independent states which now form part of Italy, on the other side Turkey, whose great power at sea was bastioned by her Ottoman outposts in Greece, Tunisia, Egypt, and Algeria. Thus Turkey had come to regard the Mediterranean as her own national inland sea, and her arrogant demands upon neighbouring countries had grown insupportable. When, in 1570, she seized the then-Venetian island of Cyprus, her action proved the last straw. Venice appealed to Pope Pius V for help in the formation of a Christian League, and Pius was moved to organise the forces of Dubrovnik, Malta, the Vatican, Genoa, Venice, and Spain. France was asked to assist, but preferred to remain neutral.

As they were assembled, the fleets of both sides became enormous. An account of the battle written immediately afterwards puts the total number of ships taking part at over 500, of which 249 were Christian and more than 270 Turkish. The latter, under overall command of the notorious Lala Mustafa Pasha, consisted of 208 galleys and 66 galleases arrayed in three squadrons. Lala Pasha's own numbered 96 assorted vessels, whilst the second squadron, under Uluch Ali, numbered 95. Mehemet Sirocco commanded 53, the remainder of the forces consisting of supply ships.

Don Juan d'Austria, who in spite of his youth was placed in overall command, divided his fleet into five groups, with himself at the head of 64 galleys and two galleases, one of the latter being, of course, *Réale*. Juan de Cordoba was given a small group of seven galleys whose task was to scout ahead. A squadron of 53 galleys and two galleases was commanded by Giovanni Andrea Doria, and another squadron of exactly the same size by Marco Antonio Barbarigo; to the rear, a guard of 30 galleys under the command of Alavaro de Bazan. The contemporary historian has Don Juan's ships armed with a total of 1,815 cannon and a force of 84,200 men: 28,000 soldiers, 12,920 fighting seamen and 43,500 oarsmen. An assumption that the Turkish fighting force was as large, if not larger, is well borne out by the vast numbers of their killed, wounded and captured, and of their Christian slaves set free.

This great Christian armada gathered at Messina in the early days of September 1571 and sailed out on the 16th, bound for Corfu, reaching the island on the 26th. Soon afterwards, whilst sheltering his fleet from storm and wind under the lee of Cefalonia, Don Juan received news of the fall and sacking of Famagusta, last Christian stronghold in Cyprus. After seizing the port in August, Lala Mustafa Pasha had carried out a series of bloody executions, murdering his Venetian captives in a particularly brutal way. The Christian ships weighed anchors and the two huge fleets caught first sight of each other, to the west of Patras and the south of Oxia, at dawn on Sunday, 7 October. Don Juan was at something of a disadvantage: Lala Pasha's ships were already drawn up in crescent-shaped battle order, whilst the formation of his own remained haphazard. Nevertheless, the young commander prepared to fight. He issued an order that every man be given an extra measure of wine and food, and that every Christian slave in his galleys be freed from his shackles, so as to afford for his spirit an easier access to heaven. Then, he hoist at the stern of his beautiful galleas a banner embroidered with a likeness of the Virgin Mary which had been blessed for him by the Pope, and went among the crew of *Réale* holding high an ivory crucifix and exhorting them to do their utmost in this, their holy cause.

The first shot was fired at 11 o'clock in the morning, and within an hour or two at most the sea all around, run red with blood, had become a scene of gigantic destruction. Don Juan, forced to deploy his fleet around a headland on the northern side of the gulf, saw both of his flanking squadrons – Barbarigo's on the right and Andrea Doria's on the left – falter and break under fierce attack by the ships of Mehemet (or Mohammed) Sirocco and those of Uluch Ali. With no hesitation, he sailed in at the head of all six Christian galleases in a direct assault upon the Turkish centre and smashed through Lala Pasha's squadron with great success. Panic spread throughout the Turkish fleet, but then the wind fell away and Don Juan's six big and heavy ships, with their crushing firepower, had to be hauled through the sea by their oarsmen.

Inspired as they were by religious fanaticism, both sides fought with maniacal fervour, and the scale of slaughter was appalling. Much of the fighting was hand-to-hand with ships locked fast together, rammer and rammed, and sinking fast. Lala Pasha, having successfully repelled three attacks by *Réale* and the Venetian admiral Veniero, personally led an ill-fated boarding party onto Veniero's galleas, and was killed. Some accounts suggest that he cut his own throat with a cry of 'Better dead than a prisoner!'. Others have it that his head was hacked off and, having first been held aloft on the point of a spear, was hoist to the top of *Réale*'s mainmast as a signal of victory.

The fighting raged fiercely until 4 o'clock in the afternoon before the alliance was assured of a resounding triumph, and for miles in every direction the calm blue waters resembled nothing more than an enormous graveyard of broken ships and floating bodies. The slaughter was almost unimaginable. Of the Turkish commanders, only Uluch Ali escaped. All in all, the Turks lost 204 vessels sunk and 11 taken, and their casualties in human terms were staggering; over 30,000 dead or wounded, 8,000 captured (among them the sons of Lala Pasha and Uluch Ali) and more than 12,000 slaves set free. Christian losses are not nearly so well recorded, but a fair consensus of various accounts would appear to put them at about 9,000 dead and 18,000 wounded.

The victory at Lepanto was utterly decisive in favour of the Christians, but it proved to be a hollow one. The Holy Alliance was never really consolidated, individual members of it failing to agree with each other. An eventual division of spoils resulted in a share for the Pope of 27 galleys and 800 'heathen' slaves. Spain got 58 vessels – galleys and ships – and 1,700 slaves, and Venice was awarded 45 vessels and 162 slaves. However, internecine quarrelling between the partners soon resulted in a splitting-up of the Christian League and Cyprus, after all, remained in the hands of the Turks.

No question, though, as to who was the hero of the Battle of Lepanto. The young Don Juan d'Austria, whose mother was a Dutch girl, returned to Holland and died there, not yet out of his twenties, in 1578.

NB Spanish, Italian, Dutch and other northern European accounts of the Battle of Lepanto differ considerably, and especially in the spelling of proper names.

RÉALE

San Gabriel

THE FLEET WHICH assembled in the Tagus at Lisbon in the summer of 1497 consisted of four ships. We know what they looked like because each was depicted in a contemporary catalogue of Portuguese ships. *San Gabriel* and *San Rafael* were splendid new *naos* of perhaps 160 tons with two large square sails on each of the fore and main masts, a fifth one under the bowsprit, and a lateen on the mizzen. The *Berrio*, smaller and lighter for work inshore, was a caravel redondo of about 90 tons. The big, sturdy carrack which served as a stores ship, a vessel of some 300 tons, had no name. All were fitted out under the expert watchful eye of Bartolemeu Dias whose own great voyages of exploration had taken him around the Cape of Good Hope, so proving that a way to the east lay open. Between them, *San Gabriel* and *San Rafael* mounted 20 cannon. The big-bellied stores ship carried sufficient provisions to allow every man in the fleet a daily ration of one pound of salt beef, one and a half pounds of biscuits, two litres of water, and one of wine. These basics were supplemented by generous amounts of almonds, dried plums, lentils, onions, honey, sugar and salt. The combined stores of all four ships were reckoned enough to sustain the crews for at least two years. Never before had any expedition been so abundantly supplied.

The man chosen by King Manuel the Fortunate of Portugal (1495–1521) to head this very costly venture was born at Sines on the coast between Lisbon and Cape St Vincent in 1460, the year which saw the death of Henry the Navigator. At 37 years old, Vasco da Gama came from a line of soldiers going all the way back to the ousting of the Moors in 1238, but his interests and skills were not only military. In addition to being a battle-hardened expert in the handling of men, he was a learned student of navigation and astronomy. There is ample evidence that he was arrogant and cruel, but those who served him well were treated with fairness and even compassion. As overall commander, or captain major, da Gama chose as the captain of his flagship a seasoned mariner called Goncalo Alvares. He gave command of the *San Rafael* to his brother Paulo da Gama, and Nicolau Coelho was made captain of the *Berrio*. The big nameless carrack was under the command of one Goncalo Nunes. Among the total for all four ships of 170 officers and men were several who had rounded the Cape with Dias, and some who could speak Arabic and/or a few of the African dialects. So, the small Portuguese flotilla which set sail from Lisbon at noon on 8 July 1497 was extremely well equipped to make what was to become one of the most momentous maritime excursions of all time.

Vasco da Gama made boldness his watchword right from the very start. He sailed on past the Canaries to make a first landfall in the Cape Verde Islands, anchoring there only long enough to take on fresh foods and water before leaving on 3 August. Spurning the coast-hugging tactics of his predecessors, he took the brave and imaginative course of heading west-south-west into the open Atlantic, and not until 10 weeks of ocean sailing had taken his ships very far south of the equator would he give the order to come about and sail east. Weeks at sea turned into months, but as his captains grew ever more afraid, da Gama remained grimly steadfast. At long last, early in the morning of 7 November, they sighted land and came to anchor in St Helena Bay, *only 1° north of the Cape of Good Hope*. It was the most audacious and spectacularly successful exercise in navigation ever accomplished.

After four months and one day at sea, the ships were in need of attention. They were hauled up onto the beach for careening; and all repairs carried out, were ready for sea again in the remarkably short time of nine days. They set sail on the 16th, rounded the tip of Africa on the 22nd, and dropped anchor in Mossel Bay on the 25th. There, secure in the knowledge that they had made the passage out of one great ocean into another, da Gama gave his people rest.

But not for long. After breaking up the stores ship for spares, and erecting a padrõe, an engraved stone column to mark the Portuguese presence, they were underway again on 8 December and sailed north up the coast until the 25th, then anchored in a bay to celebrate the holy day. Da Gama went ashore, and called the place Natal – the Portuguese word for Christmas. There could not have been much lingering over the festivities, because their next anchorage was on 11 January 1498, at the mouth of the Copper River. They stayed five days to fill up the water butts before sailing on up the east coast of Africa to reach, on 25 January, the inlet named by da Gama the Rio de Bon Signaes. Again, in those tropical waters, the ships had to be careened, and another padrõe was erected. In the meantime, a brush with the hottentot natives had resulted in da Gama receiving a spear-thrust in the leg, but the wound was not a serious one and so was quick to heal.

There followed a period of trauma. Leaving the coast behind and sailing north-east, the ships were beleagured by fierce unfavourable winds and supplies began to run low. There was still plenty of staples, but fresh foods and fruits – essential for the prevention of scurvy – were now exhausted, and for the first

time, sickness ran rife. A two-day storm drove the ships apart, and it was only by good fortune that they became united again. They ran so low on water that the daily ration per man was reduced to a quarter of a litre. The crews began to lose hope, and da Gama turned back towards the coast. Then, on 2 March, the lookout man on the *San Gabriel* sighted what he thought must be a mirage; graceful white buildings and gleaming mosques with towering minarets, and a harbour whose wharves were packed with vessels. It was the city of Mozambique.

Already a bastion of Moslem civilisation, Mozambique was just one of a whole string of East African city-states, each fiercely independent. Da Gama invited the local sultan on board the *San Gabriel*, and made the grave mistake of offering the potentate a gift of glass beads and bells. This was a land to which the big dhows of Arabia and India came to trade fine rugs, spices and rare Chinese porcelain for rare timbers, ivory and gold, a land where pearls were traded for rubies. The sultan was not amused, and barely gave da Gama leave to partly replenish his ships.

The reception he got at Mombasa, 800 miles up the coast, was even less propitious. Approaching the harbour, he interpreted a noisy celebration to mark the end of Ramadan as a form of welcome, and only realised his mistake when a mob of yelling hostiles swarmed out in boats and attempted to board his ships. Da Gama fought them off, hastily backed out to sea, and followed the coast north in search of a more friendly haven. He found it one week later, on 4 April, when he came to anchor at Malindi. The local sultan here was a bitter enemy of his rival in Mombasa, and welcomed da Gama as a friend and ally. He accepted the explorers' cheap presents with good grace, responding generously with splendid offerings of cloves, spices and six fat sheep. By far the most valuable of his gifts, however, was the service of an expert pilot to guide the Portuguese ships over the next, and final, leg of their voyage.

Calicut lay far across the Indian Ocean almost 2,500 miles to the north east and it is doubtful whether, without the help of their native pilot, da Gama's ships would have survived the passage. Their course was beset by innumerable islands, atolls and reefs, many of the ship-wrecking latter lying scant feet below the surface. But the Malindi navigator seemed to know every single one, and aided by favourable winds, he led them to the Malabar coast in the remarkably fast time of only 27 days. Even more remarkable, their landfall was within 55 miles of the port of Calicut – a truly astonishing triumph of navigation.

When da Gama's little fleet entered harbour at Calicut in India

SAN GABRIEL

SAN GABRIEL

on 20 May 1498, the great Portuguese dream at last became reality. But, to paraphrase the poet, it is sometimes better to travel hopefully than actually to arrive. A munificent welcome by the Zamorin (king) of Calicut was sadly short-lived when he discovered that, really, the Portuguese had nothing of interest to offer. To make matters very much worse, the highly influential merchants in this Hindu land were Christian-hating Moslems. They spat on da Gama's cheap trade goods, and refused to do business with him. He was reduced to having his men make small, underhand deals in the shoddy back streets of the market, and managed to accumulate a few sacks of cloves and a few dozen precious stones. It was a long, slow process during which da Gama was made painfully aware that in India, his Portuguese trinkets were useless, worth only one-tenth of what they had cost in Lisbon.

Three months of this humiliation was enough, and da Gama left Calicut on the morning of 29 August. He reconnoitred the coast to the north, looking for a sheltered cove on which to beach his ships for careening and caulking in preparation for the long voyage home, and found such a haven among a small group of islands just south of what was to become the Portuguese colony of Goa. Then, his three ships cleaned and repaired, albeit woefully under-supplied, he set out to re-cross the Indian Ocean. The native pilot had deserted in Calicut, and the passage back

through those hazardous waters took not just one month, but three. With insufficient food and water, the voyage became a ghastly nightmare. Many of the men fell prey to scurvy. Gums turned black and rotten, teeth fell out, and limbs were rendered useless by ugly gangrenous sores. Every day saw its quota of deaths and towards the end those remaining had barely enough strength to tumble corpses over the side. It was a time of awful, terrible despair.

Only the iron will of their captain major kept the survivors' spirits alive. Somehow, all three ships managed to stay together and navigate the hazardous passage, and they limped into harbour at Malindi towards the end of November. The friendly sultan there did everything possible to relieve their extreme distress, providing an abundance of fruits, fowl and good fresh meat. Sadly, however, men continued to die and those who did eventually survive were too few in number to handle all three ships. So, after stripping her of everying of use, da Gama beached and burned *San Rafael*, afterwards raking through the ashes to salvage what remained of her iron bolts and strappings.

After that disastrous westward traverse of the Indian Ocean, almost anything which followed had to be relatively easy. *San Gabriel* and *Berrio* sailed south down the east coast of Africa, anchoring at intervals to forage for fruits and water but avoiding the hostile port of Mombasa, and redoubled the Cape on 20

March 1499. In *San Gabriel*, da Gama was suffering great personal heartache. His much-loved – and much more gentle – younger brother Paulo was still desperately ill, and hoping to save his life, da Gama headed with all possible speed for the Cape Verde Islands. Paulo seemed to rally after rest and treatment on shore, but rapidly grew worse once back at sea and in a further effort to save him, da Gama made for the Azores. He put in at Terceira, but Paulo died there and was buried in the graveyard of the Franciscan monastery. He was one of many who lost their lives. Of the 170 men who set out on the venture, only 54 returned.

After parting from the *San Gabriel*, *Berrio* reached Lisbon on 10 July. Da Gama entered the Tagus on 9 September after an epic and epoch-making voyage of two years and two months and a staggering 27,000 miles. He had little to show by way of booty, but his contribution in terms of Portuguese empire-building was quite inestimable, and his personal gain in the years to follow made him enormously rich, the fourth (after King Manuel) most wealthy noble in the whole of Portugal. He sailed back to India in 1502, and came back home in 1503 to his vast estates in Evora. He was nominated the Viceroy of India in 1524, and died that same year on Christmas Eve, 24 December.

PORTUGUESE

Trinidad and Vittoria

ALTHOUGH Sir Francis Drake of England was the first fleet admiral completely to circumnavigate the world, he might never have succeeded in his quest had not Ferdinand Magellan, who preceded him by nearly 60 years, pointed out the way. Arguably the boldest navigator of all time, Magellan was the first man ever to find a western passage around the tip of South America and to sail the enormous ocean which he named the *Mar Pacifico*; and the fact that he was killed before completing the circumnavigation in no way detracts from these tremendous achievements.

The son of a portuguese nobleman, Magellan was born at Sabrosa probably in 1480, and entered the service of Manuel the Fortunate in 1495. He vastly distinguished himself at battles in India and in Morocco, but somehow fell foul of Manuel and renounced his Portuguese nationality in order to adopt that of Spain. On 22 March 1518 he was granted a Royal Charter to undertake a great expedition in the name of King Charles, and Portugal's loss was its neighbour's gain.

The famous explorer's preparations for his voyage and the actual voyage itself were very well documented at first hand, and there have been numerous subsequent accounts, most of them based on a journal kept by one of the very few survivors of the circumnavigation, Antonio Pigafetta. All the more strange, therefore, that no genuine painting of any one of Magellan's five ships has ever come to light, and although we have a very good idea of what they must have looked like, there can never be an absolutely accurate portrayal. But his flagship the *Trinidad* was a vessel of about 110 tons with a hull length of 80 feet, a beam on the waterline of 25 feet, and a draught when laden of just under 10 feet. Her tall bowsprit carried a sizeable spritsail and her foremast, set well forward in the bows, was square-rigged as was her mainmast, with main and topsails. She carried on her stumpy mizzen a single lateen sail. Her small low forecastle was set over stout blunt bows, but her quarterdeck ran up to the waist, ending just short of her mainmast. She had a high, rounded tuck and was, in other words, a fine-built Spanish carrack quite typical of her day. The *San Antonio* of 120 tons differed slightly only in size, and carried a crew of 60 against *Trinidad's* 55. The *Concepción* of 90 tons had a crew of 45, the *Victoria* of 85 tons had a crew of 42, and the *Santiago* of 75 tons had a crew of 32.

An extant, detailed list of the stores and cargo taken on board these five small ships prompts wonder as to how and where they were able to stow: 58 large and seven small cannon together with over two tons of gunpowder, and many thousands of 10-pound cannon balls; around 40 tons of assorted foodstuffs, including 984 large cheeses, 15 tons of biscuit, one and a half tons of currants and raisins, and a ton of honey in jars; 417 pipes and 253 butts of wine, and numerous casks of fresh water; some 20 tons of trade goods including six tons of lead and copper, one and a half tons of vermillion, and a ton of quicksilver; and also of course a vast quantity of spare yards, spars and cordage for a voyage of an estimated two years.

Thus heavily laden, Magellan's little fleet sailed out of harbour at Seville on the morning of Monday, 10 August 1519, knowing full well that a strong Portuguese force was lying in wait in the Atlantic bent on destroying the expedition almost before it began. Magellan brought his fleet to anchor at San Lucar, near the mouth of the Guadalquivir river, finally to prepare his ships and to wait for favourable winds. This took some time, and it was not until Tuesday, 20 September that he sailed on into deep sea. He reached Tenerife on the 26th and lay there for eight days in order to take on fresh fruit and water before heading south towards Sierra Leone. There, having reached a latitude well below that of the Portuguese fleet which lay in wait for him, he filled his sails with the south-east trade winds and made for the coast of Brazil. Juan de Cartagena, captain of the *San Antonio*, hotly disputed the captain general's course. Magellan stripped him of his rank, and clapped him in irons on board the *Trinidad*. This early seed of mutiny came to full blossom seven months later, and it might be useful at this point to examine the cause – the tendentious chain of command.

All of the five vessels, not excluding Magellan's own *Trinidad*, was captained by an Hidalgo – a high-born gentleman – who knew little or nothing about sailing a ship but whose sovereignty over life and death was utterly unquestionable. These Hidalgos spoke only to their priests, to each other, and to their individual master mariners, who were responsible for the actual running of the ships. Inevitably, jealous argument, inspired not least by the Machiavellian representatives of God, was rife. In spite of their ignorance of the sea, the 'captains' regarded themselves as in-finitely superior to all and sundry, including the Captain General himself. Magellan, however, was made of the stuff of greatness. He turned a deaf ear – not difficult when communication was often restricted to shouting from ship to ship – and led the way ever westward.

The captains had little choice but to follow and Magellan kept his fleet intact until, on 29 November, he sighted the coast of South America near the Cape of St Augustine. He followed the coast to the great bay which he named after St Julian and decided, at the end of March 1520, to winter in its sheltered waters. But for the crews there was little rest or comfort. Magellan knew he must use these months ashore to unload his ships of everything but ballast, and haul them up the beach to careen the hulls, to scrape them clean of tons of accumulated weed and barnacle, plug any leaks and re-caulk the seams. It was as this gruelling work began that Cartagena, released from irons, conspired with a priest called Pedro Sanchez de la Reina to provoke an outright, armed mutiny. They were joined by Captain Gaspar de Quesada of the *Concepción,* and Captain Louis de Mendoza of the *Vittoria*. For two whole days, the 1st and 2nd of April, those who re-mained loyal to Magellan put up a bloody resistance at the end of which the mutineers were defeated. Mendoza was killed in the fighting and his quartered corpse was strung up on a shelving beach which afterwards became known as Gallows Hill. Quesada was beheaded and his body treated in similar fashion, and Cartagena and Father de la Reina were sentenced to be marooned. They were cast ashore six months later, on 8 October, and never heard of again.

In a way, the mutiny was fortuitous. Magellan had rid himself of three of the useless and troublesome 'captains', and the most treacherous of their priests. On or about 20 May he sent the careened and repaired *Santiago* to scout a southerly course in search of a passage to the west. Two days later she ran into a violent storm which hurled her aground on a sandbank and smashed her to splinters. The crew managed to scramble ashore, and two volunteers saved the entire ship's company by strug-gling 72 miles overland in terrible, freezing winds to fetch help from the St Julian's Bay camp. With the coming of spring in those latitudes, Magellan re-launched his renovated ships and set sail on 24 August in search of the strait he felt sure must exist.

TRINIDAD AND VITTORIA

According to the log of Francisco Alvo, one of the few men who survived the circumnavigation: 'On the 21st of October I took the altitude of the sun in exactly 52° south, at five leagues from the land, and there was an opening like a bay, and it has an entrance on the right hand of a very long spit of sand. It is called The Cape of the Virgins ... and within this bay we found a strait.'

Magellan sent *San Antonio* and *Concepción* to explore this narrow passage, and they returned two days later with all flags flying and cannons booming. The entire fleet went on then to explore the tortuous 360-mile channel and emerged 38 days later at its western limit which Magellan named Cabo Deseado, The Desired Cape. But only three ships sailed on into the blue deep which lay beyond; *San Antonio* had deserted one night to put up her helm and return home to Spain. Undeterred by the loss, Magellan named his momentous discovery The Channel of All Saints; others called it The Strait of Vittoria, and it was only much later that it properly became known by the name of the man himself. As they sailed on into the vast unknown, he addressed his men with these words: 'Gentlemen, we are now steering into waters where no ship has ever sailed before. May we always find them as peaceful as we do today, and in this hope I shall name this sea the Mar Pacifico.'

And so, when he set out to cross the Pacific on 28 November 1520, Magellan hoped that the worst of his troubles were over.

He was sadly wrong. In the 98 days before his ships reached the islands he called the Ladrones he came across only two other islands; the first on 24 January, which he called St Paul's and the second, on 3 February, which he called Shark Island. Both were uninhabited and utterly sterile, and his scurvy-ravaged crews, out of food and desperately short of water, were forced to eat ox hides, sawdust and rats. Tongues turned black, gums festered, teeth fell out, and each day saw more men die. At last, on 6 March 1521, they fetched Guam in the Ladrones. Here they rested and re-victualed before sailing on to sight, on the 16th of that month, the most southerly of a group of islands which Magellan named for St Lazarus, but which are known now as the Philippines. The local overlord, King Cebu, welcomed Magellan and pretended conversion to Christianity, but very soon betrayed the great seaman's trust. Cebu encouraged Magellan in the name of Christ to lead an attack upon his enemies and it was there that Magellan, heading a force of 60 men and unaided by Cebu, fought on 27 April 1521 a force of more than a thousand natives in the Battle of Mactan. Many of the Europeans were either killed or wounded and, disastrously, Magellan himself was literally hacked to pieces.

After the slaying of their Captain General, the ships escaped to wander around the islands for months, picking up food and water, and trading where they could for cargoes of valuable spices. As they sailed from island to island, *Concepción* was found

to be leaking beyond all repair. Her crew and stores were transferred to *Vittoria* and *Trinidad,* and she was burnt. Soon, the *Trinidad* suffered a similar fate, and on 2 December the only ships' master left alive, Juan Sebastian del Gano, decided to head directly for home. It was a drastic decision, involving a 13,000-mile voyage around the Cape of Good Hope, but a necessary one if he was to avoid any contact with territories held by the hostile Portuguese. It meant sailing his rotting ship well to the south and then into the face of fierce westerly gales, and it was not until 6 May that he managed to double the Cape. By this time his few remaining victuals were putrid, his water turned foul, and his men had nothing to eat but rice. Twenty died of starvation, and the remaining few were pitifully weak and diseased. Del Gano knew that unless he could take on fresh water and supplies, both ship and men were doomed. He put into the Portuguese-held Cape Verde Islands on 9 July, but although he managed by means of a ruse to re-provision, his ruse was discovered and he was forced to sail out in great haste leaving 13 of his depleted crew still on shore.

Vittoria dropped anchor in the harbour at Seville on Monday 8 September 1522, after an incredible voyage of three years and one month, sole survivor of the five ships which originally set sail. Of the 234 men who embarked in the fleet, only 18 lived to return.

TRINIDAD AND VITTORIA

Soleil Royale

IN ALL, four ships have borne the name *Soleil Royale* but only one of them, the second, ever won renown. She wore the admiral's flag in the historic Battle of Barfleur, but would still be remembered even without this distinction. She was a work of such magnificence that those who finally razed and burned her were said to have felt ashamed at taking part in the destruction of so glorious a ship. Pride of the new French navy, the *Soleil Royale* was a mighty three-decker of 1,940 tons, marvellously designed and decorated. No other vessel in the world was so big or so splendid. This painting by Cornelis de Vries clearly illustrates the lavish, gilded carvings of her stern and quarter galleries. Her figurehead was a golden mermaid holding a golden orb, and golden crowns surmounted her three, huge, stern lanterns. All of her carving and gilding was executed by the celebrated French sculptor Pierre Puget, as is evident by the superb workmanship. The masterly lines of her hull provided for 110 gunports, but this number was reduced to 72 when it quite rapidly became apparent that the armament was overweight in any condition of sea. For this same reason, the 40 remaining 48-pounders were replaced by 36-pounders, and the other 32 guns, previously 36-pounders, were replaced by 18-pounders. All of the cannon were cast extravagantly in bronze, and every one bore the device *ultima ratio regum*.

The revolutionary design of the *Soleil Royale* combined almost all that was best in the ships of France's rivals, the English and the Dutch; but it also embodied some original features which soon were copied in turn. Curiously, however, France's naval architects neglected to emulate England's introduction of low and rounded quarters, choosing instead to retain the very high, flat stern still favoured in Holland's yards. For the rest, *Soleil* was a judicious cross between the full-bellied Dutch design and the stiff, taut lines of the English.

Although he did not live to see her launched, the second *Soleil Royale* represented a culmination in the work of one great man. Single-handed, Jean Baptiste Colbert (1619–83) actually created the modern French navy. Chief advisor to Louis XIV, who had so little interest in ships that he only ever once set foot on a deck, Colbert devoted 20 years of his life to hauling his country out of its naval doldrums and making France a real power at sea. This was his consuming dream, and he made himself unpopular in its pursuit. When he embarked on his venture, the fleet was in a state of gross negligence. France could muster only 200 ships, almost all of which were in states of such disrepair as to render them virtually useless. Ranged against this pitiful number as

merchant adversaries and potential enemies were the fleets of two great seafaring nations, the English and the Dutch. Colbert raised the money for his master plan by imposing very high taxes on all imported goods, and he ensured the manning of the warships he caused to be built by the introduction in France of what was probably the world's first form of National Service.

Also among his initial priorities was an immense refurbishing of the royal shipyards, the building of grand new docks and harbours, and the recruiting from abroad of master shipwrights and carpenters. He was obsessive and inexhaustible, and despite the indifference of Louis XIV he eventually succeeded in the fulfillment of his vision. At the end of 20 years, France had 270 first class fighting ships and could call for crews from over 60,000 seasoned mariners.

The end result of Colbert's long effort was the emergence in France of a new *kind* of ship, and one considerably superior in terms of pure design to any other then afloat. Inevitably, England and Holland were quick to recognise and adopt these innovations and France, throughout the days of sail, was never to gain that lasting ascendancy at sea to which Colbert had dedicated his life. Late 17th century French warships were unsurpassed in design, but they lacked two essential qualities; a use of first-class building materials, and crews with long experience of fighting upon the sea.

One other illustrious name is linked, and this one directly, with that of the *Soleil Royale*. Anne-Hillarion de Contentin, Comte de Tourville, commanded the great ship in her finest hour and was with her almost to the end. Tourville was a seafaring giant forced to rely on the support of, and take his orders from, a landsman pigmy. Insofar as conflict at sea was concerned, his sovereign king, Louis XIV, was a besotted ignoramus. Tourville on the other hand was a brave and worthy man who devoted himself to the sea, and one who knew far better than Louis what ought or ought not to be done. Already a captain in 1677, at the age of 35, he was promoted by stages to the rank of vice admiral and ultimately to Marshall of France. In the meantime, as a Knight of Malta, he fought and won battles in the Mediterranean against Turkish 'barbarians'. But the war during which *Soleil Royale* met her fate was an entirely different matter. France was matched against the Augsberg League, which included two nations whose fighting seamen were so far second to none as each to be equal to the other. In the event, Tourville's men fought like lions, but after one initial victory the final outcome was entirely predictable.

The war which had France on the one side and England, Holland, and Austria on the other became known afterwards as the War of the English Succession. James II of England lost the loyalty of most of his subjects by his fervent practice of Roman Catholicism, and was forced into exile. He fled to France on Christmas Day 1688. In the meantime, William of Orange had accepted an invitation to occupy the throne of England, and had landed at Torbay in November together with a large Dutch force. The force was superfluous; William was made welcome.

Aided by his friend Louis XIV, James set about regaining his lost kingdom by looking first for support in Catholic Ireland, and landed there with an army of mixed French and loyalist troops. At first, the struggle was between James and William but the latter, who had always hated Louis XIV, needed only one tangible excuse to carry the war to France and very soon, he got it. Louis was supplying James's army, and on 1 May 1689 a convoy of stores ships escorted by a fleet of 39 sail was spotted off the coast of Ireland by the commander of an English squadron, Admiral Arthur Herbert (soon to become Earl of Torrington). Herbert's 22 ships were forced to work to windward in order to engage the French force of 39, but in spite of the fact that he was beaten off, Herbert lost no ships. This action, which prompted William immediately to issue a formal declaration of war, was the Battle of Bantry Bay.

With James fighting a losing battle in Ireland, Louis planned to carry the war to the mainland of England and by the spring of 1690 he had mustered the best and largest fleet of warships that France had ever known. With Tourville in command, a mighty force of 75 ships approached the Kentish coast and England, with sea squadrons deployed in the Irish Sea and in the Mediterranean, was beset by fears of invasion. Herbert (now Torrington) was able to muster only 56 ships, 34 English and 22 Dutch. The opposing fleets came together on 30 June. To Admiral Schey's squadron, which was in the van, Tourville's armada must have appeared formidable indeed, but Dutch seamen never had anything but contempt for the French and Schey, who held the wind, sailed in to meet Tourville with no hesitation. Much to the shame of England, and to the fury of William of Orange, Torrington behaved disgracefully. He also had the wind and should have followed in close support. Instead, he held back, and the Dutch squadron lost four ships with one of them taken. William quite rightly punished Torrington by relieving him of his command.

However, this Battle of Beachy Head was no great victory for

SOLEIL
ROYALE

SOLEIL ROYALE

either side because the French, in spite of their far superior numbers, were successfully repulsed. But Tourville had lost no ships, and far fewer men, so the notion at Versailles of a second Conquest was dampened not at all and Louis continued to plan the event. Incredibly, though, he failed to press his advantage, and there was no further battle in the Channel until the summer of 1692. Meanwhile, James had been thrown out of Ireland and was exiled again in France and Tourville, under the king's orders, had spent the interval deliberately avoiding any head-on clash. This tactic of evasion gave William, and England, a breathing space in which to prepare for the invasion they knew to be imminent.

The man who succeeded Torrington as commander of the home fleet was Edward Russell, later Earl of Orford. Russell, then aged about 40 and with only 10 years experience at sea, is not now revered as an outstanding English seaman but he contrived nevertheless to win a most decisive victory at the Battle of La Hogue. First, however, came the Battle of Barfleur, and although it might be said that one is a part of the other, each deserves a separate note.

The Battle of Barfleur began on 19 May 1692, and lasted for most of two days. Tourville had sailed out of Brest with his flag hoist in *Soleil Royale* at the head of 44 ships, under a direct order from Louis which might properly be regarded as ridiculous: 'His Majesty desires him to leave Brest even should he have information that the enemy is at sea with a force superior to that in readiness to sail with him . . . . Should he meet with enemy ships,

he is to chase them back to their ports, whatever number they may be.' A commander less brave or honourable than Tourville might well have queried this recipe for suicide, but such was his unswerving loyalty to Louis, he followed this instruction to the letter.

When the allied fleet was sighted it was some way to leeward, off Cape Barfleur. Tourville had the advantage of wind, but the force which opposed him was more than twice the size of his own. As at Beachy Head, the Dutch were in the van and Tourville, doubtless mindful of their prowess on that occasion, chose to concentrate his attack on the English centre and rear. After four hours of fierce cannonading, several French ships, including *Soleil Royale*, were doubled by the English and so, caught between fire from both sides, took very heavy punishment. The French fought well with that kind of courage born of desperation, and Tourville exhibited great skill in the manoeuvering of his fleet – using, incidentally, the new English method of signalling with flags brought to France by James II – but, had it not been for the sudden looming of a heavy fog, he must surely have suffered a crushing defeat. In the event, he directed his captains to disengage and scatter under cover of the fog and so gain a measure of reprieve. The fleet split up into several groups. The first, a force of nine ships, sailed on up into the North Sea and all around the north coast of Scotland to make a safe passage home. The rest, including Tourville's great flagship, made a run for safety under the shore batteries of the fortress harbour at La Hogue.

Hotly pursued by the Anglo-Dutch allies and badly damaged by cannon fire, *Soleil Royale* never reached that haven. Next day, Tourville was forced to drop anchor off Cherbourg together with *Admirable* and *Conquerant* before transferring to *Ambitieux*. The manner in which these three ships at Cherbourg were utterly destroyed was awesome. Riddled and set on fire by cannon shot, *Admirable*'s bowsprit and beak head were driven hard into *Soleil Royale*, smashing that beautiful stern and causing an explosion in the magazine so tremendous that both ships were blown to pieces. Before she finally sank, *Conquerant* was reduced to a blazing hulk.

Much the larger part of Tourville's fleet was later to fare no better. Even as 12 of his capital ships limped into La Hogue and under what they thought would be the protection of shore fortifications, the flags of the English blue and red squadrons, and the flaming tricolours of the Dutch, were flying high on the horizon. The terrible slaughter which ensued went on for two days, the 23rd and 24th of May. In a last-stand effort to save his ships, Tourville ordered them to be run aground directly under the guns of the forts Lisset and St Vaast. Undeterred, the allied forces sent in fire ships and sailed in close behind them with cannons booming and boarding parties at the ready. Every last one of Tourville's ships was totally destroyed, and aferwards the Dutch and English turned their guns on the forts and reduced them to heaps of rubble. James II, who witnessed the carnage with his illegitimate son the Duke of Berwick, saw his hopes of regaining the English throne go up in huge palls of smoke.

SWEDISH

Vasa

WHEN, in 1611, Gustavus Adolphus I succeeded his father Charles IX to the Swedish throne, this 17-year-old youth inherited three unfinished wars. He was, however, a highly educated young man of iron character, clear and far-sighted vision, and great personal influence. He spent a large part of his short adult life fighting at the head of his armies, and was killed on 16 November 1632 at the Battle of Lützen, in Germany. In the meantime, he achieved a catalogue of outstanding victories, and won for his big, but thinly-populated, country the respect of the whole of Europe. He also built the *Vasa*.

The date at which Gustavus first commissioned the Dutch master shipbuilder Hendrik Huibertsz de Groot to make him a great ship remains uncertain, but it was probably during the autumn of 1626 because de Groot died the following year, 1627, with his work still far from done. At this unfinished stage the ship was known not as *Vasa*, but as *Ny Wassen*. She was a vessel of huge size, designed to strike terror into the hearts of Sweden's enemies. At about 1,400 tons the fine two-decker measured (in metres) 65 overall, with a hull length of 57, an average depth in hull of about 4.5, and a beam of 11.7. The tip of her mainmast rose 49 metres over the bottom of her keel, the height of a twelve-storey building. Her three towering masts were designed to carry a total sail area of about 500 square metres. The total weight of her 64 guns, every one of them cast in bronze, was close on 100 tons: two massive 62-pounders, three of 35, 48 of 24, and 11 of lesser size. She was laid down at the Royal Marine Wharf on Stockholm's Blasieholmen Island, and was to cost the enormous sum of 100,000 riksdaler. In terms of present day value, some 30 million pounds.

Fitting-out began in the spring of 1628, after *Vasa* had been towed to the royal dockyard near the Palace of the Three Crowns, and at the end of July she had all of her cannon on board. Not before time. A political storm long foreseen by Gustavus was working up into a gale. The Hapsburg Emperor, Ferdinand II, had brazenly appointed his imperial favourite Wallenstein, Duke of Mecklenburg, to the post of Lord High Admiral of the Baltic – a sea which Gustavus considered to be Sweden's own – and the young king was anxious to assert his sovereignty in a manner clear to all. 'After God,' he told his ministers, 'it is the navy which will determine the prosperity of our nation!'

Eleven days of hectic activity in the royal yards saw all of *Vasa*'s armament mounted, her ballast stowed and part of her complement embarked. She was meant to be manned by a total of 433 officers and other ranks; 133 sailors and 300 gunners and soldiers or marines. In fact, and fortunately, the vast majority of these were due to join her at Älvsnabben, where the king had ordered that '. . . there she proceed and hold herself in readiness to set sail on any such day and hour as it may please Us, for whichever destination We ordain.'

After attending a service at the big church near to the royal palace the congregation hurried down to join the huge crowd assembled on the quays to wish the great ship God Speed. At about half past three in the afternoon of 10 August 1628 the *Vasa*, dressed bravely overall with flags and pennants, was hauled away from the wall and towed to Södermalm in the hope of there gaining a headwind. When he found a light breeze from the south-south-west her captain ordered the hoisting of fore and main topsails, fore-sail and spanker. Almost at once, *Vasa* heeled over so violently that the swell rushed into her lower gunports and in only a matter of horrifying minutes she sank to the bottom of the sea.

It was a disaster of catastrophic proportions, and one which was only slightly ameliorated by the fact that *Vasa* had not yet taken on a full crew. Even so, she was carrying a party of dignitaries on their way to Voxholm, some of them accompanied by wives and children, and 30 at least lost their lives. Some accounts put the death toll as high as 50, and curiously so, because the records in every other respect are perfectly clear and detailed. *Vasa*'s commander was Captain Severin Hansson with, as his second-in-command, Lieutenant Petter Gierdsson. Identified also are all others held wholly or in part responsible for the tragedy: gunnery officer Erik Jönsson and chief gunner Joen Larsson, sailing master Jöran Matsson, and boatswain Per Bertilson. Other names which feature in historical documents are those of Hans Jönsson, Captain of the Royal Naval dockyard, and the master shipbuilder who had taken over following the death of de Groot, one Hein Jacobsson.

A court of enquiry was swiftly convened and answers sought as to exactly how and why *Vasa* had foundered. Was she badly commanded? Wrongly constructed? Improperly loaded? First to be questioned was gunnery officer Erik Jönsson, who vehemently insisted that all of *Vasa*'s guns had been mounted in the proper manner and firmly secured under his personal supervision. He stated further that in his opinion it would not have been possible to trim the ship's centre of gravity by adding more ballast, for the simple reason that the lower gunports were only 1.20 metres (about 4 feet) above the waterline.*

Petter Gierdsson, next for questioning, appears to have been exonerated too easily. He was permitted to acquit himself with a bland expression of surprise that any vessel should heel over and founder in a wind so very light.

Conversely, the sailing master was subjected to a fierce interrogation. He was accused of failing to carry out his duties in accordance with orders received, by neglecting to ensure that *Vasa*'s ballast had been correctly stowed, thereby causing the loss of His Majesty's greatest ship. Realising, perhaps, that he was to be made a scapegoat, Jöran Matsson defended himself with vigour. He firmly rejected any suggestion that the ballast had not been properly distributed, and went on to swear that he had repeatedly protested to the captain that *Vasa* was burdened with far too much top-hamper. Further, his remarks having gone unheeded, he had demonstrated his fears to Admiral Fleming when the admiral had attended *Vasa*'s roll-trials. In conclusion of this impassioned defence, he confounded his accusers by asking a simple question: if *Vasa* was incapable of standing up to a light breeze when carrying only four sails, how could she possibly have run before a strong wind under every stitch of her canvas?

Outflanked by this bombshell, his inquisitors switched their attention to the boatswain, Per Bertilsson, accusing him of having been too drunk when *Vasa* sailed to attend efficiently to his duty of checking sails and gear. Bertilsson strongly denied the canard, and produced witnesses to the effect that he had boarded the ship, perfectly sober, immediately after receiving Holy Communion.

Finally, Hein Jacobsson was called and the court asked him why, as the man responsible for completion and delivery of the *Vasa*, he had constructed a vessel with so narrow a hull and so little bluff. This was, of course, a somewhat ridiculous question, and Jacobsson's answer caused no small embarrassment. He reminded all present that he was not the designer and was able readily to prove that he had faithfully adhered to all inherited specifications. He went on to drop the second bombshell of the day, and it was one which exploded even louder than that of Jören Matsson: *Vasa*'s dimensions had been dictated by none other than King Gustavus himself.

Perceiving then that the enquiry was becoming a complete fiasco, the court officers brought it rapidly to an end with no

* *Astonishing as it may be, Jönsson's statement was quite correct.*

VASA

conclusive result. In the meantime, efforts were being made to salvage the sunken ship. *Vasa* was down off the Stockholm island of Beckholmen at a depth of 32 metres, and the divers contrived without much trouble to get her on an even keel with her mast-tops high out of the water. Raising her, however, was quite another matter, and after five months of struggle Admiral Fleming reported failure with the words 'The weight is far greater than I ever would have supposed.'

Years later, in 1664, a salvage crew under Hans Albrecht von Treibleben used primitive diving bells in a further effort to recover the ship, and managed somehow to bring up most artefacts of value, including no fewer than 54 cannon. Considering the primitive nature of von Treibleben's equipment this was a most remarkable achievement, and no-one blamed him when in the end he announced that to re-float the hull was impossible.

And so the *Vasa* lay forgotten over the next 300 years before, in 1956, interest in her was awakened and it was then discovered that she was buried in mud at a depth of 100 feet. The man who found her, Anders Franzen, headed a crew of 60 experienced divers in what was to become a very long and complex salvage operation. On 20 August 1959 *Vasa*, finally freed from her coffin of solid mud, was eased over a period of 28 days into shallow waters. Thanks to the mud and the cold Baltic sea (in which the ship-eating toredo worm cannot live), most of her hull was in an amazingly sound condition, and the crew was able to recover a vast range of objects. By 24 April 1961 her decks had been stripped bare and the hull, virtually intact, was towed into dock on 4 May. An immense, barn-like structure was built around her, and a team of marine archaeologists embarked upon the endless process of restoration and preservation. Using modern tech-

niques the experts have worked wonders, and our knowledge of life on board ship in the 17th century is enormously enriched by a museum collection of over 20,000 separate items which look and handle now exactly as they did when made.

Stillborn, as was her English counterpart, Henry VIII's great *Mary Rose*, the *Vasa* of Sweden stands now and forever unique. She is the world's oldest, and by far the most complete, example of a sailing vessel ever recovered from the sea. She revealed to naval historians an absolute mine of new information on archaic ships' architecture and today, with her masts, sails and rigging re-created from archive records of her original plans, she presents a stunning spectacle of glories ages past.

Any future tourist to Stockholm who neglects to visit the *Vasa* wharf will have forfeited an experience in life he might never be granted again.

VASA

Bluenose

BLUENOSE might appear as something of an oddity here, but no such book as this could ever be complete without her. She was a classic sailing ship in every sense of the term, a marvel of design and performance so far ahead of every other vessel in her class as to be virtually out of sight. Leisure craft apart, she was possibly the last truly great sailing ship ever built.

In 1920 Senator William H Dennis, newspaper proprietor of the Halifax *Herald & Mail,* instituted what was rapidly to become one of the most fiercely-contested sailing prizes in the world. He offered a massive silver cup, to be known as the International Fisherman's Trophy, to the outright winner of a series of races to be held alternate years off Lunenberg in Nova Scotia and Gloucester in New England, entry to be strictly confined to genuine fishing vessels such as those known and seen to earn a hard living on the salt banks of Newfoundland. When in 1919, the New York Yacht Club decided to cancel the America's Cup race because of a 23-knot wind, a disgusted Billy Dennis thought it high time to demonstrate the abilities of real professional sailors in 'proper' seagoing ships.

In reality, and although ostensibly open to all comers, the effective 'international' competition was between the big salt-bankers of New England and Nova Scotia, and the finalists in that first race of 1920 were the *Delawana* of Lunenberg under her regular skipper Tommy Himmelman, and the *Esperanto* out of Gloucester. To the utter dismay of all Canadians, *Esperanto* was a clear winner, and sailed triumphantly back home to America with Dennis's big silver cup and a cash prize of $4,000. The consolation prize of $1,000 was won by *Delawana* with a quite respectable performance, but this did nothing whatever to mollify bruised national pride, and out of the ensuing hue and cry the legendary *Bluenose* was born.

Billy Dennis, himself a keen sailor, realised that no ship in the existing Canadian fleets was likely to beat the *Esperanto* and that if his cup was ever to be brought back home, a brand new saltbanker was needed. He formed a consortium to raise funds and hired a young marine architect, William J Roue, to draw up plans. It was a staggering act of faith. Bill Roue had begun to build models of vessels seen from the windows of the family home on Halifax's waterfront when he was only five years old, but had undergone no formal training whatsoever. Everything he knew about boat design he had learned from one book, Dixon-Kemp's *Yacht Architecture,* given to him as a present after his expulsion from high school. He was, however, a natural genius, and his drawings were readily accepted. A contract for construction was awarded to the Lunenburg shipbuilding firm of Smith & Rhuland, and work began immediately.

Bluenose was launched on 26 March 1921, a 285-ton schooner of magnificent proportions. 112 feet on the waterline, her hull overall measured 143 feet and her bowsprit projected a further 17 feet 6 inches. She was 27 feet on the beam, with a draught of 15 feet 10 inches. The head of her main topmast soared 125 feet 10 inches above deck-level, that of her foremast 102 feet 6 inches. Her main boom was 81 feet 6 inches long, fore boom 32 feet 10 inches, main gaff 51 feet, fore gaff 32 feet 11 inches. Her total sail area of 10,901 square feet comprised a mainsail of 4,100, foresail 1,640, fisherman's staysail 1,305, jib topsail 966, jib 804, jumbo 770, main gaff topsail 756, and fore gaff topsail 560.

Except for her masts of Oregon pine, *Bluenose* was built entirely of local timbers – oak, spruce, birch, and pine – and the fact that there was nothing really unusual about her sail plan puzzled many uninformed witnesses as to the source of her remarkable sailing qualities. Less discernable to the onlooker were the masterly lines of her hull below the waterline and a length at straight keel of only 50 feet. This latter gave her an overhang of very nearly two thirds.

Bluenose was fitted out with all speed, and the fact that she was no ordinary fishing schooner was reflected in her final cost of $35,000. At the time, a vessel of her type and size would average around $25,000, and the very large difference represented a considerable risk on the part of her owners because *Bluenose* had to be a working vessel, and losses among the fishing fleets were by no means uncommon. Indeed, *Bluenose* came within a hairs-breadth of total disaster on her maiden voyage out to the Newfoundland banks. She was borne down upon whilst fishing by a big square-rigged ship which threatened to ram her full amidships. The bell was rung and the foghorn sounded, but the square-rigger (unidentified to this day) took no avoiding action and it seemed inevitable that *Bluenose* must be smashed apart. The desperate crew took to the boats and rowed like demons to come alongside the stranger, yelling and screaming for her to sheer off. Still the square-rigger held on course, missing the schooner's stern by a matter of inches. *Bluenose* was to survive perils much worse, but if Billy Dennis showed flair and daring in his choice of designer, he picked a skipper whose worth was unquestionable.

Angus Walters, born in 1882, began his life at sea when he was 13 years old as a deck hand on his father's fishing vessel. After serving a hard apprenticeship which included a stretch in the West Indies trade, and on rising at a comparatively early age to the command of his own ship, he quickly became renowned for his love of charging ahead under full sail. Short in stature but long on courage, he was regarded by all who knew him as being 'as good a sailor as any man alive.' Seamen vied for the privilege of serving under him, and so the *Bluenose* was always crewed by salts who were 'pick of the bunch'. And, in the light of her eventful life, they certainly needed to be.

After having qualified as a working vessel by fishing all through that summer, *Bluenose* was entered for the second International Fisherman's Trophy challenge in the autumn of 1921. She spanked home three miles ahead of her nearest rival, the *Elsie* out of Gloucester, and that only a beginning. Her record in the IFT races is so well documented as to need no description here. Year after year she won every single one of these events for which she was entered, and this in spite of the fact that frustrated American interests spent fortunes over the next two decades on the design and construction of fishing schooners built expressly for the purpose of beating the Canadian wonder. All to no avail. *Bluenose* reigned invincible, and her feats of sailing became almost mythical. Otherwise-sane people who knew and cared about sailing came firmly to believe that she was gifted with a 'soul', that some divine power had bestowed upon her an eternal right of ascendancy. In fact, no-one has ever really defined or understood the precise combination of special qualities which made *Bluenose* what she was. Could it have been some inadvertent quirk of design, or was it perhaps that unique affinity felt by Angus Walters when first he stepped on board? The more one considers the options, the more one is moved to ponder on questions to which there are no answers. Often when queried, Walters might only smile and say 'The wood for the ship that will beat *Bluenose* is still growing.' In more serious vein, he once said 'I think it was the way her masts were placed. If the rest of her is good, a vessel's spars will pretty well tell what she can do . . . I don't think there was a vessel ever came out of Lunenburg that had her sticks stepped that perfect.'

But *Bluenose* was not just a winner of races, she was a deep-sea sailer of tremendous resilience. In 1926, she was very nearly driven aground and wrecked on Sable Island, in those grim and dangerous waters known throughout the fishing fleets as the Graveyard of the Atlantic. Anchored off a lee shore to ride out a raging gale, she was hit by what Angus Walters later described as a 'grandfather sea'. Her cable snapped and she was hurled towards the rocks, 14 stanchions ripped away together with parts

BLUENOSE

BLUENOSE

of her rails and bulwarks. Walters and his 20-man crew fought like tigers to bring her head up into the gale, and somehow denied to Sable Island this addition to its long list of victims. In 1930, she made another miraculous escape. Grounded on the rocks of Newfoundland's Placentia Bay, she withstood four days and nights of endless battering which snarled her rigging and smashed her lifeboats. Once again she survived the tempest, and lived to sail away.

These great triumphs of design strength and seamanship were soon to pale into insignificance. In 1935, *Bluenose* was appointed official Canadian representative at the Silver Jubilee celebrations of King George V and Queen Mary. After a 17 day passage across the Atlantic, evidence that her fame had spread far beyond home waters was made manifest by a tumultuous welcome from the crowds of island seafarers lined up to await her arrival first at Plymouth, and then at Cowes on the Isle of Wight. Later, when King George reviewed his Home Fleet at Spithead, *Bluenose* lay there at anchor, a tiny dwarf among giants. But the dwarf did not go unnoticed. Angus Walters was summoned by his monarch to board the royal yacht, and was honoured by a private audience with the king and queen, and their three sons, the Prince of Wales, the Duke of York, and the Duke of Kent. Walters never revealed what passed in that long conversation between himself and the royal family, but it is safe to assume that the talk was most probably all about ships and the sea.

This proud happening in Walters' life was followed not long afterwards by what was to prove his worst nightmare. Barely out of Falmouth in Cornwall on her long passage home, *Bluenose* ran into a towering rain-lashed gale. She weathered it for three days and nights before being hit by a mountainous sea which thundered up out of the dark black night and struck her broadside-on, slamming her over onto her beams-end. This one gigantic hammer blow smashed and tore away both lifeboats, the deck house, fore-boom and main-boom jaws, and all of her portside bulwarks. Her decks below were flooded by countless tons of water, and in that hellish, raging darkness every man on board resigned himself to a final resting place in Davy Jones's locker. Then, as seconds passed like minutes and minutes passed like hours, *Bluenose* began, as though by magic, slowly to right herself. With her seams aft split open by the pounding seas, she came painfully back onto an even keel, and her subsequent saving was due entirely to the superhuman will of Angus Walters. All amidst that raging hell, he rallied and bullied crewmen and passengers alike to raise her flooring planks and shift tons of pig-iron ballast up for'ard, and *Bluenose* limped back into Falmouth for well-won rest and repair. One old salt on board at the time recalled the storm as being far and away the most terrifying experience in a lifetime spent at sea. Angus Walters merely remarked (of *Bluenose*) 'I was never more proud of her.'

The Second World War put an end to races for the International Fisherman's Trophy and so, in a way, to *Bluenose*. Not, though, before she sang a glorious swan-song one sunny September morning when Lunenburgers were enjoying a Fisherman's Exhibition. Four young saltbankers were racing neck and neck in the final leg of a scheduled contest when suddenly, on the horizon, a fifth big schooner hove into view. It was *Bluenose*, returning heavy-laden with a huge catch of fish. As she was recognised, the crowds gave vent to a full-throated roar, and although he could not possibly have heard it, Angus Walters responded. *Bluenose* was low in the water, and without her topmasts, but Walters hoist all the sail he could and made what seemed like a valiant but fruitless effort to join in the race and win. Incredibly, *Bluenose* overhauled the leaders to barrel across the finishing line *minutes* ahead of her closest follower.

No longer her skipper, Angus Walters was by no means alone among the millions of radio listeners stunned and shattered by a bland announcement, one dismal afternoon in January 1946, that the famed Canadian schooner *Bluenose* had been wrecked and lost off the coast of Haiti, her beautiful back broken on a coral reef and her bones abandoned to rot away in waters so far from home.

In 1961, the old Lunenburg firm of Smith & Rhuland was commissioned by an American film company to construct a replica of HMS *Bounty,* and the replica was built on the very same ways on which was built the *Bluenose*. This event inspired a campaign by the brothers Brian and Philip Backman (co-authors of the book *Bluenose,* published in 1975 by McClelland & Stewart of Toronto) with headlines in local newspapers shouting 'If another *Bounty*, why not another *Bluenose*?' The Backman brothers were strongly supported by Billy Roue and Angus Walters, both of them into their 80s, and *Bluenose II* was launched eventually on 24 July 1963 at a cost to her sponsors of $300,000, nearly ten times as much as the original.

But, and to paraphrase Browning, old raptures are never recaptured.

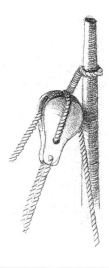

Bibliography

Allen, O E (Editor) *The Windjammers*. Time Life Books, Amsterdam 1979.

Andrews, K R *Elizabethan Privateering*. London 1964.

Andrews, K R *Drake's Voyages*. London 1967.

Archibald, E H H *The Wooden Fighting Ship*. London 1968.

Ashley, C W *The Yankee Whaler*. New York 1926.

Backman, B and P *Bluenose*. Toronto 1975.

Barjot, Admiral, and Jean Savant *Histoire Mondiale de la Marine*. Paris 1961.

Barrow, Sir John *The Mutiny of the Bounty*. London 1831.

De Blauwe Wimpel Various issues.

Bligh and Bowker *Mutiny!!*

Blok, P J *Michiel Adriaanszoon de Ruyter*. Amsterdam 1928.

Blussé van Oud Alblas, A *De Geschiedenis van het Clipperschip*. Amsterdam 1972.

Bosscher, Ph M *Een nuchter Volk en de Zee*. Bussum 1979.

Bowness, E *Ships & Shipsmodels*. London 1937.

Brandt, Gerard *Het Leven en Bedrijf van den Heere Michiel de Ruiter*. Amsterdam 1746.

Burgess, R H *The Great Age of Sail*. Lausanne 1967.

Catalogue; *Scheepsmodellen en scheepsbouwkundige tekeningen 1600–1900*. Nederlandsch Historisch Scheepvaart Museum. Amsterdam 1943.

Chapelle, Howard I *The search for Speed under Sail*. Bonanza Books 1967.

Clark, A H *The Clipper Ship Era*. London 1911.

Copper, F S *Racing Sailormen*. London 1963.

Coppens, T *Maurits, zoon van de Zwijger*. Baarn 1984.

Corbett, Sir J S *Drake and the Tudor Navy*. London 1898.

Cotton and Fawcett *East Indiamen*. London 1949.

Cutler, Carl C *Greyhounds of the Sea*. Winconsin 1930.

Domizlaff, Hans *Das Grosse Buch Der "Passat"*.

Enc Brittanica Various editions.

Enc De Kleine Winkler Prins Amsterdam 1980.

Feenstra, Anno *De Clippers*. Amsterdam 1945.

Feiling, Keith *A History of England*. London 1950.

Fraser, Antonia *King James*. London 1974.

Histoire de la Marine Paris 1934.

Howarth, David *Sovereign of the Seas*. London 1974.

Howe and Mathews *American Clipper Ships*. Salem Mass. 1927.

Humble, R (editor) *Naval Warfare*. London 1983.

Jebens, H *"Passat"*. Hertford 1969.

Jobé, Joseph (editor) *The Great Age of Sail*. Lausanne 1967.

Kähre, Georg *Under Gustaf Eriksons Flagga*. Aland.

Keble-Chatterton, E *Ship Models*. London 1923.

Kemp, P *The History of Ships*. London 1978.

Ketting, Herman *"Prins Willem"*. Bussum 1979.

Kitson, Arthur *Captain James Cook*. London 1907.

Lacey, Robert *Henry VIII*. London 1972.

Laing, Alex *American Sail*. New York 1971.

Landström, Björn *The Ship*. London 1961.

Landström, Björn *Regalskeppet Vasan*. Stockholm 1980.

de Lavarende, J *La Navigation Sentimale*, translated into Dutch Romantische Scheepvaart, by F W Michels.

Leclercq, W L *De Laatste Nederlandsche Zeilschepen*. Utrecht 1966.

Lubbock, Basil *The China Clippers*. Glasgow 1919.

Lubbock, Basil *The Blackwall Frigates*. Glasgow 1922.

Lubbock, Basil *Log of the 'Cutty Sark'*. Glasgow 1926.

Lubbock, Basil *The Down Easters*. Glasgow 1929.

Lunshof, H A *De Stuurman of "De Groene Leeuw"*. Amsterdam 1941.

MacGregor, David R *Fast Sailing Ships*. Lausanne 1973.

MacGregor, David R *Clipper Ships*. London 1979.

Macintyre, D *The Adventure of Sail*. London 1970.

Martinez-Hidalgo Y Terán, José Mª *Lepanto La Batalla, La Galera "Real"*. Barcelona 1971.

Mathews, F C *American Clipper Ships*. 1927.

Metzelaar, A C *Europa Ahoy!* Amsterdam 1945.

Moerman, J J *Der Vaderen Erf*. Zaandam 1952.

Moerman, J J *Neerlands Vlag aan vreemde Kust*. Zaandam 1955.

Mollema, J C *De Nederlandse Vlag op de Wereldzeeën*. Amsterdam.

Moore, Sir Alan, *Sailing Ships of War*. London 1926.

Oderwald, J *Nederlandsche Snelzeilers*. Amsterdam 1940.

Petrejus, E W *Het Schip vaart uit*. Bussum 1975.

Rodger, N A M *The Wooden World*. London 1987.

Schaüffelen, O *De laatste grote Zeilschepen*. Bussum 1972.

Smit, L and H Hacquebord *Nederlandse Zeilschepen 1813–1880*. Alkmaar.

Stanford, M J G *The Raleghs Take to the Sea*. Mariners Mirror 1962.

Thomas, Geo Malcolm *Sir Francis Drake*. London 1972.

Trease, Geoffrey *Samuel Pepys and his World*. London 1972.

Tryckare, Tre *Lore of the Ship*. Gothenburg 1975.

Vere, Francis *Salt in their Blood*, translated into Dutch Zout in hun Bloed by F. Muller van Brakel.

Warner, Oliver *Great Sea Battles*. London 1963.

Warner, Oliver *Nelson*. London 1975.

Whipple, A B (editor) *The Whalers*. Time Life Books. Amsterdam 1979.

Williams, Neville *Elizabeth I*. London 1972.

Williams, Neville *Francis Drake*. London 1973.

Williamson, J A *The Age of Drake*. London 1938.

Willison, George F *Here they dug the Gold*. London 1950.

Wyatt, H G *The Tale of the Bounty*. London 1940.

Zee van der, Daan *Vermetel Voorgeslacht*. Deventer.

Index

Page numbers in *italics* refer to illustrations.